W9-AZB-521

The Ax-Grinders

CRITICS OF OUR PUBLIC SCHOOLS

The Ax-Grinders

by Mary Anne Raywid

New York THE MACMILLAN COMPANY 1962

First Printing

The Macmillan Company, New York
Brett-Macmillan Ltd., Galt, Ontario

Printed in the United States of America

Library of Congress catalog card number: 62-11356

To Veev

*Who was filled with enthusiasm and delight,
and made all things possible*

The author gratefully acknowledges the editorial assistance of Lynne Young Ianniello.

ACKNOWLEDGMENTS

Many people have contributed a great deal to this book. I should like particularly to thank Richard B. Kennan and his staff of the National Education Association's National Commission for the Defense of Democracy Through Education. The information made available to me by the Commission was invaluable, since much of it is unpublished and would have been obtainable in no other way. Dr. Kennan, Edwin Davis, Henry Butler, Richard Morgan, and Robert Mukai offered a number of valuable suggestions, and I am indebted to Bernice Brigham, Dorothy Calhoun, Naomi Stout, and Jane Goostree for their many kindnesses and frequent assistance.

A number of others at NEA were also most helpful. I particularly want to thank Opal Jackson, Grace Brubaker, Virginia Stephenson, and David Barnes—all of the Research Division—and Irene Jacobs, former Librarian, for their help with my many questions. David Iwamoto, Robert Leeper, Gerald Van Pool, Bob Luke, Shirley Cooper, Harrison Sasscer, Merrill Hartshorn, and Walter Hess kindly made materials available. Eric Rhodes and Roy Wilson read parts of the manuscript and contributed valuable suggestions.

I also owe a great many thanks to the Anti-Defamation League of B'nai B'rith—particularly to Jack Baker, Director of International Affairs; to Milton Ellerin and Jerome Bakst, Director and Assistant Director of Fact-Finding; and to Nissen Gross, Midwest Director of the League's Civil Rights Division.

Robert Skaife, Executive Secretary of the Affiliated Teacher Organizations of Los Angeles, offered assistance and advice in the planning of this book. James A. McNeil, Superintendent of the Pascack Valley Regional High School, Hillsdale, New Jersey, very graciously made his files available to me, and read portions of the manuscript. Clara Stratemeyer, former Elementary Education Supervisor in the Montgomery County Schools; John Anderson and Irwin Knowle of the *Washington Post & Times Herald*, and the staff of the Montgomery

County Education Association, all offered information important to the preparation of Chapter V. John Nelson, Director of Teacher Education at Grinnell College, read several chapters and offered a number of excellent suggestions. The late Harold Rugg of Teachers College, Columbia University, and Arthur Rice, Editor of *The Nation's Schools,* offered help as well as interest and encouragement.

The study and the original manuscript culminating in *The Ax-Grinders* were initially prepared as a doctoral dissertation submitted to the University of Illinois. I should like to thank the members of my doctoral committee, Professors Harold C. Hand, Ray H. Simpson, B. Othanel Smith, and William O. Stanley, all of the College of Education, and Professor J. Austin Ranney of the Department of Political Science. Professor Archibald Anderson, though not a member of the committee, repeatedly gave assistance and advice.

A number of my friends and some of my relatives were also pressed into service. I want to thank Marian Telford and Mary Jane Aschner, particularly, for their frequent help and encouragement. Peggy Dye, Katherine Ascher, and the late Ardene Stephens helped in various ways with the original manuscript, and my colleagues Vera Tarr and Robert Guttchen have made suggestions on the revision. My brother, Alan Raywid, and his friend John Wilson contributed generously of their legal knowledge. And my mother, the late Vivian T. Raywid, offered assistance as well as constant moral support.

Of course, the responsibility for faults is mine.

MARY ANNE RAYWID

CONTENTS

The Ax-Grinders

1. *Education Under Fire*

An irate citizen storms into the educator's office, demanding that a "subversive" textbook be censored. An equally angry visitor insists that "money is being spent foolishly." A group descends upon the superintendent to plead for a "return" to the three R's. A minister lambastes the schools from his pulpit, while a politician builds his criticism into his platform. Patriotic organizations bemoan the lack of fundamental Americanism, and college professors decry the lack of fundamental learning.

Not only is American education under fire; the practice of criticizing our schools is well on its way to becoming a national pastime. For some, it is already a favorite armchair sport. For others, it has become a full-time career.

Since World War II, there is virtually no aspect of public education that has gone unquestioned by one source or another. Undoubtedly, at least a portion of this criticism has been earned. It is no more reasonable to assume that the educational profession is free of failure, of inept members, than it is to assume that all doctors or lawyers are perfect at what they do.

It is clearly the right of citizens to protest where schools are failing to accomplish the right things, or where they are succeeding in accomplishing the wrong things. The wise educator looks to the community's opinion as a valuable source of help.

But while some criticism has been warranted and helpful, not all has been. A prominent feature of the postwar period has been a rash of criticism which is neither accurate nor designed to improve. There have been abundant charges, some patently untrue, some containing a seed of truth enlarged and distorted to grotesque proportions. Perhaps even more serious are the charges which are not concerned primarily with facts, but with values that mirror or proclaim purposes that could destroy public education. Charges of this type have split entire communities into hostile factions, have led to school systems in which educators are so busy combating or adjudicating among factions that there is little time or energy left for educating, have driven teachers to place self-preservation first and teaching a poor second, and have made true teaching impossible among youngsters who have been goaded to defy those from whom they might otherwise learn.

Of course, criticism of public schools should not be stifled. Legitimate criticism must not only be preserved but also actively encouraged. The public, however, must have a way of evaluating specific charges, of determining the acceptability of criticism, of judging claims of failure or transgression.

In the course of examining the critic and some of his charges against public education, it is hard to escape concluding that a large part of the contemporary educational debate has never been limited to education and that the attacks have not been confined to school practices alone. Often it is our way of life that is being challenged rather than our theories of education.

An obvious starting point in assessing educational criticism is the critic's formal affiliations and affirmations, the resolutions officially adopted by an organization in its charter or constitution. But another kind of statement may prove an even more reliable index to the group's beliefs and the kind of surprising effects it may bring. Though organizations officially commit themselves to acceptable, if not exclusively laudatory, goals, the day-by-day efforts of many critics seem concentrated on enterprises bearing little relationship to their commendable declaration of purpose. It is assumed throughout this book that the daily activities of a group make a useful and legitimate measure by which to judge the critics.

The relevance of critics' associations is also assumed—not as a basis of finding guilt by association but rather as grounds for "guilt by collaboration." As we shall see, few of education's more determined detractors work alone. The forms of cooperation range all the way from informal assistance, such as the exchange of mailing lists and materials, to such official and extensive commitments as sharing identical personnel and office space. Still another tangible and vital form of cooperation is the exchange of financial aid. Since it can be true that "he who pays the piper calls the tune," the source of critics' support is pertinent to our inquiry.

We must, for the sake of our schools and children, recognize the undesirable critic, and determine why the attacks on our schools have reached such epidemic proportions. Can patterns be traced? Is each attack unique? What kind of effects have resulted? What can be done?

This book deals with these questions. In a sense it takes the form of an argument. First, some of the groups which comprise the nation's school critics are reviewed, their diversity illustrated, and the nature and extent of their complaints examined. Then comes the important question of how to distinguish the valid from the invalid charges. Next, accounts of actual attacks demonstrate the critics' methods and the way that many national organizations help. The final chapters attempt to make sense of it all: to discover the causes, and explore the means of prevention and cure.

Nowhere does this book attempt to answer or refute the charges of critics. Such a task is important, surely, but it is the topic of quite another book. This one focuses on the critics themselves, because often, in the chaos of their abuse, there can be discerned a hidden ax which needs exposing. Many who are highly critical of our schools will deplore this grinding of axes.

In this country there are approximately a thousand groups that are highly critical of public education. Yet even with a daily heightening of their vocalism in newspapers, books, and magazines, there persists the lethargic assumption that it is the sound of a noisy little group of disgruntled professors, publicists, and admirals. But by virtue of numbers alone, the critics of educational policy and practice are a force to be reckoned with.

To identify the critics, and to let them air their complaints, a questionnaire (see page 222) was sent to nearly three hundred of their groups. It was an unusual instrument that might easily be called "loaded." Respondents were given no opportunity to comment favorably on the schools. The most they could do was to express a belief in the *absence* of certain undesirable features and conditions. Furthermore, the questionnaire permitted no shades of opinion, but allowed only a flat "yes" or "no" on highly generalized questions. The cautious observer, concerned with accuracy, might well have hesitated to reply to any of the questions.

The document consisted of twenty-three questions on which respondents were invited to indict or exonerate public schools, and covered virtually everything that pertains to schools—books, curriculum, teachers, administrators, methods, goals, and so on. Thus, a "yes" response to all the questions amounted to an exhaustive indictment of public education. A number of respondents made just that indictment.

Eighty-three organizations and individuals agreed to answer.* We can surmise, but we cannot of course be sure, that their replies are typical of the views of the nation's numerous critics. But even if we obstinately assumed them to be *atypical,* these replies make startling reading. And the fame and prestige of some of these respondents perhaps provides an even better index to influence than sheer numbers. Those who have followed the printed and spoken words of today's educational critics will find many of the most prominent among the list of questionnaire respondents.

One of the most striking features of the list of responding organizations is the number of "patriot" groups present. About half the names suggest a primarily patriotic orientation. When all the groups endorsing a particular political and/or economic viewpoint are added, roughly two-thirds of these critical organizations are represented. Four on the list have names suggesting a primarily religious concern. Only about 20 per cent of the names even suggest that their foremost interest is public education. Even this figure may be misleadingly high, for several of this group have been accused of controlling purposes not nominally evident. To one, for example, has been attributed the chief motive of holding taxes down by defeating school-consolidation legislation. Others openly exist to oppose consolidation on the exclusive ground that it increases government centralization.

These organizations whose primary *raison d'être* is not education

* More than half the forty-one additional organizations who wrote that they could not reply because their groups took no official stand on education nevertheless proceeded thoroughly to denounce public schools. It is unfortunate that legal considerations make it impossible to include them.

add a great deal of numerical strength to the school critics. If all those seeking membership in a "Council of Christian Laymen" thereby become school critics, the ranks of the critics are considerably swelled. There may be council members who dissent on such tangential issues as education, but, to judge from its president's report on the organization's official position, such members must be in a minority.

To be fair, we do not know the membership totals of responding organizations. We have reason to suspect that one group from which correspondence was received represents no membership beyond its "president." Others appear to be mere publishing devices with only small staffs. On the other hand, two of the organizations on the list—the American Coalition of Patriotic Societies, and We, The People!—are national federations representing several hundred autonomous affiliates. Another—Liberty Lobby—serves before Congress the common interests of a large number of sympathetic organizations. Two of the three groups just named affirmed every charge on the questionnaire, and the third all but a bare few.

Such a community of interests involves a danger that much of this book is devoted to pointing up. Americans have always believed that public education was separate from political affairs, and, in this century, that the public schools should be immune from sectarian influences. Yet the very names of some of the organizations listed suggest trends counter to these traditions. As we shall see in subsequent chapters, a very specific view of public education and its faults is becoming increasingly identified with an equally specific set of political and economic ideas.

Our questionnaire survey also served to show the extensive cooperation among education's critics. For example, the source of a poem, "The Little Red Hens," enclosed with the reply of the Keep America Committee, is evidently the Committee for the Preservation of the Constitution, *and* the Minute Women.[1] (The "little red hens" in question are the members of the Parent-Teacher Association, an organization that takes blows from some of education's critics and occasionally from schools as well.) It is obvious that through the overlapping and cooperative efforts of at least the three groups implicated, "The Little Red Hens" has been widely circulated. Such cooperation suggests the remarkable efficiency that is obtained from a single effort to discredit.

While several themes clearly are shared by most of the organizations that responded, there appears at first sight to be no single theme common to all or most of the *individuals* who replied to the questionnaire. But gradually similarities emerge. About a third, for instance, are, or have been, professors of liberal arts. And a third are journalists. In addition, on many matters of public policy there is a wide agreement that will be investigated in later chapters.

The denunciations are generally unqualified and wholesale. One organization sums up its own position in the comment "a rotten public school system." Others less dramatically express the same view through their replies to all or most of the questions. The official replying for the Beverly Hills Freedom Club wrote a note, not untypical, that is worth quoting:

> I am not a teacher here in California, but the system has been impregnated so long with "Unesco" and you know what it is and has done to any system indoctrinated with it.
>
> I came from Ohio about eight years ago and can say with absolute (ly) *[sic]* candor that the totalitarian system has had a great helper in the "Progressive System."
>
> The Godlessness, disloyalty, lack of teacher background, poorly educated teachers; teachers who ought not to be teaching as they have no interest in their work, only salary; many systems Red infiltrated; money spent on wrong things in school systems; Superintendents not interested in the basic work, some who emphasize frills to the exclusion of basic work; those who favor "soft" curricula and pass pupils on the number of years spent in the grade.
>
> We need to begin at the first grade and on up through to revise the whole system. The parents also should be "reborn" to realize that they too must be interested in a sound educational system. The Parents and Teachers Ass'ns. should be renovated and Red Infiltration drained out of it *[sic]*.[2]

The sincerity of these comments is obvious. One may speculate that the respondents may not be aware of their real motives, but conviction and belief burn through almost every reply. So does a genuine abhorrence of public education. Twelve per cent of the group felt schools to be wanting in every respect named. Twenty-four per cent served up an indictment on twenty or more of the twenty-three questions. On the other hand, only 24 per cent were willing to clear the schools on as many as *half* the charges named.

What features of public education are the most popular objects of complaint among these critics? Here are the targets of respondents' objections, in descending order of the frequency with which they were named:

Curriculum (received the most criticism)
Costs
Aims and values
Methods
Professional organizations
Administration
Teacher education
Textbooks
Teachers
Religion (the fewest indictments)

Virtually all complained about the curriculum. Running a close second was the specific charge that money is being spent on the wrong things. One critic sums it up with the claim, "There is [*sic*] adequate funds for essentials. Too much trimmings use up funds." An impressive number were willing to push the cause of economy much further: 42 per cent stated flatly that we spend too much money on public schools. Teachers themselves, however, despite their central function in the institution which critics are ready to denounce wholesale, afforded a surprisingly unattractive target for complaint. As for religion, more respondents found "godlessness" than found "sectarianism." Inexplicably, twenty-one critics see them both prevailing simultaneously.

With the possible exceptions of school spending and religion, the questions composing the questionnaire can be divided into two general themes. One set elicits the general charge that the schools are in some manner subversive; the second, that they are anti-intellectual in purpose or effect, or both. In the statements of almost any given critic, one or the other of these themes is clearly dominant.

There has been a tendency to draw a sharp distinction between the two types of criticism and between the critics voicing them. Many people envision one kind of critic as the extreme, perhaps misguided, patriot who finds conspiracy lurking everywhere, and the other kind as a man of great learning—an erudite, if slightly fusty, professor. Some have even drawn chronological distinctions, believing that the patriotic critic carried the day from about 1945 to 1953 and that the professor has done so ever since.

But perhaps the case for the "two types" is weaker than would appear on first glance. Because of the "buckshot" character of the extreme patriot's criticism, it is not startling to find claims of anti-intellectualism scattered among his charges of subversion. (According to some critics schools are simultaneously guilty of successfully inculcating un-Americanism and of failing to do *anything* successfully.) But we hardly expect the reverse to be true. The professor is not usually thought an exponent of the "conspiracy" brand of educational criticism. Yet replies to our questionnaire do not bear out this widely held assumption. Overwhelmingly, the respondents who charge anti-intellectualism also suspect subversion. There is only one exception: the Council for Basic Education, which speaks for those critics who find schools anti-intellectual. But even the council's leadership does not completely exclude subversion from its criticisms. Professor Arthur Bestor, its well-known first president, believes that schools have adopted aims inconsistent with the American tradition. And two groups welcomed and lauded by the Council[3]—Michigan's Association for Rural Education and the Committee for Home Rule in Vermont—believe that teacher organizations are conspiring to control society. One of these also finds subversion in textbooks, and educational aims that undermine our national tradition.

Certain other conclusions can be drawn from the survey. Because the questionnaire was so clearly "loaded," inviting the most general denunciation of the schools, we might have expected considerable hesitation on the part of anyone to reply at all. This should certainly have been the case with the twelve scholars, professors, and school superintendents who responded. Even more curious are the replies of those who, perhaps afflicted by a "protest syndrome," were so willing to denounce, but left a blank in preference to exonerating the schools on even a single charge. In Exhibit I, pages 12-17 the ratio of "guilty" to "innocent" is thus approximately twelve to one. Indeed, 28 respondents served up 114 indictments without showing they had made the slightest investigation of the issues.

* * *

The charts which follow show the replies of the various organizations and individuals responding to our questionnaire. A "yes" answer to a question—constituting an indictment or a vote of "guilty"—is represented on the charts by a plus (+) sign. A "no," or "not guilty," answer is represented by a minus (—) sign. An encircled reply indicates that the respondent gave no evidence of having looked into the matter at issue. Numbers on the charts refer to qualifications added by respondents, and to sidelights on the reply. These comments, which appear on the pages immediately following each exhibit, reveal a great deal about the critics.

Exhibit I consists of the replies of organizations. When possible, the name and title of the responding official are also listed.

Exhibit II contains the replies of individuals. A brief identification of each appears on pages 223-225.

A copy of the original questionnaire appears on page 222. Note that the last four questions (items 20–23 on Exhibits I and II) pertain to the professional organizations of teachers and administrators.

CRITICS AND CHARGES

EXHIBIT I: ORGANIZATIONS

Is the situation in public schools generally UNDESIRABLE with respect to . . .	1. Subversive textbooks	2. Other unsuitable text material	3. Teacher loyalty, patriotism	4. Un-American, anti-Christian content	5. Life adjustment, nonessentials	6. Impractical, soft curricula	7. Teachers' beliefs	8. Teachers' activities	9. "Progressive" education methods	10. Aims contravening American tradition	11. Other improper educational aims	12. Godlessness in schools	13. Sectarianism in schools	14. Preparation given teachers	15. Subject emphasis in teacher education	16. Too much money spent on schools	17. Money spent on the wrong things	18. Unsound administrative practices	19. Administrative aimlessness	20. Indifference to sound education	21. Indifference to American tradition	22. Desire to control society	23. Domination by anti-intellectuals
American Coalition of Patriotic Societies Milton M. Lory, Pres.[1]	+	+	+	+	+	+	+	+	+	+	+	+	+	+	+	+	+	+	+	+	+	+	+
American Council of Christian Laymen, Verne P. Kaub, Pres.	+	+	+	+	+	+	⊕	⊖	+	+	+	+	+	+	+	+	+	+	+	+	+	+	[2]
American Economic Foundation R.[3]	+								+					+									
American Education Association Mrs. Cathryn L. K. Dorney, Dir.	+	+	+	+	+	+	+[4]	+[4]	+	+	+	+	+	+	+		+	+	—				

American Viewpoint, Inc.[5]	—	2	⊖	2	2	2	2	2	2	2	2	2	2	2	2	2	2	2	2	2	2	—	2
Americanism Education League		+	—	⊖	⊕	⊕		+[4]	+			+		2				+			+		
Anti-Communist League of America John K. Crippen, Exec. Sec.	+	+	—	+		+			+	+	+			+	+		⊕	+	—		+	+	
Arkansas State Chamber of Commerce[6]				—	+	+								+	+	—	+	+					
Association of Citizens' Councils of Mississippi Robert B. Patterson, Sec.	+	+	+	+	+	+	+	+	⊕	+	+	+	+	⊕	⊕	+	+	+	+	+	+	+	+
Association for Rural Education Mrs. Howard Hewson, Ass't. Editor	+	+			+	+			+	+	+			+	+	—	+	+	—	+	+	+	—
Beverly Hills Freedom Club Dorothy M. Seeger, Sec.	+		+[7]	+[7]	+[7]	+[7]			+[7]		+[7]	+[7]		+[7]	+[7]		+[7]			+[7]			
California Anti-Communist League Wesley Swift, State Dir.	+	+	+	+	+			+	+	+		⊕	⊖				+	+		—	+	+	—
California League of Christian Parents, Walter Blount[8]	+	+	+	+	+	+	+	+	+	+	+	+	+	+	+	+	+	+	+	+	+	+	+
Christian Nationalist Crusade Gerald L. K. Smith, Dir.	+	+	+	+		+	+	+	+	+		+	—		+	—	+	+		+	+	+	—
Christian Party, The J. B. Stoner, Archleader	+	+	+	+			+			+	+	+				+	+						
Citizens for Better Education Mrs. E. Whitley	+	+	—	+	+	+	+	+	+	+	+	⊕	⊕		+	⊖	⊕	+	2	+	+	+	2
Colorado School Protective Association, Robert Donner[9]	+	+	+	+	+	+	+	+	+	+	+	⊕	⊖	+	+	+	+	+	+	+	+	+	+
Committee for Home Rule in Vermont, Herbert G. Ogden					+	+			+		+						+	+		+		+	

All notes begin on p. 20.

EXHIBIT I: ORGANIZATIONS

Is the situation in public schools generally UNDESIRABLE with respect to . . .	1. Subversive textbooks	2. Other unsuitable text material	3. Teacher loyalty, patriotism	4. Un-American, anti-Christian content	5. Life adjustment, nonessentials	6. Impractical, soft curricula	7. Teachers' beliefs	8. Teachers' activities	9. "Progressive" education methods	10. Aims contravening American tradition	11. Other improper educational aims	12. Godlessness in schools	13. Sectarianism in schools	14. Preparation given teachers	15. Subject emphasis in teacher education	16. Too much money spent on schools	17. Money spent on the wrong things	18. Unsound administrative practices	19. Administrative aimlessness	20. Indifference to sound education	21. Indifference to American tradition	22. Desire to control society	23. Domination by anti-intellectuals
Constitution Clubs of Illinois, Inc., E. S. Powell	+	+	+	+	+	+	+	+	+	+	+	+		+			+	+					
Constitution Party of California John E. Castle[10]	–	+	⊕[11]	[2]	+	+	⊖	⊖	+	⊕	⊕	⊕	⊖	+	+	+	+	+	+	+	+	+	[2]
Constitution Party of Indiana A. G. Blazey, State Chm.	+	+	–	+	+	+	+	+	+	+	+	+	+	+	+	+	+	+	–	+	+	+	–
Constitution Party of Virginia B. M. Miller, State Chm.	+	+	+[4]	+	+	+	+	+	+	+	+	+		+	+	+	+	+	+	+	+	+	+
Council for Basic Education James E. Koerner, Exec. Sec.					+	+			+		+			+	+			+	+	+			+

Defenders of American Education Mrs. J. J. McLaughlin, Chm.	+	+		+	+	+	2	2	+	+	+			+	+	+	+	+	−	+	+	+	
Defenders of the American Constitution, J. P. Horton[12]	+	+	+	+	+	+	+	+	+	+	+	+	+	+	+	+	+	+	+	+	+	+	+
Defenders of State Sovereignty and Individual Liberties	⊕	⊕		+	+	+			+	+	+			+	+					+	+	+	+
Facts in Education[13] Mrs. Frances P. Bartlett, Editor	+	+	+	+	+	+	+	+	+	+	+	+	+	+	+	+	+	+	+	+	+	+	+
Fairfax Citizens Council Mollie Ray Carroll[14]	+	+	+	+	+	+			+	+	+	⊕	⊖	+	+	+	+	+		+	+	+	+
Fifty Million Americans Edward Whiteside, Chm.	+		⊕			+			+[7]	+	+					+	+	+					
Friends of the Minnesota Schools Association Mrs. Paul Schouweiler					+	+			+		+			+	+	⊕	⊕	+		+		+	
Friends of the Public Schools of America, Inc. Wilbur Helm, Pres.	+	+		+	+	+	+	+	+	+	+	+	+	+	+	−	+	+	+	+	+	+	+
Institute of American Citizenship[15]	⊖	⊖	⊖	−		+	⊖	⊖	+	−	+	⊖	⊕[2]	−	+		⊕	⊖	⊕	⊕	⊖	⊖	⊕
Iowa School Organization Riley Clark, Pres.	⊕	⊕	⊖	+	+	+	⊖	⊕	+	+	+	⊖	⊖	⊕	⊕	+	+	+	+	+	+	+	+
Keep America Committee	+	+	+	+	+	+	+	+	+	+	+	+	+	+	+	+	+	+	+	+	+	+	+
Liberty Lobby, Willis A. Carto	+	+	+	+	+	+	+	+	+	+	+	+	+	+	+	+	+	+	+	+	+	+	+
Michigan Coalition of Constitutionalists Mrs. Mary Streit	+	+	⊕	+	+				⊕	+		+				+	+			⊕	⊕	⊕	
National Information Service L. L. Muncy	+	+	+	+	−	+	+	+	+	+	−	+	+	+	+	+	+	+	+	+	+	+	+

All notes begin on p. 20.

Exhibit I: ORGANIZATIONS

Is the situation in public schools generally UNDESIRABLE with respect to . . .	1. Subversive textbooks	2. Other unsuitable text material	3. Teacher loyalty, patriotism	4. Un-American, anti-Christian content	5. Life adjustment, nonessentials	6. Impractical, soft curricula	7. Teachers' beliefs	8. Teachers' activities	9. "Progressive" education methods	10. Aims contravening American tradition	11. Other improper educational aims	12. Godlessness in schools	13. Sectarianism in schools	14. Preparation given teachers	15. Subject emphasis in teacher education	16. Too much money spent on schools	17. Money spent on the wrong things	18. Unsound administrative practices	19. Administrative aimlessness	20. Indifference to sound education	21. Indifference to American tradition	22. Desire to control society	23. Domination by anti-intellectuals
National Sojourners, Inc. Capt. John E. Wright[16]	2		+	+	+	+	2	+[4]	+	+[4]	+[4]	+[4]	—	+	+	2	+	+[4]	+[4]	+[4]	+	+	+[4]
Ohio Coalition of Patriotic Societies, Col. William E. Warner, Chm.	+		+	+		+		+	+	+	+	+		+		+	+	+			+	+	
Organization to Repeal Federal Income Taxes, Inc. D. B. Lewis, Pres.[17]	+	+		+					+	+				+			+	+	+	+	+	+	
Patriotic Research Bureau Elizabeth Dilling	+	+	+	+			+	+	⊕	+	+	+					⊕	⊕	⊖		+	+	2

1789 Club, The, Mrs. Virginia Hedrick, Exec. Sec.	+	+			+	+			+	+	+			+	+		+	+		+	+	+	
Tacoma Study Club[18] Mrs. Virginia Shackleford, Pres.					+				+		+		+	+	+		+	+				+	
United States Chamber of Commerce, John R. Miles, Mgr., Education Dept.					+	+				+	+					−	+						
We, The People![19] Harry T. Everingham, Exec. Dir.	+	+	⊕	+	+	+	+[2]	+[2]	+	+	+	⊕	⊕	+	+	−	+	+	[2]	[2]	+	+	[2]
Wisconsin School Association, The, Lyle Emmerton, Dir.	+	+			+	+				+	+	+			+		+					+	
World Union of Free Enterprise National Socialists Lincoln Rockwell, Comm.				⊕									+[20]										+[21]
Anonymous[22]	+[4]	[2]	−[4]	+[4]	+[4]	+[4]	+[4]	−[4]	+[4]	+[4]	+[4]	[2]	−[4]	[2]	[2]	+[4]	+[4]	+[4]	+[4]	+[4]	+[4]	−[4]	[2]

All notes begin on p. 20.

EXHIBIT II: INDIVIDUALS

Is the situation in public schools generally UNDESIRABLE with respect to . . .	1. Subversive textbooks	2. Other unsuitable text material	3. Teacher loyalty, patriotism	4. Un-American, anti-Christian content	5. Life adjustment, nonessentials	6. Impractical, soft curricula	7. Teachers' beliefs	8. Teachers' activities	9. "Progressive" education methods	10. Aims contravening American tradition	11. Other improper educational aims	12. Godlessness in schools	13. Sectarianism in schools	14. Preparation given teachers	15. Subject emphasis in teacher education	16. Too much money spent on schools	17. Money spent on the wrong things	18. Unsound administrative practices	19. Administrative aimlessness	20. Indifference to sound education	21. Indifference to American tradition	22. Desire to control society	23. Domination by anti-intellectuals
Haskell, Mrs. Katherine for Marilyn R. Allen[23]	+	+	+	+	+	+	+	+	+	+	+	+	+	+	+	+	+	+	+	+	+	+	+
Benson, George	[24]	+			+	+			+														
Bestor, Arthur	⊖	⊕	⊖	⊖	⊕	⊕				⊕	⊕	⊖	⊖	⊕	⊕	⊖	⊕	⊕	⊕	⊕		⊖	⊕
Buckley, W. F., Jr.		+		+	+	+			+	+	+	+	+	+	+		+	+	+	+	+	+	
Chodorov, Frank					+	+			+				+		+			+	+	+	+	+	+
Cleveland, L. Victor	+[4]	+[4]	+[4]	⊕[4]	⊕[4]		⊕[4]	[2]	+[4]	+[4]	+[4]	+[4]	[2]				⊕[4]				+[4]	+[4]	
De Forest, Lee	⊕	⊕	⊕	⊕	⊕	⊕	⊕	⊕	⊕	+	+	⊕	+	⊕		⊖	⊖	—	—	⊖	⊖	⊖	⊖
del Valle, Lt. Gen. P. A.	+	+	+	+	+	+	+	+	+	+	+	+	+	+	+	+	+	+	+	+	+	+	+

Dodge, Homer	⊕	⊕	⊕	⊕	⊕	⊕	⊕	⊕	⊕	⊕	⊕			⊕	⊕		⊕	⊕		⊕	⊕	⊕	
Evans, Medford	+	+		+		+	+		+	+	+			+	+	+	+	+	+	+	+	+	+
Gordon, Rosalie		+		+	+	+			+	+	+			+	+		+	+	+	+	+	+	
Haake, Alfred P.	+	+	⊕[2]			+	+	+	2	+		+		+	+	+	+	+			+	+	
Hall, Wallace	+[4]	+	−[2]	+	+	+	−		+	+	+	+	−	+	+		+	+	+	+	+	+	+[25]
Haney, Lewis	+	+			+	+			+	+	+												
Hoiles, R. C.	+	+		+	+	+			+	+	+	+		+	+		+	+	+	+	+	+	+
Hoyt, J. Curtis	2	+			+	+			+		+	−	−	+	+	+	+	+	−				
Speroni, P., for John G. Keenan	−				+	+			+					+	+		+		+	+			
Kendall, Willmoore	+	+	+	+	+	+	+	+	+	+	+	+	+	+	+	−	+	+	−	+	+	+	+
King, Willford I.	⊖[26]	⊖	⊖	⊖	⊕	⊕	⊕	⊖	⊕	2	⊕		⊖	⊕	⊕	⊕	⊕	⊕	⊖	⊕	2	⊖	⊕[27]
Kirk, Russell	+			+	+	+	+		+	+	+	+	−	+	+	+	+	+	+	+	+	+	+
Lee, J. Bracken	+	+	2	+	+	+	2	+	+	+	+			+	+		+	+	+	+	+	+	+
Le Fevre, Robert T.	+	+		+	+	+			+	+	+	+	−	+	+	+	+	+	−	+	+	+	
MacLean, Donald	+	+			+	+			+	+	+			+	+	−	+	+	−	+		+	
Manning, Walton	−	−	−	−	+[4]	+[4]	−	−	2	+[2]	+	−	−	+	+	−	+	+	+	+	+	+	+
McGinley, Conde	+	+	+	+				+	+	+		+					⊕	+			+	+	
Morley, Felix	−	+	⊖	+	+	+			+	+	+	+	−	+	+	−	+	+	+	+	+	−	+
Pavey, Charles W.	+	+	+	+	+	+	+	+	+	+	+	+	2	+	+	+	+	+	+	+	+	+	2
Pomeroy, Col. E. C.	+	+	+	+	+	+	+	+	⊕	+	+	+			+	⊕	⊕	+		+	+	+	+
Regentin, Edward	+	+	+	+	+	+	⊕	⊕	+	+	+	⊕	⊕	+	+	+	+	+	+	+	+	+	+
Rudd, Col. Augustin G.	+	+	⊕	+	+	+	+	−	+	+	+	⊕	⊖	+	+	+	−	+	−	+	+	+	+
Tucker, Mrs. Cornelia	−	−	⊖	−	+	+	⊖	⊖	+	⊖	⊕	⊖	⊖	⊕	⊕	⊕	⊕	⊕	⊕	⊕	⊖	⊖	⊖
Van Der Hoeven, E.	−	+	⊕	+	+	+	+	+	+	+	+	⊕		+	+	−	+	+	+	+	+	+	+
Wallin, Adm. Homer N.	+	+	+	+	+	+	+	+	+	+	+	+	+	+	+	−	+	+		+	+	+	
Williams, John R.	+[4]	−	+[4]	−	+	−	+	−	−					+	+	−	+			−	+	+	−
Zube, Mrs. Arnold	+		+	+	+		+			+	+					+	+	+		+	+	+	

All notes begin on p. 20.

TABLE NOTES

[1] Mr. Lory's reply to the questionnaire is stated in an accompanying letter where he indicates that his organization's answer is "yes" to every question.
[2] The respondent indicates that he is unsure how to reply.
[3] The initial, which was entered on the questionnaire, suggests that the reply was written by Morgan S. A. Reichner, Executive Director of the American Economic Foundation.
[4] The respondent qualifies his reply to apply to *some* cases only.
[5] The respondent indicates that there is positive evidence on most counts, but refuses to make any indictments applying so broadly.
[6] There is no indication of who submitted this reply. The questionnaire returned by the Arkansas State Chamber of Commerce had been addressed to the Arkansas Public Expenditure Council. It was returned with that organization's name deleted and replaced by "Arkansas State Chamber of Commerce." No explanation was added.
[7] This reply is inferred from material enclosed by respondent.
[8] Questionnaires were addressed to "Mr. Walter Blount, c/o Christian Parents for Better Education," and to "Mrs. Alice Blount, President, California League of Christian Parents." Both Mr. Blount and Mrs. Blount (presumably his wife) replied. Mr. Blount indicated that the two names denote a single organization. Interestingly, the replies differed. Mr. Blount's was selected, since it was fuller.
[9] Mr. Donner's position in the organization, though not revealed on his reply, is that of founder.
[10] Mr. Castle's title is difficult to determine from his correction of our letter addressed to "Col. William P. Gale, State Chairman." Either Mr. Castle is State Chairman and Colonel Gale is his assistant, or vice versa.
[11] To judge from the respondent's deletions, response applies only to a lack of patriotism and not to the question of teacher loyalty.
[12] Our inquiry was addressed to Mr. Horton, but a note appended to the reply is signed "Eugene C. Pomeroy." It is not clear whether Colonel Pomeroy was answering for Mr. Horton or in his own official capacity.
[13] We addressed this inquiry to Mrs. Bartlett as editor for Pasadena's famous "School Development Council." Her letter suggests, however, that the council is no longer active and that *Facts in Education* is an independent publication.
[14] Miss Carroll's title is not known. She writes that she replied to the questionnaire at the request of Manning Gasch, President, to whom it was addressed.
[15] Evidently this institute is defunct. However, our questionnaire was completed and returned with the following unsigned note: "This Institute 'died' a quiet death some years ago. I am familiar with two groups 'offshoots' in some respects. So here is an 'idea' of its *[sic]* response."
[16] Captain Wright's reply suggests that he is the ex-chairman of this organization's National Americanism Commission.

[17] Apparently Mr. Lewis authorized this reply, but it is not certain that he wrote it. According to a note jotted on the questionnaire, it may have been completed by Dr. Alleson.

[18] The questionnaire returned by this organization was originally addressed to "Mr. Frank W. Clark, Back to the Republic." Mrs. Shackelford does not indicate why she came to receive the inquiry, other than noting that her organization has been active in the field of education.

[19] Mr. Everingham's revisions penned on the questionnaire serve to limit his "yes" replies to cover "many cases," rather than "the general situation," and to raise the question of whether he is stating the official We, The People! position.

[20] This response applies to a revised, or new, question inserted by Mr. Rockwell. It constitutes an indictment of schools on the grounds that they submit to Jewish pressure.

[21] Mr. Rockwell's revision of this question implies that educational organizations are dominated by Jewish elements.

[22] The individual returning this reply specified that his responses were to be identified neither by name nor by organization.

[23] Actually, it is not clear whether Mrs. Haskell was replying for Miss Allen, or in her own right. Mrs. Haskell notes only that Miss Allen—to whom our inquiry was addressed—requested that she complete and return the questionnaire.

[24] Dr. Benson checks neither reply but notes that textbooks are "deluded and misled." He further suggests that his objections are largely directed at teaching materials rather than at teachers.

[25] Mr. Hall has revised the original question so that this indictment of educational organizations is on the grounds of their *political* domination.

[26] Mr. King notes that his investigations of all issues have been "indirect."

[27] Mr. King has revised the original question so that this indictment of educational organizations is on the grounds that they are "misled."

WHO IS A CRITIC?

2. In Search of a Definition

American schools belong to the American people, and the citizen has the right, even the obligation, to try to correct evils in public institutions. Furthermore, because it might prove helpful, any public employee should listen to criticism. Virtually without exception, today's educators feel that some of the criticisms of public schools are sound and valid complaints. But there is also the feeling that some of the criticism is unjust and has little basis in fact—and that the people who level this type of charge are being unfair and, apparently in some instances, knowingly dishonest.

It is important to know how to recognize in advance the opprobrious critic and the unjust attack. To be able to do so, we need definitions of "unjust attack" and "opprobrious" or "illegitimate" critic. Constructing such definitions is no simple task. To see why, let us examine some of the many definitions now used.

Most current definitions of "critic of the schools," or "destructive critic," offer little help in separating the sheep from the goats. According to one that is widely quoted, the "Subversive or Dishonest" group of critics "attracts emotionally unstable people," "uses smear literature," and "accepts rabble-rousing techniques."[1] Not one of these statements would aid us in determining whether a newly formed "Parents Council" is a "Subversive or Dishonest Group." We are unwilling to call its membership "emotionally unstable," its publications "smear literature," and its methods "rabble-rousing" until *after* we have decided that the organization is up to no good. In short, the definition offers no help in determining whether a new voice comes from friend or foe. Just as it is impractical to define TNT in such a way that it can be recognized only *after* the explosion, it is unwise to define "foe" in such a way that he is recognizable only after a full-scale battle is under way.

Most formulations distinguishing the respectable from the disreputable critic link specific practices and procedures with one type or the other. But some of the particular practices listed seem questionable. There is, for example, an unfortunate association of the "undesirable" critic with all the effective techniques of influencing public opinion—apparently denying effective measures to the respectable critic! The undesirable critic is often associated with the use of the sensational, the emotional, the general, and a reliance on the press.

Supposedly another indication of the "bad" critic is that he deals in personalities, that he is guilty of the *ad hominem* argument. Such is often the case, but how can we distinguish between the illegitimate critic who attacks the personality of his victim and the legitimate critic who is also concerned with personalities, and justifiably so? After all, character and personal behavior are often important considerations. If a school superintendent is a thief or if a teacher is a prostitute, then attacks on their character may very well be relevant.

Some definitions focus upon the critic's motives: "Criticism is constructive to the extent that it is motivated by a desire to improve the existing situation." The obvious trouble with this approach is that motives are complex, intangible, mysterious things. Sometimes the critic himself doesn't know why he does what he does. Furthermore, the critic's intentions may be irrelevant to the real problem: what effects he may produce. It is not his intentions which cause the difficulties, but his results. Whether a critic is sincere in wanting to improve schools, or whether his interests lie exclusively in his own fortunes, is, after all, not the schoolman's problem. Conversely, it gets us nowhere to label "sincere" or "honest" the bumbling citizen whose misguided efforts produce disaster—however pure his motives may be.

These are some major difficulties in the current ways of identifying the undesirable critics who concern us. There are other problems, too, in constructing a definition. One of the pitfalls is to judge sinister those who would do away with what one approves, or uphold what one abhors. The problem here is that this is precisely what the schools argument is about! We have few, if any, universal agreements on educational aims or values. We can hardly then judge hostile to public education anyone who simply has values differing from our own. To do so would commit us unqualifiedly to hundreds of definitions of the "hostile critic." Certainly even educators would not be able to agree among themselves. There could be only the chaos defiantly defended by Humpty Dumpty: "When *I* use a word, it means just what I choose it to mean—neither more nor less." The point of course is that we need a definition of the illegitimate critic acceptable to two people who do not agree as to the proper ends of education.

Suppose we avoid the battle over educational values. Are there, then, values outside education that can legitimately be used? In other words, what are the values most of us accept as legitimate in judging others and their actions?

First, in all practical affairs we reject a declaration of fact unless it is arrived at according to certain rules of evidence. If an individual knowingly violates these rules, we condemn him for it. *Second,* in both private and public affairs we condemn an individual for an unalterable determination to carry out his will irrespective of the judgments and wishes of others. In personal relationships such an individual is said to violate the integrity of the personality of others; in public affairs he is said to violate the rules and requirements of democracy. *Third,* we also condemn an individual who violates procedures that define common decency and civility in our society—our rules for dealing with one another.

We accept these rules of evidence, of democratic procedure, of decency and civility, in theory as well as in practice. We follow them and believe we *should* follow them. We accept them as guides in virtually all our experience, from informal relationships with friends to formal dealings with strangers and even institutions. Even more, we seek to instill them in children. And if we violate them as adults, most of us do so with the feeling that we have done the wrong thing. Since we accept these three sets of rules for *other* purposes, they should be at least potentially acceptable as a basis for judging educational critics and their charges.

Criticisms of education can be divided into two types: charges primarily involving facts, and charges primarily involving values. The rules of evidence are immediately applicable to the first type—to examining the merit of claims or charges involving facts. We have accepted ways of determining the truth or falsity of factual claims. We have rules for gathering and interpreting information. When an individual arrives by *other* methods at what he claims to be true, we tend to view him as ignorant, dishonest, or a bit odd. There is sufficient agreement in our society to deem indefensible the position of one who ignores these rules in arriving at his charges against education. Six rules of evidence are particularly relevant to judging criticisms brought against schools.

First are the rules of generalization. No matter how tempting it may be to act otherwise, we know that one can tell little about all the schools in Toledo, for instance, after observing just one or two. On this basis a visitor might conclude that "all pupils are below thirteen years of age" and that "no schools teach geometry." The observer has obviously seen only one type of school—an elementary school—and assumed it to be typical of all schools. Should he visit a number of the city's elementary schools, he might be in a position to make a general statement to the effect that "Toledo elementary schools do not teach geometry"; but no amount of observation in Toledo alone will equip him to make the broader claim that "today's schools do not teach geometry." To do so would be gravely to overstep his evidence.

If these errors seem obvious, they are no more so than some of those actually committed in various charges against education. Rudolf Flesch, the author of *Why Johnny Can't Read—and What You Can Do About It,* taught one child reading for six months, and observed another child to be similar to his pupil. He then concluded that his method was "the only natural system of learning how to read" and that "the teaching of reading—all over the United States, in all the schools, in all the textbooks—is totally wrong and flies in the face of all logic and common sense."[2]* It would appear that Mr. Flesch is

* To be fair, Mr. Flesch does allude broadly to some additional evidence: "I have worked my way through a mountain of books and articles on the subject, I talked to dozens of people, and I spent many hours in classrooms, watching what was going on."[3] Since he does not reveal which mountain of books and articles, what people, which classrooms, we cannot be expected to judge his case on the bases of these. His "mountains," like his conclusions, could be somewhat overstated!

guilty of the grossest overgeneralization possible. His sweeping, all-inclusive "truths" have been divined from a *single* case. He has arrived at his conclusions on the basis of "anecdotal" evidence—the kind in use in the announcement, "Operations are fatal because Betty Smith, down the street, died from hers."

A second rule of evidence requires that we accept demonstrable fact. Facts seem to exist independent of our personal like or dislike for them. One cannot deny their existence merely because he simply would prefer things to be otherwise. The ridiculous position of the person refusing to admit what is obviously the case reminds us of an old line of Wallace Beery's in which he indignantly accused a companion, "You'd believe yer damned old eyes before you'd believe me."

Yet some of the charges against education put their advocates in just about the same position. Recently, no less a scholar than an emeritus professor, former dean of liberal arts, and the ex-president of the American Chemical Society refused not only to admit what is demonstrably true today but also stated in effect that he would not accept the claim, regardless even of *future* evidence in its favor! After having ridiculed the organization of subject matter into teaching units, this scientist was apprised of a considerable amount of evidence indicating that the unit method of teaching produces results superior to those of other methods. The professor replied that he would continue to criticize this means of presenting material, ". . . even though the unit organization is shown to be superior by 225 studies."[4]

A third and closely related rule of evidence requires the recognition and tentative acceptance of what is less certain but is nevertheless indicated by the weight of present evidence—that is, what we now know. We cannot suspend action until all the evidence is in. Several generations may need to learn arithmetic before we arrive at the "best" way of teaching it. Meanwhile, the only sensible course is to act in accord with what present evidence suggests.

One of the problems of research in the social sciences is that the educational research specialist's predictions are less certain than those of the natural scientist. He is wrong more often. But the critic who wants to dismiss all educational research on these grounds offers us no sensible alternative. Those educational critics who demand that the present—or even an earlier—*status quo* be maintained in the absence of absolute, incontrovertible proof are demanding impossible guarantees. To make such a demand violates the rule of evidence requiring tentative acceptance of what research now tells us.

A fourth rule of evidence requires only that a man be honest. He must not distort the evidence. We do not arrive at facts by setting out to show that white youngsters are brighter than Negroes, and by concealing any inconvenient evidence to the contrary. Investigators can do this by commission or omission: by falsifying or lowering test scores for Negro youngsters, or by deliberately omitting bright Negroes from the testing program. Deliberate errors of commission seem to be one of the most popular means, among school critics, of distorting evidence. In one case, a junior high school principal's statement that his school had ten remedial reading groups serving 100 pupils somehow became his confession that he had "100 children who could neither read nor write."[5] Of course, since many facts of education are expressed in statistics, there may be misunderstanding and honest error. But in other instances a plea of ignorance hardly constitutes a valid excuse. Such would appear to be the case with the critic who reported that the Los Angeles County high schools offer a course on how to be well groomed, when no such course has ever existed.[6] Other instances include the "researcher" who quotes a statement and by blatant deletions utterly reverses the author's intent.

Many of the critics who denounce public schools as "godless" are violating a fifth rule of evidence; namely, the rules of logical inference. W. S. Fleming, the author of *God in Our Public Schools,* is one among many who claim that the comparatively low crime rate in certain states is a direct result of the daily Bible reading in the classrooms of these states. Of course, even though the Bible is widely read in prisons, it still may be that Mr. Fleming has drawn a correct relationship. But he has seriously violated the rules of inference in failing to examine and eliminate other possible explanations of crime in these states. For instance, the fact that the states in question are primarily rural might be the reason for their low crime rate. Bible reading may be completely irrelevant to the incidence of crime.

The same sort of thing is evident in a pronouncement by Professor Arthur Bestor of the University of Illinois. Giving short shrift to factors experts have found crucial, Professor Bestor offered an interviewer this bit of reasoning:

We have wasted an appalling part of the time of our young people on trivialities. The Russians had sense enough not to do so. That's why the first satellite bears the label "Made in Russia."[7]

The sixth rule of evidence determines what can legitimately be considered as evidence at all. It is sometimes difficult to discover what offers support to a claim. But it is not difficult to isolate those means of persuasion which rarely if ever constitute evidence. Emotion and humor are two.

Many who talk about education and the schools appeal to our sentiments toward children. Though this is a time-honored device of orators, certainly it is by itself an untrustworthy means of supporting a factual conclusion. When a rousing speaker floods us with compassion for a child's helplessness, and reminds us of our great hopes for him, this scarcely proves that his teacher is a Socialist.

Attempts to substantiate claims of fact by appeals to emotion have been rampant. Other critics tend instead to support their claims through humor or ridicule. We are not suggesting that the telling jibe, the biting innuendo, and the general ability to make one's opponent appear ridiculous are not "cricket." Rules of evidence have nothing to do with Marquis of Queensberry rules for sportsmanship. But the efficiency of naked persuasion is quite another matter from ours. Humor alone, like emotional appeal, has nothing to do with evidence.

In general, there are two ways to support a claim of fact. The first and preferable way is by empirical evidence. But when this is not available, an "appeal to authority" can be made. Of course, it is hardly legitimate to cite an authority when there is on hand a body of information that amounts to empirical evidence. A number of sailors and geographers might once have been quoted to support a claim that the world was flat. But once Magellan's men returned from their global trip, the argument became ridiculous. Similarly, it is idle to claim on Dr. Arthur Bestor's authority that today's children are not so well educated as those of fifty years ago, when extensive evidence to the contrary is available.

When a claim *can* legitimately be supported by an appeal to authority, a far more complicated question is raised: Who is an authority? Obviously, an authority on one subject may know next to nothing about another. Admiral Rickover, for example, is undoubtedly an authority on reactors and the harnessing of atomic energy, but it is difficult to see why this qualifies him as an expert in education. It is the intrusion of such men into the educational controversy that has complicated the question of authority. For although no sane citizen would seek medical advice from a man simply because he happens to be an excellent lawyer, a portion of our citizenry seems more than willing to listen to Rickover's pedagogical advice simply because he knows a great deal about atomic submarines.

Of course, one does not have to be an educator to determine if a man is educated. This is a favorite and legitimate posture assumed by many critics. (One version: "I'm not a hen, but I know when an egg is rotten.")[8] But though it does not take a mechanical engineer to judge when a car won't run, more exact diagnosis and the prescription of a cure are quite another matter.

Educators who maintain that it always takes a schoolman to judge the success or failure of schooling have talked themselves into a vulnerable corner. All who have gone to school know something about education—in roughly the same way that we naturally know something about health and medicine because we have bodies. And, of course, there *are* specialists in fields outside pedagogy who are in a unique position to make certain judgments on education. The college professor of English, for instance, knows whether the high school graduates in his classes are articulate and grammatical, and a scientist is equipped to evaluate evidence supporting the claims of schoolmen and their critics. But it is only the professional educator who is in a position to offer specific *diagnoses* and *prescriptions*.

So much for the six rules of evidence. They aid us in evaluating claims of fact—such charges as: "High school graduates can't read"; "The only way kids learn to spell is through constant drill"; "The author of that textbook is a member of the Communist party." But there are other kinds of criticisms to be examined. There are charges which are primarily matters of value, such as: "Schools ought to undertake nothing more than the teaching of reading, writing, and arithmetic"; "Education courses should be eliminated from our colleges"; "Controversial issues should not be discussed in the classroom." The difficulty is that there is no generally accepted body of values to govern the specific functions of our schools.

But though we lack widely accepted educational values, we have others that can be used in weighing the legitimacy of demands or protests. These values are procedural: they consist of our convictions on how public decisions should be made. Formally, policy decisions are made for schools by boards of education that are, in most communities, elected. Unofficially, the decisions are made by public opinion—or "the majority." If a community really wants its youngsters taught to swim, sooner or later swimming finds its way into the curriculum. Conversely, in those communities where public opinion comes to hold that the school's only legitimate purpose is teaching the standard academic subjects, courses such as music appreciation or dramatic arts are eventually weeded out.

Thus, since what is done in the schools roughly corresponds to what the majority thinks *ought* to be done, the critic of educational values represents a minority viewpoint. Now, our form of government is based on majority rule. The assumption is not that the majority is always right—or that truth is a matter of counting noses, as school critics have scornfully suggested.[9] It is assumed simply that over a period of time the "people" will make more wise decisions than would result from any other decision-making formula.

Along with its right to rule, the majority assumes certain obligations toward the minority: it must be allowed the means—free speech, petition, assembly—to attempt to muster a majority. But the minority, too, enjoys its rights and privileges only by assuming the concomitant obligation to uphold the form of government that permits its very existence; that is, it must *allow* the majority to rule.

Traditionally, those who have concerned themselves over democracy's fate have worried over the future of minority rights. Today, however, it may often be the majority that is threatened. Technology and other factors have made it possible for a very few to exert a degree of power that once could only be exerted by the numerically strong. As a result, a growing fear of minority domination has stimulated more and more government regulation of private interests. We deliberately set out to curb the strength of powerful groups. Political scientists writing on lobbies and pressure groups reflect our concern in the very titles they select: "The Unorganized Majority *vs.* the Organized Minority" and "Concentrated Private Interest *vs.* Diffused Public Interest."[10] And nowhere is the danger of powerful minorities shown more vividly than in investigations of lobbying interests.

The problem which pressure groups create for government is precisely the problem contemporary critics have created for schools: as minorities, both have frequently managed to frustrate democratic procedure by exerting power and influence far greater than their numbers entitle them to do. The educator has often joined with the public in assuming that the issue involves only the minority's right to be heard. But there is another question: that of who will run our schools, the majority or the minority. To raise this question is to recognize the critics for what they are: pressure groups. And at this point, a reminder is in order: the public, too, has rights. By definition, democracy ends the minority's privileges where they begin to impinge upon the well-being of the community. This is true whether the minority be a political organization, a religious sect, or a group criticizing schools.

A number of critics violate the first commandment of our form of government: that the majority decides. They are willing and eager to assume enormously greater power over decision than that to which they are entitled. They make considerable and tortuous efforts to suggest that they *have* a majority, or are well on the way to it. More importantly, they deny the principle of majority rule in seeking to impose their will on a public that rejects their judgments. A congressional committee found the ambition of the Conference of American Small Business Organizations to be "nothing less than the establishment of CASBO's philosophy as *the standard* of educational orthodoxy . . ."[11] Had the group been successful in the attempt to function as the national criterion of truth and value, the right of the public to make such decisions might well have become history.

Many organizations critical of education have sought in this fashion, not merely to influence public opinion, but virtually to mint it from their own molds. The practitioners of "government by intimidation," as Dr. James Conant has called it, have forged and presented as the sacred truth a narrowly orthodox interpretation of Americanism. All who resist it are charged with "un-Americanism" and "subversion"—even when conflicting interpretations have time and again been sanctioned by a majority of Americans. What are their methods?

For one, the careful cultivation of "ideological conflict and public confusion," through the use "of a charged public opinion as an instrument of pressure":

Men need slogans, catch-phrases, and generalizations to reduce their experience to understandable terms. But these slogans should not be a substitute for thought; when they are, men have lost the first part of their ability to govern themselves. Yet this is precisely what the pressure groups and their public relations experts are about . . . at the expense of the general welfare of all Americans [they] use terms like "socialism," "statism," and "welfare state" to forestall rational analysis of . . . [what] . . . they oppose. We are prepared to risk our national existence against totalitarianism, yet there are those among us who live by the totalitarian principle of the great distortion, endlessly repeated. Political freedom cannot live in an atmosphere of such hysterical oversimplification.[12]

Indeed, as subsequent chapters show, many critics of education give every evidence of wholehearted contempt for "political freedom." They do not try to hide it. The annual meetings of patriot coalitions probably attract more contemporary educational critics than are ever otherwise gathered under one roof. Observers at the meetings of one of the largest of these coalitions report the frequency of the claim, "You can't depend on majority vote to accomplish or settle anything." And, by way of explanation, "None of the great things which we cherish were accomplished by the majority."[13]

In addition to such outright declarations, there is other evidence of contempt for democratic procedure. Many critics are unwilling to assume the responsibilities of office, or to find someone who is. A willingness to stand for election to local school boards would imply a genuine desire to correct faults; the reluctance to do so suggests no more than delight in the pleasure of finding them. Or perhaps the critics distrust the methods of democracy as too sluggish for, or even hostile to, their purposes. The democratic system obligates the critical minority to bid for overt control, thereby rendering themselves accountable to the public. Should they nominate school board candidates who are repudiated in an election, democracy's procedures require that they *permit* majority rule even though its outcome is not to their liking. Instead, many enjoy the advantages of power without having to submit to the only process by which the public is willing to confer it.

Finally, democracy imposes on all groups seeking to influence public decision the obligation to disclose information to which the public is entitled: the group's purpose and program, the names of all its members, and the sources of its support. A number of the organizations most bitterly criticizing public education are clearly "front" groups with "real purposes, clientele, methods of operation . . . [and] . . . sources of financial support . . . different from those stated . . ."[14] We have often failed to insist that educational critics fully and accurately describe themselves—perhaps out of the charitable but disastrously mistaken belief that the educational critic stands to make no personal gain from his success. But most of these critics have a great many wholly tangible interests at stake. As for the rest, we should not underestimate the genuine appeal of purely ideological satisfaction.

There is, finally, another rather obvious set of criteria for judging critics—namely, the rules of common decency. Between individuals they may be well enough defined, but they are not so clear where impersonal relationships—that of an individual to an institution, for instance—are involved. Just as many who would never condone lying to one's friends have no scruples about misrepresenting their income to the Bureau of Internal Revenue, so we cannot automatically trust the critic to use rules of personal behavior in his dealings with the schools. But there are standards of "fair play" essential to the effective operation of every institution.

In local education circles, it should be axiomatic that complaints first be addressed to school officials. Of course, a public announcement of charges before they are known to those responsible will give a critic the advantage over his unsuspecting opponents. But, as the mayor of a town where this occurred observed, "unfortunately, this is not a game. The . . . education of children is at stake."[15] And the failure to take complaints first to the schoolman has injured schools where there was no disagreement on values and no evidence of corruption or incompetence. Despite conscientious efforts, evils can and do creep into any large-scale enterprise. But if he *is* making conscientious efforts, the schoolman can only assume, in the absence of severe criticism, that there is no intense dissatisfaction. His only other alternative is an extremely expensive one: constant canvassing of the entire community.

In an increasingly complex society, it is ever more vital to agree upon moral standards by which to govern impersonal relationships. We recognize as essential those rules of behavior whose violation threatens an obvious danger—the laws of the highway, for instance. Though the danger of a besieged school system may not be so dramatic, an established procedure for registering complaints against schools may be as important as an established procedure on the highway. Of course, should a critic approach an incompetent or nefarious school superintendent, he probably would obtain little satisfaction and be forced to turn elsewhere. But it is neither fair nor expedient to assume that school authorities are incompetent or nefarious until they have been given the opportunity to investigate alleged evils.

Collectively, these three sets of rules—rules of evidence, democracy, and common decency—constitute the definitions we have sought and should enable us to distinguish between legitimate and illegitimate critics, and between kinds of criticism. Throughout this book, any critic found to be violating these rules is considered an "illegitimate" critic.

THE FIRST WAVE

3. *Tenafly and Kitty Jones*

Attacks on school systems often follow a specific pattern. Many of those that occurred in the late forties and early fifties developed this way: A leader emerges as the initial critic. Then "peripheral" personnel appear—a parent with a private grievance decides to follow the leader. Next come demands made on the board of education, or grievance letters to the editor of the local newspapers. That done, parents' or citizens' groups may organize to "look into the schools situation." Literature appears, often unidentified, unsolicited, and highly critical of public education. By this time the original charges may have grown to include vague criticisms of "progressive" education, warnings of subversion in schools, and protests against specific educational methods.

Frequently, the leader of the attack finds his influence extended to other communities. A "professionalization" of the critic takes place as he is invited to meet and advise other disgruntled citizens. In this stage the critic may become affiliated with national organizations espousing his own points of view on schools.

This is how it happened in Tenafly, New Jersey. The attack on Tenafly schools that began in December, 1952, has been selected as fairly typical of those made between 1948 and 1954. It seemed to follow a two- or three-year rash of school attacks in northern New Jersey towns. The first was in Englewood. Others, receiving far less publicity, took place in East Orange, Summit, Montclair, Red Bank, Nutley, and Millburn. The towns are all located within an approximate radius of twenty miles of one another. All are primarily residential suburban communities with families of above-average incomes.

The first whisper of trouble in Tenafly came over an administrative code adopted by the local school board several years earlier. A feature of the code which proved objectionable to at least one Tenafly citizen was the authority given the superintendent of schools.[1] The protesting citizen was a Mrs. Kitty Jones.

Developments in the Tenafly story were described by a local school official. In a letter to the National Education Association's Defense Commission, he reported:

> . . . [The] attacks started sometime . . . [in] January [1953] by attacking . . . [the] Superintendent along philosophical lines, mainly . . . [on grounds of his] professional training at Teachers College, Columbia University. From there it went to the Board of Education, which she [Mrs. Jones] claimed was merely rubber stamping . . . [the superintendent's] recommendations and the policy of Teachers College.
>
> After several open letters to the Press and leaflets which appeared all over our town, the attack changed to the philosophy of John Dewey and progressive education as dominating the school administration and the teaching staff, and from here it continued along these lines with several publications pertaining to progressive education, a socialist curriculum, etc. . . .

Mrs. Jones was not previously unknown in Tenafly. She had worked with Frederick G. Cartwright, the man credited with launching the earlier attack on Englewood schools. After his efforts failed, Cartwright established the Englewood Anti-Communist League. Mrs. Jones apparently became an ardent supporter.[2]

Although rumblings of trouble in Tenafly did not become obvious until midwinter, the school attack had been some months in the making. According to a *Chicago Tribune* story, "it started as the concern of a parent over what she felt was harmful de-emphasis of the traditional methods and aims of elementary school education in America. . . ." According to the article, Mrs. Jones's misgivings over the school progress of her twin stepdaughters led her to "books, pamphlets and articles on modern theories of education particularly those emanating from Columbia University's Teachers College." Then Mrs. Jones began to focus on alleged socialistic or leftist influences in education.

In October, 1952, she registered for a Public Relations Workshop conducted by Columbia's Teachers College. After this workshop, Mrs. Jones turned out six publications, in as many months, on modern education and its many evils.

Perhaps significant is the fact that eight months before the start of this writing career, Mrs. Jones unsuccessfully sought membership on the Tenafly school board. After her defeat, she removed the twins from the public schools, enrolled them in a parochial school, and devoted her efforts to a series of pamphlets. Her husband, Theodore A. Jones, immeasurably aided her publishing career through the purchase of a Varitype machine.

In April, 1953, Mrs. Jones presented a twelve-page printed "Report" on the Public Relations Workshop to the two Home-School Associations that had sponsored her attendance.[3] The report not only contained a session-by-session résumé but also five personal conclusions, four of which dealt with Teachers College rather than with the workshop itself, and were critical of the institution. A month later a twenty-eight-page pamphlet, "What Do We Want for Our Children?"[4] appeared. In it, Mrs. Jones builds a powerful case against certain educational leaders—many of them associated with Columbia Teachers College—who she claims are plotting to subvert the United States. Her solution—sure to "strike a death blow to the undertakings of these men"—is at best anticlimactic: the whole problem is to be solved merely by offering history and geography as separate subjects! According to Mrs. Jones, this pamphlet was mailed to five hundred parents, and attempts were made to distribute it in the schools.

In September, Mrs. Jones printed a list of forty-seven "articles and books pointing to (1) the growing illiteracy of the products of our public schools, (2) the subversive infiltration of textbooks and curriculum development and (3) the efforts of the educational monopoly to silence the objectors."[5] The list was more than two feet long. It showed that Mrs. Jones was, by this time, well acquainted with the work of the Guardians of American Education, the American Education Association, the National Council for American Education, the *Educational Reviewer*, and the Church League of America—all groups highly critical of education. Her second September effort, also more than two feet long, became what is perhaps her best-known publication. Entitled "How 'Progressive' Is Your School?" this piece contrasts something called "up-to-date traditional education" with "education for socialism."[6]

Curriculum, promotion practices, grading policies, and homework all are examined. Mrs. Jones deals kindly with "up-to-date traditional education," but of course "education for socialism" is the whipping boy. She applies the latter label somewhat broadly to an assortment of practices many of which are openly followed in many public schools. In fact, a number of the practices she equates with progressive education, and calls "education for socialism," are followed in schools which certainly do not view themselves as "progressive."

Later in the month, Mrs. Jones temporarily abandoned her writing for more active protests. At the school board meeting she appeared with Frederick G. Cartwright and Frederick H. Grein (vice president of Cartwright's Englewood Anti-Communist League) in a public demonstration against progressive education and its alleged domination of the Tenafly school program. According to a local paper, Mrs. Jones came armed with a prepared statement in support of her thesis that there is a direct relation between juvenile delinquency and progressive education. The newspaper describes her as "a frequent and voluble critic."

The same newspaper issue also carried the first official school board reply to the critics. Acknowledging the attack and its general charge of "progressiveness," the board listed four specific practices as the focus of the hullabaloo:

1. Manuscript rather than cursive writing is taught in the first grade.
2. Addition and subtraction are not taught in the first grade.
3. History and geography are not taught separately.
4. Competition in classroom learning has been eliminated in the lower grades by changing the marking system.

The board acknowledged and defended each practice. It also distributed its reply in a mimeographed letter to "The Citizens of Tenafly." The introduction included the statement that "the Board of Education strives to provide for Tenafly's children the best possible educational program."

Soon after—in October, 1953—came a new Jones literary effort called "Is This What Is Meant by 'The Best Possible Educational Program'?" For the first time the document's identification read "Mr.

and Mrs. Theodore A. Jones." It judges nine Tenafly textbooks to be "slanted," gives a list of 131 Tenafly high school library books "which favor the Welfare State and Socialism, . . . follow the Communist line, and . . . are written by Communist sympathizers and . . . members . . . ," and recommends a list of books and periodicals to be added to the school library.

Mr. and Mrs. Jones's charge of subversive books was echoed by Cartwright in the October 23, 1953, issue of the Englewood Anti-Communist League's bulletin *Reveille To Wake Up America.* The exposure of 131 "slanted" library books was claimed to constitute "a veritable *Who's Who* of persons identified with the International Red Conspiracy."

At her request, the Tenafly board of education granted Mrs. Jones an open hearing on the matter of the subversive books. At the hearing, where she and Mr. Cartwright presented their "documentary evidence," they were routed: Parents insisted that they *wanted* their children acquainted with various points of view. But despite this reaction within the community, resolutions began to pour in charging that the school administration was ultraprogressive and "Red."

As the attack on Tenafly schools approached a climax, it was complicated by the convergence of two other issues: a building bond issue pending in the fall of 1953 and a controversial high school principal. Some school officials felt that the bond issue plus attempts to increase teachers' salaries provoked a group of new homeowners. But, fortunately, there seems to have been no fusion between the followers of Mrs. Jones and those specifically worried over school costs. Although Mrs. Jones shared their concern (at least once during her unsuccessful campaign for board membership, she claimed that school maintenance costs could be lowered), the two groups seem to have worked separately. In this respect, Tenafly schools were more fortunate than other school systems in similar straits, where two or more critical groups merged and completely joined forces. Even so, the Tenafly schools were caught in a cross-fire from two distinct sources.

Quite apart from the work of Mrs. Jones and that of the cost-conscious taxpayers, a small group of teachers and parents began claiming that the high school principal was being "attacked." This man's views had apparently conflicted with those of Tenafly's central administration and school board. Soon, the cudgels were taken up for him by Mrs. Jones. She suggested that the Tenafly principal was being victimized and that his case was analogous to a *fictional* principal, "belittled because he is 'conservative,' 'scholarly,' 'dignified,' because he objects to the 'core curriculum' and because he is in the confidence of many of the parents."[7]

A letter to "Taxpayers and Parents" appeared in late December or early January urging a wholesale investigation of the schools. And at the board meeting following the surprise resignation of the controversial principal, a citizen sympathetic to the Jones point of view asked for the resignation of the Tenafly superintendent of schools. But the community was lining up behind the central administration. At the same board meeting the superintendent received a standing ovation from a capacity audience, following a tribute paid him by a retiring member of the board:

> It is about time . . . that Messrs. Jones, Cartwright and Grein recognize that in our minds their viewpoint was that of biased, distrusting, narrow-minded crusaders. It is also time that they realize that neither the Superintendent, the Board of Education or Tenafly citizens intend to have them tell us what we want our children to read. . . .[8]

This vote of confidence given the superintendent had followed a one-page diatribe entitled "Superintendent Approves Communist Works for School Use," printed by Mr. and Mrs. T. A. Jones. It condemned the superintendent for recommending that the *Nation* be retained in the high school library. It denounced the editors of this magazine and then took several swipes at the superintendent and at the board: "Here is either a case of deliberate oversight or administrative incompetence. . . ." Further, ". . . the Board of Education is derelict in its duty to the children and the parents if it accepts the judgment of the Superintendent in this matter and permits this periodical, which features so many Communist-inspired articles, to appear each week on the High School magazine rack. . . ."[9]

A month or so later, Dr. Robert Skaife of the NEA Defense Commission was invited to address a PTA meeting on "Attacks on Our Schools." Cartwright went back into action. The day before the meeting, a mimeographed letter from the Englewood Anti-Communist League, addressed to "Fellow Citizens," raised (and underlined) this question: *"Has Robert Skaife been sent by the* N.E.A. *to do a hatchet job on those citizens of Tenafly who are dissatisfied with teaching methods in their school system?*" The single-page communication also warns of the nefarious nature of the PTA: "Wearing the mantle of sanctified respectability and purporting to speak for the majority of parents and teachers (a claim greatly exaggerated), they exert tremendous influence upon public opinion and school authorities to accept subversive and un-American doctrines."[10] (Here the role of "school authorities" seems to have shifted from villain to victim. Sometimes it is difficult to tell the sheep from the wolves.)

The following night, at the meeting itself, the sword was again wielded directly by Mr. and Mrs. Jones when they distributed a statement on "The background of Speaker Skaife." This exposé consisted largely of denunciations of the NEA and its Defense Commission, which Skaife represented. Despite little reason to expect a favorable reception, the Joneses were back again at the administration by the end of the month with the one-page query "What IS the Educational Aim of Our Superintendent?" and the question-answer, "To Stifle Honest and Constructive Criticism?" The occasion for this piece of literature was the superintendent's recommendation of a book—*How We Fought for Our Schools*[11]—to board members and other citizens. The query goes on to attack the book, its author, and the Tenafly superintendent.

But the critical forces in Tenafly seemed definitely to be losing ground. The spontaneous vote of confidence given the superintendent at the end of January was one indication. The passage of the building bond issue by Tenafly voters on February 9th was another. Gradually, as 1954 wore on, the trouble began to die. It is difficult to say just what caused it to expire, but it is plausible to assume that the board's statement, listing and answering the only really specific charges, had something to do with it. Doubtless some citizens were enraged by the wholesale denunciations in the charges. Possibly others grew weary of the views and vague assertions of Mr. Cartwright of neighboring Englewood. Perhaps those who made plain their desire to expose Tenafly youngsters to various viewpoints managed to convince the rest of the community. Perhaps the extreme position taken by Mrs. Jones worked to alienate some who might otherwise have tended to see things her way. In any event the crisis gradually disappeared. Mrs. Jones suddenly stopped attending the open meetings of the board of education.

To make it even more final, Mr. and Mrs. T. A. Jones moved to neighboring Woodcliff Lake in the spring of 1954.

That is the end of the Tenafly story. It is not the end of the Kitty Jones story. Although she may be illustrative of the educational critic who flourished in the early fifties, Mrs. Jones's career was most decidedly not limited to that period. If anything, her efforts since then have become more diversified. The career of Kitty Jones, since the move to Woodcliff Lake, has followed three separate paths. The first consists of locally centered endeavors. The second consists of newspaper writing, which seems to have replaced the pamphlets and one-page Varityped letters of earlier days. The third is an even more sustained literary effort: a book of some two hundred pages.

We find that the Joneses took an active interest in a proposed high school in their new community of Woodcliff Lake. The eruption, however, did not occur until a year after the new school opened. And then, the name primarily associated with the fracas was not that of "Jones," but "Hoyt." The J. Curtis Hoyts had been neighbors of the Joneses in Tenafly and had participated in the Jones attack on Tenafly schools.[12] The Hoyts also moved to Woodcliff Lake, to a home close to the Joneses. In May, 1956, approximately three hundred letters criticizing the new Woodcliff Lake high school were sent out over the signature "J. Curtis Hoyt, Chairman, Pascack Study Group on Education."[13]

The trouble broke with absolutely no warning. No criticism had ever been brought to the school board or the administration, and Mr. Hoyt was a newcomer to the community. Unknown to board members and administrators alike, he had no children in the high school.[14]

The lengthy Hoyt document (six pages of single-spaced typing) makes both charges and recommendations. The major target is " 'sex education' " or " 'sex influence,' " though numerous charges run the whole gamut of contemporary educational criticism: students are not learning anything; books are poor (thirty-five—named—"traditional and modern books of accepted literary merit" are not used); the school runs " 'rehearsed workshops' . . . purely for indoctrinational purposes . . ." and follows a " 'progressive' " ideology (as evidenced by the frequent use of the word *democracy*); and finally—apparently with no relevance whatsoever—Columbia Teachers College harbors "educators for socialism." Five specific recommendations follow, on the use of class time, test construction and content, textbook selection, and what should and should not be taught. Finally, the board is invited to submit "a progress report on these matters by the end of the month."

The letter raised a furor. Not only was the school new and untried, but a bond issue referendum to enlarge it was coming up in less than a month.* Hoyt was deluged with questions about the group and its membership. He would say only that it was "not the kind of group that holds monthly meetings and elects officers." The group's membership never became known, but the letter strongly suggested the guiding hand of Kitty Jones. She denied membership but admitted helping to formulate the group's objections.[15]

Hoyt denied that the criticisms were in any way related to the proposed bond issue. He denied that he was even aware of the proposal. The board of education questioned this, as did at least one local newspaper editor who pointed out that the subtle timing of the attack made it impossible for the victim to reply before the bond issue vote. Fortunately, the editor was mistaken. The board of education immediately mailed a reply to 4,000 homes in the area. And on June 5th the bond issue was approved by a 2 to 1 majority.

The Pascack Study Group on Education then refused an invitation to present its views at a regular board meeting. Instead it requested a *private* hearing, and was turned down. In refusing the request, the board noted that the charges had been "broadcast . . . yet the . . . group requests private discussion on these public charges." It stated that as a public body, elected by and responsible to all citizens of the District, its discussions should be open to the community.

The following fall, a letter signed "Kitty" was distributed in Woodcliff Lake.[16] The letter, estimated to have had a distribution of approximately one hundred copies, is one of Mrs. Jones's cleverest efforts. It discards a direct onslaught for an oblique approach. The misleading remark "We had no idea how wonderful it would be to have our girls in High School," is followed by one indictment after an-

* We cannot pass up the opportunity to point out the exorbitant costs of inadequate school-construction financing. The Pascack Valley Regional High School opened in September, 1955, with a first-year enrollment of 560. The original bond issue was for $1,250,000. The board of education made it plain at that time that the facilities would soon be inadequate. Within one week after the school opened, it was necessary to launch plans for enlarging it.

other. After "Even a Dale Carnegie class wouldn't teach our children 'how to get along at home' but our fine school does!" Mrs. Jones condemns English and home economics instruction as well as the testing program.

But even this more subtle approach failed to win converts near home. It seems to have been Mrs. Jones's last local effort. With little success in Woodcliff Lake, she next turned up in distant Evanston, Illinois, a residential community similar to Tenafly, located on Chicago's well-to-do North Shore.

In the fall of 1956, residents of Evanston received invitations to an "American Seminar on Education." The seminar was to be a two-day affair, consisting of four sessions. Mrs. Jones was to carry three of the sessions unaided, and was to serve as a panel participant at the fourth.[17] The seminar, however, fell short of expectations. Shortly before it was to convene, the panel moderator withdrew; only about half of the reservations for the dinner preceding the panel-discussion were filled; and the two local school administrators who had agreed to participate in the panel managed to balance the impact of Mrs. Jones and Donald Raihle, a Minneapolis businessman whom we shall meet again later.

In her "grass roots" activities, Mrs. Jones seems to have been little more successful in Illinois than in New Jersey. Her second route toward "professionalization" as a critic of modern education consisted of newspaper writing. For a while, these outpourings almost constituted a career of writing letters to the editor. Although this was not a new field to Mrs. Jones, her real newspaper career was launched with an article in the *Tablet*, early in 1957.

The *Tablet* describes itself as a Catholic weekly, though many Catholics seem ardently to oppose it. The paper takes a highly specific stand on many secular issues, and is recognized as *the* authoritative source on Father Coughlin—the man who warned us in the late thirties of the "international plot of Communists and bankers to hand the world over to Jews."[18] Coughlin's Sunday-afternoon radio talks were regularly reprinted in the *Tablet*, and long after he had retired from the national scene the paper continued to urge that we make a holiday of his birthday.

We do not know how the *Tablet* and Mrs. Jones came together, but early in 1957 the paper printed an article by Kitty Jones titled "Are the 'Iowa Tests' Mere Indoctrination?"—the "Iowa Tests" being achievement tests widely used throughout the country. Mrs. Jones opened her piece with "Secondary schools throughout the country, both private and public, should discard entirely the 'Iowa Tests of Educational Development. . . .' " She went on to explain: "Their use can do no less than slant immature minds subtly and insidiously, toward the collectivist state." The lengthy article further condemns the secrecy the publishers urge for the test, questions whether it measures what it purports to measure—and what it *ought* to measure—and asserts that questions and answers are left-wing, or produce "left-wing thinking."[19]

Without explaining how a test might indoctrinate, Mrs. Jones's article would seem so filled with irrelevancies and *non sequiturs* as to convince no one. Such was evidently not the case. Three days after the article was published, a resident of Long Beach, New York, read portions of it at a school board meeting and submitted it to the board for "appropriate action." The superintendent was instructed to investigate the charges made in the article.

At the next meeting of the board, Superintendent David Salten presented a skillfully compiled twenty-four-page memorandum in answer to the charges. Dr. Salten also gave attention to one of the more threatening aspects of Mrs. Jones's article. As reported in the minutes of the meeting, he said:

> Mr. Dolan in his presentation of the Kitty Jones article made the point that *The Tablet* was a Catholic publication. . . . A considerable number of citizens in the audience left the meeting under the misapprehension that *The Tablet*'s position was the official Roman Catholic position on the subject. This can hardly be the case. . . .

Salten then listed twenty-four New York area Catholic schools using the Iowa tests. There was no further trouble in Long Beach.

The article itself was answered in a letter to the *Tablet*'s editor from Lyle Spencer, president of the company that published the tests, in which Mr. Spencer pointed out Mrs. Jones's errors of fact. The following week Mrs. Jones was back with a lengthy reply controverting Mr. Spencer's facts and telling him what questions the tests *should* have asked.

A few days later Mrs. Jones returned to writing to local editors. The purpose this time was to instruct citizens to warn their congressman against a pending federal-aid-to-education bill, on the grounds that public school children's minds would be controlled by Washington if the bill passed.

The following month, the *Bergen Evening Record* heard from Mrs. Jones in still another letter to the editor. This time she identified the *real* motive behind the program for gifted children: ". . . an insidious movement to segregate leaders who will be the workers in a socialist state." The program was also condemned on the grounds that it "calls for much expensive equipment." And an anachronistic *coup de grâce* concluded that ". . . this program . . . leaves the bulk of the children forgotten and discriminated against."[20]

Several months later, Mrs. Jones was back in the *Tablet* with an apparently unsolicited analysis of a *Tablet* story. The analysis took to task a *Tablet* writer, and used the occasion to point out that schools were actually planned by an "interlocking educational directorate" not willing to to be bound by a majority, but anxious instead to " 'dupe' " a school board into falling in line. To top things off, in the extravagant school building construction resulting from this process, "education has been relegated to second place"—with the effect that "the curriculum likewise reflects the policy of making education secondary. . . ."[21]

By the time this letter was written, Mrs. Jones was describing herself as a "non-professional teacher" and as a "known critic of current educational trends. . . ."[22] The latter part of her claim may have been based on the publication of her book in 1956. The book *Progressive Education Is REDucation* bears the joint authorship of Kitty Jones and Robert Olivier (or "Oliver"—his name is spelled both ways on the book's cover).[23] The book concentrates largely on the experiences of Mr. Olivier, who is described in the publisher's announcement as a man who ". . . taught in the public schools for thirty years, took a vocal stand for sound American education and was promptly dismissed."

How Mr. Olivier and Mrs. Jones got together is unknown. But *why* each found the other receptive can be illustrated in a single sentence from Olivier's testimony at his hearing before the board of education: " '. . . many teachers . . . do not understand the evil philosophy of progressive education, the monster that threatens to devour the souls of our young citizens and eventually destroy the wonderful public institutions and the wonderful country that it professes to love.' "

Much of *Progressive Education Is REDucation* is devoted to this general theme. Into the story of Robert Olivier's personal difficulties in Washington, Louisiana, is woven the theme that the "progressive education" he opposed is un-American and sacrilegious. Olivier's troubles ostensibly sprang from ideological differences with the central administration and board of his school system. The actual charges against him, however, had to do with "wilful neglect of duty" and suggest a somewhat different kind of difficulty. At the close of the hearing, the board voted to dismiss Robert Olivier:

> Olivier was dismissed by the school board on June 25, 1954. . . . His dismissal followed a public hearing by the board, which charged him on eight counts with wilful neglect of duty. He was charged with encouraging and instructing students at Washington High School to be disrespectful to and disobedient of the faculty and school authorities, of arousing and attempting to arouse the students to be rebellious and riotous, committing acts of insubordination to the superintendent and other school authorities, setting a bad example to his students by being critical of school officials, failure to cooperate with principal and faculty, making statements and accusations and taking actions designed to confuse the students and parents and faculty; displayed an attitude of defiance of authority; and made statements about faculty and school officials designed to create a distrust and hatred of them.[24]

Considerable research underlies several portions of the Jones-Olivier book. Chapter III, for instance, "Making Little Socialists," suggests the author(s)' familiarity with various professional books, official curriculum guides, and the most popular phonics arguments. The lengthy Appendix also indicates a familiarity with some of the classic attacks on American schools: Scarsdale, Pasadena, Schenectady. The bibliography suggests a knowledge of the work of such critics as Mary Allen, Verne Kaub, Russell Kirk, Merrill Root. But the chapter titled "Dewey and the Devil" reveals an appalling ignorance of the particular devil exorcised therein. The real meat of the chapter—and the aim of the entire book—is the attempt to fuse progressive education with Communism. This occurs through efforts to show Communist support for progressive education; Communist propagandizing on the part of the NEA; the "Urging [of] School Children to Tattle on Their Parents' Beliefs"; progressive educators' advocacy of force and violence; and finally, the "Philosophy of John Dewey Equated with Communism."

To date, this is the major part of the career of Kitty Jones. Little is known of her formal education, although she claims a "background" in engineering.[25] As far as instruction in pedagogy is concerned, her participation in the public relations workshop seems to be her only official contact with a teachers' college or department of education. And the fact that she had been a party to a school attack in Englewood prior to this experience makes it at least plausible that some of her ideas about education were formulated before she registered for the workshop. In fact the Englewood incident might even lead one to conclude that Mrs. Jones's main purpose in attending was to gather ammunition.

Mr. Jones, who seems to take an active interest in his wife's career in education, is an electrical engineer and an active political conservative. Early in 1956, along with Messrs. Cartwright and Grein, he unsuccessfully filed as a candidate for delegate-at-large to the Republican National Convention. The three, calling themselves "Conservative Republicans," claimed Senator Jenner as their choice for the Republican presidential nomination. Later in the year, Mr. Jones is reported to have supported the Conservative party platform and candidate.

It is difficult to suppose that her efforts have brought Mrs. Jones much satisfaction. She clearly sees herself as a crusader unselfishly paying the price exacted by the "smear" tactics of the unprincipled opposition. A part of this price was paid in Tenafly. Mrs. Jones had been a Sunday-school teacher in the Episcopal Church, but she was asked to resign, according to the blurb sheet of her book, because of her attack on the public schools. The Tenafly community rejected the Joneses' views on education. Woodcliff Lake's intellectual climate proved no warmer. And the individual who persistently urges views which a group has examined and rejected is unlikely to find a warm personal reception among its members.

What are the convictions to which Mrs. Jones is dedicated? For what beliefs is she martyring herself? Here are what seem to be the major ones:

1. John Dewey must be "permanently laid to rest."
2. The " 'activity' program" and " 'projects' " must be eliminated.
3. The organization of subject matter for presentation should be " 'logical' " and not topical.

4. History and geography must be taught separately.
5. Grammar, composition, and literature must be taught specifically (not included in " 'projects' " or " 'activities' ").
6. The instructional method used must be that of " 'teacher question-pupil response.' "
7. The "committee-group-gang climate" must be eliminated.
8. Parents must "define the function of the school."
9. School-sponsored (or school-inspired) workshops are indoctrinational, and must go.
10. "Collectivist"-minded textbooks, and books written by collectivist-minded authors should not be used, and must be eliminated from school libraries.
11. The pupil must learn as much as possible from the textbook; additional aids to be used are "recitation, blackboard work, review and individual help from the teacher." "An occasional formal debate" is permissible.
12. Textbooks should be "objective with a degree of nationalistic bias." Maps, charts, pictures, slides, and films may be used occasionally, "for illustrative purposes."
13. Instruction in cursive writing must be given in the first grade.
14. After a general introduction of "the two hemispheres," the sequence in geography should be the United States and then the world.
15. A "period" should be devoted weekly to "aesthetic development."
16. "The teacher's position is that of authoritarian."[26]

THE FIRST WAVE
4. Aiders and Abettors

It is not surprising, of course, that the news of a school attack carried from one community to another, or even that a critic in New Jersey should seek and find his counterpart in Minnesota or California. But, as we shall see, the collaboration among education's critics was not carried out on such a casual and informal basis.

During the late forties a number of national organizations were formed for the primary purpose of dealing with alleged shortcomings of the public schools. In addition, groups organized primarily for other purposes assumed the function of publicizing and curing school ills. These organizations offered assistance to one another and to the amateur "grass-roots" critic as well. The pattern of operation was laid out in the widely quoted "Michigan statement" of Allen Zoll: " 'We form hell-raising groups to find out what is being taught in the schools, and then we raise hell about it.' "[1] Zoll claimed that his own organization, the National Council for American Education, had 400 local affiliated groups—plus 10,000 direct memberships.[2]

Mutual assistance need not be formal to be successful. Kitty Jones may have belonged only to the local anti-Communist league. Yet she had no trouble in finding national organizations to endorse, promote, and distribute her publications throughout the country. The two groups that have helped most in this regard are the Guardians of American Education, and America's Future.

Mrs. Jones's best-known work was the chart, prepared in Tenafly, contrasting "up-to-date traditional education" with "education for socialism." The Guardians of American Education circulated this chart in its original form, under the two titles "How Progressive Is Your School?" and "Elementary School Education." GAE charts bear the declaration "Copyright, 1954." Since Mrs. Jones has no by-line on the GAE-distributed charts, and since she claimed no copyright on her early Varityped literature, it is possible that the Guardians circumvented her completely. But regardless of formalities that may or may not have been observed in the "adoption" of the chart, one thing is certain—in so doing, the GAE clearly bestowed its stamp of approval.

The Guardians of American Education was born in 1940, "at a meeting of 54 citizens and parents, disturbed by some aspects of teaching material used in the public schools."[3] A brochure describing GAE quotes its charter on the matter of purposes:

> To preserve among the principles of public school education the ideal of upholding faith in the American form of government and of maintaining belief in our traditional tenets of social and economic freedom.

The basic premise is more plainly stated in GAE's first publication: "How long shall we continue to permit our public schools to be used as a breeding ground for alien ideologies?" (Cf.: "When did you stop beating your wife?") Even more specifically, GAE was established to combat "left-wing . . . educational leadership . . . [which is trying to replace] our American way of life . . . [with] a 'new social order' based on the principles of collectivism and socialism."

Prior to World War II, GAE's major target was Professor Harold Rugg, of Teachers College, Columbia University. They attacked Rugg and his books for expressing the viewpoint of the "Frontier Thinkers" who in turn were alleged to peddle the "old Marxian concept, streamlined with 20th Century verbiage." Citizens were urged to act:

> Examine your child's textbooks. Demand to see the teacher's guides. . . . Look for subversive material in . . . books or courses.
>
> . . . Write letters to your local newspapers, calling attention to the situation. Take the matter up with civic and patriotic bodies. Have committees appointed to see the evidence for themselves.
>
> . . . Be sure to call on your American Legion and other veterans' organizations. This procedure has been most effective in scores of communities where un-American teachings have been eliminated.

Watch for Federal legislation designed to fasten this "new social order" brand of education on the entire nation.

GAE proudly claims to have distributed more than 100,000 copies of *Undermining Our Republic,* which contained this call to action. A copy went to every newspaper in the country.

The organization reports that it suspended operations throughout World War II. Following its reactivation in 1952, GAE reprinted and distributed several attacks on education published in the *American Legion Magazine*. All bore the message that our schools and teachers constitute a sore threat to Americanism.[4] Since that time GAE seems to have been dormant and did not reply to our questionnaire. But although little is known of the *organization's* current activities, we do know more about the work of one of its founders.

Recently GAE's long-time chairman, retired Army Colonel Augustin G. Rudd, wrote a book titled *Bending the Twig*. Because of his long association with GAE and because of the book's theme, we are probably safe in assuming that it reflects GAE views. Moreover, it may also indicate something of the policies of the New York Chapter of the Sons of the American Revolution, named as the publisher on some copies of the book, and of the Heritage Foundation, which is named as the publisher on other copies.[5] Colonel Rudd himself is chairman of the SAR Educational Committee.

On the book's jacket, the Heritage Foundation proclaims that "Colonel Rudd is generally recognized as the first layman to undertake a national campaign to return common sense to the public education of our children." Although several other organizations and individuals claim that distinction, Rudd has certainly attempted a more thorough analysis than the somewhat sketchy efforts of many critics. Furthermore, his tone is often reasoned and restrained. For instance, his concise five-point exposition of "The Activity School, the Project Method, the Child-Centered School, etc." [*sic*] is scholarly and objective prose. Only those familiar with the lengthy and controversial attempts to define *each* of these educational positions would realize the impossibility of doing the whole job in a five-point, one-page statement. This has its ludicrous aspects even before we get to the "etc." of the title.

Rudd calls his book a "study," and documents his claims with extensive footnotes at the end of each chapter. Of course, only the initiated are prepared to separate the sheep from the goats in his list of sources including such names as Milo F. McDonald, Russell Kirk, R. Freeman Butts, A. E. Bestor, and Michael Demiashkevich. But Rudd doesn't take an extreme approach. Rather than damning *all* educators, he claims his charges apply only to "some." It is this restraint that lends surface credence to his book.

Bending the Twig reflects a position popular in some circles of American educational criticism. We have already seen the view as it was expressed in Tenafly. Rudd, too, seems genuinely worried that a sinister and conspiratorial educational profession is trying to make education an indoctrinating process for the collectivist point of view. To support his claims of the radical views of educators, Rudd turns to the writings of the "Frontier Thinkers" of the thirties. He believes that this group got its start with the American Historical Association's investigation into the teaching of social studies. The last of the committee's many-volumed report, the volume titled *Conclusions and Recommendations*,[6] is alleged by Rudd to contain the "Master Plan." It provides ". . . the working plan of the Frontier Thinkers for rebuilding society . . ." and "the design of the leftist educators for a collectivist society." According to Rudd, Columbia's Frontier Thinkers afterward proceeded to enlarge and sell the plan. Their efforts, he implies, were successful. They allegedly enlisted National Education Association support; NEA is "the most authentic voice of the public school teacher"; *ergo*, educators are trying to deliver the country into the hands of Socialism—or worse.

Although we are not concerned here with refuting charges, it would be misleading not to look a bit further into this one. Recall Mrs. Jones's message, and her persistent equating of progressive education and "education for socialism." Colonel Rudd echoes the same theme. Much of the evidence Rudd and his confrères repeatedly cite as "proof" of educators' socialistic tendencies is their predictions. A group of Columbia professors (the group known as the Frontier Thinkers) predicted, during the Depression years, the modification of our economic system. But surely, the weatherman who forecasts a tornado cannot be accused of having revealed his secret hopes. Yet this is the sort of argument Rudd and his friends offer.

Actually, they could offer a much better one, because it is obviously true that many of the Frontier Thinkers *were* in favor of far-reaching changes in the structure of our economy. The traditional whipping boys, Professors Rugg and Counts, have made no secret of their beliefs, or of the programs they advocated. And perhaps many of their colleagues, by failing to recognize or even acknowledge the existence of these clearly formulated positions, did everyone concerned a grave injustice. But they also failed to defend the right of these men to espouse their convictions.[7]

But where the critics have erred most seriously is in alleging that these have been the views of the *educational profession*. The Frontier Thinkers comprised only a small fraction of those involved in American education. Rudd himself credits a single magazine as the "spearhead" and the organ of the group.[8] The magazine—discontinued more than fifteen years ago—never had a circulation of more than 5,000.[9] Membership in the society which published it has never exceeded 900.[10] Not a terribly significant portion of the profession, even if one rashly assumes that all readers were sympathizers.

Critics have cited only one other evidence of commitment within the profession to allegedly socialistic ideas, and this one is blatantly false. Rudd claims the National Education Association has "taken over the fight." The enlistment of NEA is alleged to have occurred with its "capture . . . by the leftist-liberal faction . . . accomplished by winning over the controlling NEA officers. . . ." These "officers" are then reduced to one—Willard Givens, NEA's Executive Secretary from 1935 to 1952. Dr. Givens' radicalism is demonstrated in this way:

> In the 1934 NEA Convention, the leftist-liberals scored a monumental victory in the adoption by the NEA Department of Superintendence of a declaration, *Education for the New America,* which called for socialization of the "credit agencies, the basic industries and [the] utilities." Dr. Givens chaired the reporting committee.

Now, here are the facts. First, this was not the NEA Convention, it was simply a meeting of the Department of Superintendence. Second, Givens had nothing to do with the preparation of the report. Instead, his chairmanship made him responsible for collecting reports from the meeting's twenty discussion groups, summarizing them *as submitted,* and handing them over to the organization's president. Third, none of these reports ever came before the NEA Board of

Directors, its Representative Assembly, or any other official body. Hence, according to NEA bylaws, they *could not* express the organization's position.[11]

Rudd might have avoided echoing the six-year-old misstatements of another critic, namely, the *Educational Reviewer*, if he had but determined their veracity before quoting them.[12] He is not alone in the error. A large number of organizations charging schools and teachers with subversion use the false 1934 NEA Convention report as evidence. They continue to repeat it—despite documented denials and the fact that those echoing the claim can easily check the facts for themselves.

We have said that many of the groups critical of education enjoy a well-coordinated system of cooperation, and we have tried to show some of the strands of this network: how the Guardians of American Education picked up and distributed Mrs. Jones's material; how a GAE founder's book, *Bending the Twig*, was received in two quarters—the New York Chapter of the Sons of the American Revolution and the Heritage Foundation. Now see how the favors are returned: Kitty Jones, whose chart had been distributed by Rudd's GAE, gave the Colonel's book a warm welcome in the *Tablet*:

> *Bending the Twig* not only serves as a devastating expose of the New Illiteracy . . . but also presents, in a scholarly manner, its philosophic fallacies and its socialistic objectives. The book could very well be used as one of the texts in the History of Education or the Philosophy of Education in teacher-training institutions not dominated by the entrenched educational bureaucracy.[13]

Still another group greeted the book with considerable enthusiasm. According to an announcement in *National Review*, the Donner Foundation purchased 20,000 copies of Rudd's book to distribute to "school board presidents and educational leaders" throughout the country.[14] An investment of such magnitude calls for a look into the Donner Foundation. It appears to be a personal extension of one Robert Donner who for some years served as both its president and director. Donner is a retired steel industrialist who has been described as the "millionaire 'angel' of countless ultra-rightist causes. . . ."[15]

Among other activities, he founded a Colorado Schools Protective Association in 1949. At a meeting in which the "Protective Association" advocated a school tax rebate for all Colorado parents who sent their children to private schools, Donner said:

> . . . public schools do not, with some exceptions, teach the importance of keeping intact the great fundamental principles of the declaration of independence *[sic]*, our private enterprise and free initiative system.
>
> Nor do they teach the fallacies of socialism, collectivism or the advantages of our free economy which has been regimented in the last 20 years into a giant federally controlled octopus of bureaucracy.[16]

An editorial commenting on the Colorado Schools Protective Association said the group's major activity was campaigning against school district consolidation. The editor then charged, "If children in various parts of Colorado have only second-rate schools they can blame the 'protective association. . . .'" It sized up the group "as an organization dominated by larger-than-average taxpayers who are more interested in their tax bills than in education."[17] Of course, there is nothing evil about stumping for lower taxes. But, if the editor's interpretation of dominant interests is correct, surely we can ask why the group calls itself a "Schools Protective Association."

Donner also belonged to and served as the executive for a "Colorado Citizens Committee for Education." As such, one of his official acts was the mailing of a circular urging recipients to

> . . . please make it your business to cooperate with those who are trying to eliminate . . . [the] subversive movement, trend, and philosophy from the schools and also to rid the schools of the left-wing and radical educators from the administrators and teachers in the schools here and elsewhere in the Republic. . . .[18]

This could be a worth-while aim and plea, depending on what Mr. Donner considers a "subversive movement, trend, and philosophy." Clues to his definition appear in his activities. These include his demands that the Colorado College library remove the *Nation, New Republic, Christian Unitarian Register, Commonweal,* and various books by John Dewey.[19] In connection with these demands, Donner circulated the GAE pamphlet *Undermining Our Republic,* "exposing" Harold Rugg. Donner was obviously acquainted with and sympathetic to Colonel Rudd and his work, prior to the Donner Foundation's magnificent purchase of *Bending the Twig.*

Donner likened the government to a giant octopus, but the same metaphor can be used to describe his many associations with educational critics. He contributed to Allen Zoll's National Council for American Education, and distributed some of its materials.[20] The House Select Committee on Lobbying Activities disclosed a close relationship between Donner and the National Economic Council. This council has been a strong critic of public schools and has been accused of attempts to discredit "those who oppose its objectives by appeals to religious prejudice. . . ."[21] Donner has also cooperated closely with at least one more educational critic—Joseph P. Kamp, and his Constitutional Educational League—by distributing Kamp's pamphlets and contributing funds.[22]

The well-coordinated system of cooperation used by many of education's critics takes us down a labyrinthine path. We have already moved from GAE's distribution of Kitty Jones's chart to GAE's program; to the "program" of its executive; and on to the programs of those who gave him succor. GAE is only one of the two major organizations which have distributed Mrs. Jones's "How 'Progressive' Is Your School?" The second group, America's Future, billed the Jones work this way: "Progressive education—what it purports to be, and what it actually is . . . NOW . . . is easy to understand. . . . A 16-page pamphlet boils the whole thing down. . . ."[23] The America's Future organization has also distributed Mrs. Jones's *Progressive Education Is REDucation.*

America's Future refers to itself as "a non-profit educational institution dedicated to upholding the principles of free, competitive enterprise and constitutional government."[24] In its several publications it opposes high taxes, wasteful government spending, foreign aid, the United Nations, "encroaching" Socialism in government and schools, radical teaching in schools and colleges, progressive education, and federal aid for education.

The activities of America's Future have largely consisted of a four-part program: radio, book, pamphlet, and newspaper efforts. Radio activities have consisted largely of a weekly commentary by John T. Flynn, which has reportedly been carried by 535 Mutual

Network stations. The book program includes a quarterly review of "All-American Books" which can then be purchased directly from America's Future. There is also an *All-American Book Digest*, published four times yearly, "for those who lack the time or the money for full-length, full-price editions. . . ." The first issue of the *Digest* was devoted to John T. Flynn's *While You Slept* and Mary L. Allen's *Education or Indoctrination*.[25]

According to America's Future, pamphlet offerings have dealt with "such timely topics as: Income Taxes, Progressive Education, Social Security, States Rights, Supreme Court, etc. . . ." One of the pamphlets on progressive education is presumably Mrs. Jones's. Another, *What's Happened to Our Schools?*, was prepared by the organization's secretary and is called "Rosalie Gordon's clear analysis of a very serious condition."[26] The gist of the answer to the title question is stated on page 4:

> . . . it is difficult to believe that it ["something drastic"] has happened by accident, *that there has not been a planned, slyly executed and almost successful attempt to deliberately under-educate our children in order to make them into an unquestioning mass who would follow meekly those who wish to turn the American Republic into a socialist society*.

Miss Gordon is versatile. She has also written on the "timely topic" of the Supreme Court. Entitled *Nine Men Against America*,[27] the theme of this work may be summarized in the author's own words:

> . . . all those who are devoted to our American way of life, and who believe it is worth saving against the encroachments of the collectivist sappers, are agreed that if it is to survive something must be done about the Supreme Court.[28]

In support of her argument, Miss Gordon analyzes many Roosevelt, Truman, and Eisenhower appointees to the Court—a group that she finds lacking in ability, experience, and character. She considers eight "major" proposals as to what "must be done about the Supreme Court," giving John T. Flynn's suggestion the influential final position:

> It is that all decisions of the Supreme Court, from 1937 to the date of the adoption of the proposal, should be declared to have no force and effect as precedents in judicial or other proceedings. . . .

So much for the pamphlet program of America's Future. Its newspaper activities consist of sponsoring a "700-word editorial by John T. Flynn [which] goes to 4,016 weekly newspapers in 'grass roots' America . . . [and] carries the America's Future message to an estimated 20 million readers. . . ."

The history of America's Future is obscure. An earlier New York corporation of the same name was apparently either abandoned or laid to rest immediately prior to the incorporation of the present America's Future, Inc., in Delaware. If the first organization still exists, the second disclaims association with it, for America's Future, Inc., prominently announces and reiterates that it was founded in 1946.[29] Today's AF makes repeated efforts to prove itself a completely independent, unaffiliated organization. But hearings held by the House Select Committee on Lobbying Activities of the Eighty-first Congress suggest that such is not the case. Part V of the Committee's lengthy report comments on "the great wealth of seemingly independent groups which are actually created for special purposes by going organizations":

> The Committee for Constitutional Government has been especially prolific in this regard, having spawned at last count no less than four subsidiary organizations: Fighters for Freedom, America's Future, Constitution and Free Enterprise Foundation, and Features for America. One group specializes in the distribution of literature, another in political action within congressional districts, a third in syndicated columns and releases, a fourth in contacts with educational institutions. But what appears to be a number of distinct groups is in reality the Committee for Constitutional Government operating in several different ways. The Committee for Constitutional Government has learned well what has been called the first rule of successful pressure politics: to wit, never admit that it is only you who is talking.[30]

According to Edward Rumely, the Executive Secretary of the Committee for Constitutional Government, "America's Future was organized as a New York corporation by Frank Gannett in 1938 or 1939," and its purpose was to serve as the "radio" or "radio arm" of the Constitutional Government group.[31] A clue as to how it took on the publishing and distributing functions is provided in the minutes of a CCG trustees meeting:

> To avoid the possibility that large purchases of books or literature from the Committee may be interpreted by the Government as being contributions to the Committee, it would seem desirable to have a separate selling organization to deal with the large purchases. Preferably, this selling organization should be a reliable, established concern. If it did not conflict with its other activities, America's Future might take on the function.[32]

In the light of this evidence, it is curious that America's Future is so anxious to represent itself as an entirely independent organization. And why did Executive Secretary Rumely of the Committee for Constitutional Government seem equally anxious to portray his Committee, America's Future, Fighters for Freedom, the Constitution and Free Enterprise Foundation, and Freedom for America as five separate and distinct organizations?

Two explanations seem highly plausible. The House Lobbying Committee suggested one in that "first rule of successful pressure politics . . . never admit that it is only you who is talking." Perhaps the leadership of the five organizations hoped to give the impression of many groups, representing many people, all seeking similar ends. A second possible explanation is suggested in the minutes quoted above: perhaps certain economic advantages were anticipated from an appearance of complete independence.

Despite denials, there have been connections between the five organizations. As the Lobbying Activities Committee pointed out, "Not only do different groups draw support from common sources but they also frequently share common personnel as well. This tendency is especially marked with respect to interlocking directorates."[33] So it is interesting to note that in 1950, Frank Gannett (the founder of both the Committee for Constitutional Government and the original America's Future) was on the board of trustees of at least four of the five organizations. We have been unable to obtain information about the personnel of Features for America, but we do know that four men held executive positions in three of the *other* four organizations. Nine additional men held such positions in two of the four groups.[34]

Furthermore, as of 1950, three of the five groups were located in one building; the other two were located in a single building nearby.

And according to Rumely's testimony, the Committee for Constitutional Government and the Constitution and Free Enterprise Foundation shared the same offices with America's Future. The three organizations shared a common mailing room, and some of America's Future files were kept in the Committee's offices.[35]

There has been, then, more than a casual relationship between America's Future and the other four groups. Indeed, if the House Committee is correct, America's Future is merely a "creature" of the Committee for Constitutional Government. The Lobbying Committee described CCG this way: "The group's three major activities appear to be raising money, stimulating letter and telegram campaigns on pending legislation, and distributing books, pamphlets, and other printed matter to members of Congress, state legislators, other public officials, and private institutions, organizations, and individual citizens. . . ."[36]

The CCG thinks of itself this way:

> . . . the Committee for Constitutional Government fights for economic freedom as against encroaching big government. It strives for lower taxes, for reducing the number of Federal employees by 600,000, for curbing the power of labor monopolies, and for restoring equality before the law to all citizens, and for ending confiscatory upper-bracket taxation. . . .
>
> It has been effective in opposing socialized education, socialized housing, socialized medicine. . . .[37]

These positions, flickering with conviction and self-righteousness, are equated with truth:

> The Committee for Constitutional Government, Inc., regards itself as strictly an educational organization. It attempts to teach the public sound economics and the principles of constitutional government. Its position almost exactly parallels that of the economics department of a college or university. . . .[38]

The Constitution and Free Enterprise Foundation, which the Lobbying Committee dubbed a "subsidiary" of the Committee for Constitutional Government, publishes and distributes books—mainly to colleges and universities. Its *raison d'être* is clearly revealed in the minutes of a CCG meeting:

We have . . . been faced with the difficulty that the . . . income-tax authorities have refused to rate the Committee for Constitutional Government as a strictly educational institution, and, hence, contributions . . . have not been made deductible for tax purposes. . . .

We are now confronted by the fact that all contributions of $500 or over . . . must be reported. . . . In order to place the committee in a thoroughly safe position, and also to maximize its revenues, it is suggested . . .

1. The foundation should be activated at once. Its activities should be confined to matters which are unquestionably educational in nature, and which cannot possibly be construed as attempts to influence legislation. At the earliest possible moment, a ruling should be secured that contributions . . . are deductible.

2. The make-ups of the . . . boards of trustees of the foundation and of the committee should be so arranged that personnels do not overlap widely. . . .

3. The field men should immediately be furnished with blanks for subscriptions to the foundation. . . .

4. Publication of strictly educational literature . . . should be the work of the foundation. . . .[39]

Features for America, an admitted subsidiary of CCG,[40] has seen to syndicating columns written by CCG's Dr. King and by Ralph W. Gwinn, then a congressman from New York. Since the CCG retained control of Features for America,[41] the aims of the latter were of course those of the parent organization.

Although Fighters for Freedom is also a division of the CCG,[42] it too is independently incorporated. According to a release from the group, its purpose is " 'to fight highly organized left-wing movements which are pressing our government deeper into socialism.' "[43] Its announced platform has consisted of the following:

1. Pitilessly expose communism . . . and stop the march to fascism or socialism.
2. Restore the American incentives to work, own, and save. . . .
3. Protect every individual's right to work where he will. . . .
4. Safeguard our system of free, untrammeled, competitive markets. . . .
5. Stop using taxpayers' money to compete against private enterprise.
6. Build down Washington's swollen bureaucratic Big Government. . . .
7. Protest against politicians' buying votes by promising Federal Aid for education, socialized medicine, and public housing, which results eventually in Federal control.

8. Stop inflation. . . . Stop deflation. . . .
9. Abolish or reduce immediately those taxes which especially hinder saving and capital accumulation. . . .
10. Preserve the Constitution with its Bill of Rights, and oppose all attempts to violate it by legislation, usurpation, or evasion.[44]

The total picture emerging from the beliefs and activities of the five organizations suggests that all five are political pressure groups sharing identical viewpoints and dedicated to identical aims. It is obvious that neither America's Future nor the other four organizations have interests which are limited to the schools. The slant of their shared purposes is clearly toward extreme political conservatism. All five appear to be political action groups in one sense or another, and so the "rule of successful pressure politics" advanced by the Lobbying Committee may explain why each maintains a separate identity.

The fact that these and other organizations critical of education are predominantly political in purpose has produced one of the gravest and most ominous features of contemporary attacks on education. Compare America's Future's *What's Happened to Our Schools?* with the Guardians of Education's *Undermining Our Republic*. The message is identical: schools are socialistic with the intent of rendering the nation socialistic. But though the Guardians of American Education may be aided by individuals and organizations whose major interests lie elsewhere, it is an organization primarily concerned with *schools*. America's Future, on the other hand, is a group primarily devoted to promoting a specific political program. The successful fusion of the two interests—politics and education—suggests a threat of tremendous gravity to public schools.

The danger lies in the fact that America's Future—along with numerous groups of comparable scope and persuasion—has managed to intertwine condemnation of the schools with a specific political outlook: the credo of political conservatism. The result is that those subscribing to extremely conservative economic, social, or political views form what is perhaps the largest, most vocal amalgam of educational critics in the country.

In identifying extreme conservatives as prominent school critics, we are led to still another organization, We, The People! This is one group that does *not* try to create the impression of absolute independence. At the 1957 We, The People! convention, it was announced with pride that the 1,000 people in attendance represented more than sixty organizations in thirty-two states.[45]

We, The People! is one of four major coalitions of extreme conservatives in this country. The other three are the Congress of Freedom, the Campaign of the 48 States, and the American Coalition of Patriotic Societies. Together, the four can claim the support of well over two hundred separate organizations.[46] Although this reveals little about the actual number of people involved, it is nevertheless significant that a little publication entitled *First National Directory of "Rightist" Groups, Publications and Some Individuals in the United States (and Some Foreign Countries)*[47] lists 992 entries. Further, just one *segment* of the extreme right—the "racists"—can claim more than 3,500,000 in the United States![48]

Thus, not only do the views of the far right characterize a larger, more significant minority than we may generally assume, but it is also evident that the group shares a common, negative outlook on public education. We know that We, The People!, a prominent spokesman for the political right, has taken a distinct stand on education. The twentieth plank of its 1957 "Platform and Action Program to Save America from Socialism, Communism and World Government" consisted of these statements:

> We are unalterably opposed to the control of American public education by any Federal agency or national or international organization, such as the National Education Association (N.E.A.), the United Nations, UNESCO, and the organizations which they dominate.
>
> The control of our schools must be returned to the parents and communities whose traditional right it is to exercise such control.
>
> We demand that the advantages of the American system of Constitutional Government and private enterprise be taught at all levels.
>
> The indoctrination of American youth in un-American ideologies, such as socialism, Communism, world government, and collectivism, must be stopped.[49]

We, The People!—or its director who answered our questionnaire—believes schools to be guilty on almost every possible score.* Obvious

* It is not entirely clear whether the We, The People! reply represents the organization's position or its director's personal views.

in the responses is the conviction that American schools are not genuinely American. Since We, The People! is openly political, the organization might be expected to have ideas of what government should be and do. Thus it might be expected to take a stand on the finance and control of education, and even on what schools teach about political, economic, and social affairs. But We, The People!'s questionnaire responses show criticism of teaching methods, teacher preparation, and even subject matter where there is no question of political implications.

Questionnaire replies generally show a high correlation between political conservatism and criticism of the schools. But is there a logical reason for it? Such a reason is clear enough in some cases. For example, the rightist who defines patriotism as "the uncritical acceptance and approval of the past acts of the United States" could be expected to criticize the history teacher for pointing out that this country has added territory through open aggression. Is there also a logical connection between the conservative political orientation and the teaching methods of today? teacher preparation? apolitical as well as political content? We believe the relationship exists. Although we explain its general nature in Chapter XI, the reader may here examine for himself the extreme conservative position as stated in the creed of We, The People!

The creed is a twenty-four-plank platform, the education plank of which we have already quoted. This platform was prepared at the organizational We, The People! convention in 1955; it was revised in 1956, and has apparently been reaffirmed since. Here are some highlights from the lengthy Preamble that precedes the platform:

> We, the people of the United States, shall actively oppose all attempts to substitute atheism, alien idealogies *[sic]* or anti-Christian traditions . . . [p. 4].
> . . . government of men is being craftily substituted for government of law; powers not delegated to the Federal Government are being grossly usurped; countless unauthorized functions are being undertaken and we are rapidly approaching the very dictatorship by Federal Government which our Constitution . . . was specifically designed to prevent [p. 5].
> . . . it is necessary that we, the people . . . take action to regain the rights usurped by the Federal Government and demand that they be returned to the states and to the people [p. 6].

Here are detailed excerpts from the platform itself:

1. There must be returned to the states the rights, privileges, duties and responsibilities which have been usurped by the Federal Government . . . the states must have the power to regulate such matters as (1) the conduct of their schools, (2) racial problems, (3) the voting qualifications of their citizens, and (4) the enforcement of their own criminal and anti-subversive laws which they shall have the sole power to enact.
2. . . . To prevent a continuance of . . . abuse of power, we favor an amendment . . . providing that the power of Congress to regulate commerce . . . shall not extend to the relationship between employer and employee or the conditions under which . . . goods are produced within a state, or to the prices charged therefor, or to the carrying on of any business by the Federal Government directly or indirectly [pp. 6-7].
3. There must be a drastic reduction in Federal spending. . . [p. 7].
4. . . . The heavy progressive rate features of our income tax laws can and must be eliminated. . . [p. 7].
5. The method of electing a President and Vice-President . . . should be changed . . . to take away the excessive power now exercised by the larger cities in the present electoral college, thus removing the unduly great influence of minority groups. . . .
6. We favor the adoption of an amendment . . . giving to the States power to amend the Constitution . . . without any action by Congress. . . [p. 8].
7. We favor the adoption of the original Bricker Amendment. . . .
8. The use by the Government of the taxpayers' money and Government credit to compete with any form of private enterprise must be stopped. . . .
9. The Constitutional powers and duties of each branch of the Government . . . shall be exercised and performed only by such branch, and may not be delegated, even in time of war. . . .
10. The Courts' practice of rewriting the Constitution must be stopped . . . [p. 9].
11. Communists and Socialists must be completely eliminated from the public payrolls.
12. The Federal Government's powers and duties must be reduced. . . . Aid in such matters as housing and education is not the function of the Federal Government. . . .
13. We favor the equal application of anti-trust laws to all monopolies, whether of business, labor or agriculture. . . .
14. . . . we affirm that the wage earner has the same rights, duties, privileges and responsibilities as other persons or organizations. This includes the right to organize and to work or not to work, free from interference by any individual, organization or government agency. . . .
15. We believe in the equal rights of all under our laws, including the

right to choose one's associates. We condemn the so-called Fair Employment Practices Legislation.
16. Indiscriminate immigration cannot be tolerated. The McCarran-Walter Act must be preserved and enforced [p. 10].
17. . . . We are opposed to subsidies of all kinds. . . .
18. Under the Constitution Congress has the sole power to coin money and regulate the value thereof, and of foreign coin. We demand that Congress resume its Constitutional power.
19. . . . We are opposed to the direct or indirect confiscation of the property or income of any individual or group through taxation, price or rent control, or otherwise.
21. Ownership or control of the most economical sources of electrical energy by the Federal Government is the ownership or control of the means of production, i.e., socialism. Accordingly, we favor (1) the abolition of the Atomic Energy Commission; (2) the transfer to the Defense Department of the functions . . . necessary for producing . . . nuclear weapons . . . and (3) the transfer and release to private American enterprise of all other functions and facilities of the Commission.
22. Billions of dollars of the taxpayers' money have been . . . given away to foreign countries . . . foreign aid should be confined to strictly essential military purposes . . . in the interest of the United States [p. 11].
23. The present Reciprocal Trade Agreements Act delegates. . . [the imposition of tariffs] to the Executive contrary to the provisions of the Constitution. We demand its repeal [p. 12].
24. . . . We should without further delay withdraw from the United Nations, demand removal of the United Nations' headquarters and all its agencies from American soil and terminate diplomatic relations with the Soviet Union and her satellite countries. . . .[50]

Since the purpose of We, The People! is to bring together people active in other organizations, we find among its leadership a number of names encountered elsewhere. For example, the 1958–1959 president was the Honorable Ralph W. Gwinn, who recently retired from the House of Representatives when his party did not back him for renomination. He is the same Ralph Gwinn who, as a member of Congress, received a monthly compensation of $350 from the Committee for Constitutional Government, for "research expenses," and who used his franking privileges to mail almost three million pieces of CCG literature in a three-year period.[51] He is the same Ralph Gwinn whose congressional career was described this way by John Fischer:

During his fourteen years in Congress, Mr. Gwinn has accomplished precisely nothing. No legislation bears his name. No idea of his has made the slightest impress on any administration. His influence with his colleagues is nil. When he rises to speak in the House, the floor empties as if somebody had pulled a fire alarm.[52]

Fischer goes on to explain something of Mr. Gwinn as a person and as a thinker:

In private life Mr. Gwinn is an earnest, gentle person who gives large sums to worthy causes. He loves to deliver little homilies, to anyone who will listen, about the Great Seal of the United States which appears on every dollar bill; . . . Mr. Gwinn . . . regards it as a talisman of all the virtues.

His piety is phenomenal. . . . His main trouble seems to be that somehow he got the Four Gospels all tangled up in his mind with the economics of John Stuart Mill and the political dogmas of James A. Garfield. To him, they are all Holy Writ.

Consequently he has devoted his public career to a frenzied, if ineffectual, battle against practically everything that has happened in the last quarter century. . . .

Next to unions, he hates and fears the federal government, which is undermining our moral fiber and filching our liberties. . . .

The National Advisory Board of We, The People! includes Willis Carto, the late Lee De Forest, Robert Le Fevre, Eugene Pomeroy, Alfred Haake, John Crippen, Merrill Root, General P. A. del Valle, Frank Chodorov, B. M. Miller, and Verne Kaub. The views of all of these individuals appear in the replies to our questionnaire. Their charges, or the charges of the organizations they represent, testify eloquently to the nature of much contemporary educational criticism.

THE SECOND WAVE

5. *Montgomery County*

If the motif of the First Wave of contemporary attacks on education can be summed up in the charge of "un-Americanism," the motif of the Second Wave is "anti-intellectualism." This second wave, however, did not wait for the first one to abate, and, of course, critics typical of the late forties and early fifties are still most active. But beginning about 1950, a new group began to make its appearance and since about 1954 it has in some measure eclipsed the earlier critics.

The typical member of the new group is the liberal arts professor. The group that has most loudly and frequently replied to his charges consists mainly of professors of education. The complaints still pertain both to educational aims and values, and to content and methods, but this time the values urged are a little different. The current critic typically insists that the purposes of schooling should be primarily, if not exclusively, intellectual. The questions he poses can be summed up this way: Should the schools undertake anything that is not primarily intellectual in aim and content? If not, what is to be done with youngsters incapable of absorbing this exclusively intellectual fare? The criticisms of content and methods derived from this theme are thus leveled at "non-essentials," "soft" curricula, "spoonfeeding," and the alleged lowering of academic standards.

The nature of the *entire* group involved in making and publicizing charges is not easy to identify. The liberal arts professor has been the typical originator of the charges, but as earlier events have already shown, the critic rarely has the opportunity to broadcast his charges widely without help from other sources. Are there organizations providing help to the liberal arts critic, comparable to the groups that helped Kitty Jones? Since this Second Wave of criticism is currently taking place, it is too early to answer the question fully and finally. But tentative answers are emerging.

First, a number of national magazines seem to be aiding the liberal arts professor, but whether they are doing so by actual design or by mere "coincidence of interest" is hard to determine. Periodicals offering comparable assistance to the critic of the first wave were usually limited to patriotic magazines (the *American Legion Magazine*, for instance) or to periodicals of the extreme right (such as *National Republic*). Current educational critics get their views publicized in the organs of the literati and of the more restrained right (*Harper's* and *U.S. News & World Report*, respectively). While the situation may seem comparable, the *effect* is not. The magazines that helped the earlier critic have a relatively small circulation and go to special-interest groups. The critic and his reader frequently were two like-minded individuals talking to each other, and it is unlikely that the articles made many converts. In today's situation, the magazines giving considerable space to school critics and their charges are magazines of mass circulation. Some are "prestige" periodicals that the well-informed must be acquainted with, even though one disagrees with their editorial policies. Under such circumstances, "conversions" are not unlikely. Thus the magazine editor is extending a weapon to the current educational critic which was not available to his earlier counterpart.

To date, formal networks of cooperation binding second-wave critics are harder to trace. But one prominent form of mutual assistance consists in the overlapping of charges. For instance, the academic critic is aided by those organizations concerned with cutting school costs—hence taxes. The link is discernible when the academic critic insists that money won't help and that what is needed is a general overhauling of school policy and practice.

A third source of succor to the academic critic has been the extreme conservative. Of course, some critics are themselves identifiable with both groups: they are academicians and they embrace that world view which has been described as "approximately 300 miles to the right of

Chester A. Arthur."[1] Often, extreme conservative support has come to critics who do not necessarily share the "rightist" view in matters political. Extremist organizations have occasionally distributed the academician's speeches or articles. The Foundation for Economic Education, for example, has long distributed Professor Arthur Bestor's "Aimlessness in Education" address, under the more alarming title "Education for 1984," and the extreme conservative has lent the academician support in the form of numerous references and citations. In *Progressive Education Is REDucation,* Kitty Jones refers frequently to the works of a number of academic critics. Of the thirty-five books named in her "Bibliography for 'Education in a Free Society,' " fourteen are by educational critics prominently associated with the academic attack on public schools.

Although this kind of support need not mean overt collaboration, it nevertheless constitutes assistance. Thus, when one of the best known of the professor-critics attempted to go on record disassociating himself from the efforts of the Zoll-type critic,[2] he may well have been sincere, but despite his intentions, both he and his confrères *have* received tangible aid from the critic of the First Wave.

Of course, an author is not responsible for all the uses made of his work. He may not always be consulted, and when he is, his permission to quote does not necessarily reveal an endorsement of the purposes to which he is quoted. But there is much to be said for judging an endeavor good or bad in terms of its consequences as well as its intent or motive: the road to hell may indeed be paved with good intentions. If we hold the liberal arts critic accountable for the results he helped produce, then he is burdened with much more blame than he has been willing to accept.

Now, much of the academic criticism to date has been made at the national level: through books or magazine articles with nation-wide circulation. The effects of the nation-wide discussion are just beginning to be felt at the local level, and the attack on the individual school district is relatively new. It is our unhappy conviction that it may be reenacted many times throughout the country, within the next five to ten years. If this prediction is correct, we need to be familiar with the charges, the kind of situation that has proved conducive to them, and the events which have led to this kind of attack on public schools. Although it may be too early to see a pattern, the story of what has happened in one community may serve as warning for what can happen in others.

Montgomery County, Maryland, has been the victim of a great deal of educational criticism. Its severe school problems go back at least as far as 1948, and the area's school system has often been called a "fever spot." Like Tenafly, Montgomery County consists in large part of a suburban community. The bulk of the county's population lives in the highly built-up residential area close to the borders of Washington, D.C. Forty years ago the area was almost completely rural. Until 1952 the county board of education—which, in Maryland exercises a degree of control not vested in the county boards of most states—was appointed by the governor. Since that time, board members have been elected.

One of the first portents of trouble was a petition addressed to the board of education in March, 1948. Signed by 150 parents, the statement protested the emphasis on social studies and the neglect of the three R's. The board was given fifteen days to indicate what it intended to do "to improve the conditions."[3]

In early summer further restlessness crystallized with the formation of a Parents League for Curriculum Improvement. A member—who was also currently serving on the county board of education—described the group's purposes this way: "The league's principal concern has been the failure of the public schools to place adequate emphasis on the fundamental skills, i.e., reading, writing, spelling, arithmetic, and the social sciences."[4] The League soon drew up a twenty-six point petition demanding, among other things, curriculum revision, more homework, and less freedom in the classroom.[5]

During the same period Montgomery County schools were under fire from at least two additional sources. In early June a county commissioner had charged that "school officials are attempting a 'socialistic' school system with . . . 'wasteful frills . . .' " and, perhaps more to the point, that "school leaders are using 'rabble-rousing and scare propaganda in order to pressure the county government out of more funds.' "[6] Several days later, the county commissioners received a complaint about textbooks containing Communist propaganda.[7] The instigator of the complaint, a local attorney, was to become the Montgomery County writer of letters to the editor. He modified his charges about the textbooks, following an official investigation of them, but soon thereafter charged that the board " 'approves of outright un-American and subversive indoctrination. . . .' "[8] At least one event that may have grown out of these charges was the announcement of a local veterans' group that a "program to promote Americanism in Montgomery County schools . . . [would be] its major activity of the year. . . ."[9]

In the fall, the Parents League claimed credit for several distinct improvements in the school program. Perhaps League members were satisfied with the additional homework assignments and the increased distribution of textbooks, which they maintained had come about only at their insistence. At any rate, the group seems to have dropped from public view for several years thereafter. In the fall of 1950, however, the League began to publish a *Bulletin*. An angry passage from the first issue suggests that the two-year silence had not indicated truce:

> If more parents would let the Board of Education know in no uncertain terms, how fed-up they are with today's teaching methods, with the waste of their children's time on non-essentials while the important, basic subjects are skipped over lightly and not really taught—perhaps we could force even unwilling "educators" to inject some common sense into our county school educational program.[10]

Comments like these suggest that the Montgomery County Parents League may have been something of an anomaly of the period 1948–1953. The dominent theme of the educational criticism of those years was patriotic in nature. Despite the letter-writing attorney's efforts to launch un-Americanism investigations, the League seems to have remained aloof from such attempts. In 1951 the group corrected the oversight.

Several features of a March, 1951, meeting of the Parents League indicate that the organization was rapidly enlarging its concerns. These new interests definitely associate the League with the critics of the First Wave of criticism. Here is a part of what took place at this meeting:[11]

1. A discussion of the group's correspondence with individuals or groups in Pasadena; Portland and Eugene, Oregon; Denver; and Houston [all of which had, by this time, suffered attacks on local schools].

2. A report of a visit from a "Mr. Raihle of Minneapolis." [This Mr. Raihle is the same Minneapolis businessman who later was to aid Kitty Jones with her "American Seminar on Education." At home, Mr. Raihle had served as an officer of the Parents Council organized to oppose the "common learnings" program in the Minneapolis schools.][12]
3. A distribution of material written by Augustin Rudd of the Guardians of American Education.
4. An urge to "support the petition in Congress to investigate socialism in the public schools."
5. A discussion of the need to get into every PTA, "to convert the Board of Education and to attack Dr. Broome" [then Superintendent of Montgomery County Schools].

Despite the rather ominous portent, the Parents League did not create a great stir. The PTA-infiltration plan was not successful, and in fact Superintendent Broom denied in 1951 that Montgomery County Schools were even under attack.[13]

Nor was the League wholly successful in its plan "to attack Dr. Broome." He retired in 1953, after thirty years in the county schools. The new superintendent, Forbes Norris, inherited several sets of problems. The Parents League seemed to take little official part in the controversies besetting board and administration, but it is obvious that its viewpoint was well represented.

Some of the turmoil was reflected in the bitter campaign for school board membership in 1954. One of the candidates was a member of the Minute Women organization which had spearheaded the attack on Houston schools culminating in the removal of a deputy superintendent. Another was Wylie Barrow, the member of the Parents League whom we quoted a few pages back. And one candidate for reelection aroused comment when, by disavowing school board minutes, he attempted to deny measures he himself had introduced. One stand he sought to modify was his resolution which had the effect of permitting the American Legion, the DAR and others to review copies of school text books. . ."[14] An observer recalls that this was "the McCarthy election," fought largely on the purely academic issue of whether UNESCO materials should be used in schools—an academic issue because no such materials *were* used in Montgomery County schools.

While the campaign was under way, a columnist also reported:

. . . the Chicago Tribune group wants to undertake a private study of the school system!

Bernie Harter, former managing editor of the old Washington Times-Herald when owned by the Chicago Tribune, has been approached by "friends" to make a quiet unofficial survey of the school system.

Harter was a crack editor. . . . But following up a crime story or figuring out whether to put a rape headline on the front page is a lot different from surveying the school system and books. . . . The school board, of course, knows nothing about this proposed survey. It's all been kept very hush-hush . . . if any school survey is to be made, it should be done by properly authorized officials, and with all the people knowing about them, not by unqualified people with secret axes to grind.[15]

Following a fiery three years, the Montgomery County School Board voted, in 1957, not to reappoint the superintendent. Among the reasons listed were the "textbook censorship controversy"; an administrative decision suspending seven high school students for fraternity membership; and general " 'administrative lack of judgment.' "[16] While the board denied that racial integration had anything to do with its decision, one report stated "it was integration that set off the biggest rifts, with Dr. Norris insisting on a middle-of-the-road course while factions of the board sought either swift integration or no integration."[17]

Restlessness in the community was reflected in the board, where disagreements were so frequent and severe "that it seriously considered a resolution regulating seating of members, as a move to create harmony at board meetings." The local Citizens Committee for Fair Play in Public Service spoke of " 'the school board's scheme to saddle Dr. Norris with most of the controversial headaches of its administration,' " and interpreted charges against Norris as " 'a self-righteous attempt to cover hopeless splits among board members themselves. . . .' "[18]

One further problem added to Montgomery County's difficulties: that of financing schools. When Dr. Norris was appointed superintendent in 1957, he faced budget troubles in his requests for the following year. Only 85 per cent of a budget he deemed essential in the light of anticipated enrollment increases was granted. His predictions came true. The fall of 1957 found 1,500 pupils in double classes, with some classes meeting in nearby churches and, in one case, three classes meeting simultaneously in a single "all-purpose" room.[19]

This is the background for the situation that existed in Montgomery County in late 1957, when a Second Wave of educational criticism began. Possibly such a background may prove an integral part of the pattern of most Second Wave attacks. In any case, events in Montgomery County strongly point to these conclusions: attacks on schools do not come to maturity in a vacuum. Rarely if ever are contemporaneous charges limited to one or two specific demands or protests; rarely do they develop without relation to issues of a political or quasi-political nature—and the most frequent single problem which seems tied to educational criticism is that of paying for schools.

The 1948–1957 events in Montgomery County laid the foundation for subsequent school problems. These events revealed a core of vociferous objectors—not all of whom can safely be assumed to have moved, lost interest, or changed their minds. But since the Parents League for Curriculum Improvement—the apparent nucleus of the fundamentalist group—lived about ten years without gaining wide local support, it would seem that the fundamentalist point of view was not particularly strong in Montgomery County.

Late in 1957, however, the county's educational fundamentalists received a boost from a brand-new source: a recently formed "Conservative Club." A number of the views expressed earlier by the Parents League jibed neatly with those expounded by the new group:

> We believe that the most important concern of the local community is the education of its youth. But it is the *kind* of education that is important: we believe that bad education is worse than no education. We favor the highest standards of administration and instruction; and we favor curricula that emphasize the basic disciplines and that encourage respect and devotion for traditional American institutions and values. We are opposed to so-called progressive education. We also oppose attempts to indoctrinate our youth in moral relativism, welfarism, one-worldism, disrespect for Constitutional government and other tenets of the Liberal orthodoxy.[20]

In November of 1957, the Conservative Club sponsored a meeting featuring an address by Mortimer Smith, Executive Secretary of the Council for Basic Education. Some of the 125 people attending the meeting had the distinct impression that several other organizations had a share in sponsoring Mr. Smith.[21] Two of these organizations were the Parents League for Curriculum Improvement and the Montgomery Petition Group whose *raison d'être* is apparently identical to that of the White Citizens Councils of other communities.

The title of Mr. Smith's talk was "Planned Mediocracy in Our Schools." The double-barbed title—not plain "mediocracy," but deliberately *planned* mediocracy—expressed an idea that is not foreign to the organization with which Mr. Smith is associated. His talk also reiterated the message of his several books in advocating that "Liberal Arts people . . . take the leadership in education away from the 'professional educators.' "[22]

The Conservative Club has been labeled by its president as a " 'political action' group." A look at its "Declaration of Principles" clearly confirms the aptness of the designation. The group's position on a few major issues is as follows:

> . . . "Co-existence" with Communism is neither desirable, nor possible, nor honorable. . . .
>
> We deplore the tendency to subordinate United States foreign policy to that of the United Nations. . . .
>
> We favor a constitutional amendment, in the nature of the original Bricker Amendment. . . .
>
> We believe that it is the job of government to protect its citizens' lives, liberty and property. All other activities of government tend to diminish freedom and hamper progress. . . . We believe that Big Government is inherently, bad government. . . .
>
> . . . We believe . . . that public education is the exclusive concern of State and local governments, and that any form of federal aid to education imperils this principle. . . .
>
> We oppose the income tax . . . it is discriminatory and confiscatory. . . .
>
> . . . We reject "middle of the roadism" as a political philosophy because we believe it implies a denial of principle. It is an expression of political timidity and moral emptiness.

Although this might suggest that the interests of the Conservative Club are limited to national affairs, its "political action" was to take place at the local level as well. The Club's president announced that the group would " 'approach' " candidates to run for the county school board—and indeed, the organization began campaigning months in advance for the November elections. On January 30, 1958, political scientist Willmoore Kendall of Yale University was the Conservative Club's speaker. Professor Kendall's topic was so highly reminiscent of Smith's message to the group, delivered not two months earlier, as to suggest a certain collusion of intent, if not collusion by actual design. And two meetings in two months devoted to education—only one of many interests stated in its four pages of "Principles"—tends to suggest considerable Conservative Club emphasis on education.

Kendall's title was "Who Should Control Our Public Schools?" His general theme was virtually identical with that of Smith's, but markedly less temperate: Professional educators, and the NEA as their official organ, are conspiring to exercise authoritarian control over public schools—and in fact, have already succeeded. Control of education is completely in the hands of left-wing liberals, and the NEA and educators are using the schools to indoctrinate. Professor Kendall issued a call to action: "The 'ordinary people' should stage a revolt against professional educators and recapture control of the public school system."

While Professor Kendall's diagnosis was definitive enough, his prescription was less clear. With respect to a positive educational program, the speaker stated only that " 'ordinary people' " know the subjects needed to educate; what we must do is to weed out all incapable pupils and then require of the balance the mastery of " 'hard' " subjects. Professor Kendall closed with the telling comment, "I am skeptical . . . of any report that any public school system is much good."[23]

When one person in the audience of 225 attempted to defend the Montgomery County School Board as conscientious and alert, he "drew hoots of derisive laughter." Obviously, the Conservative Club's crowd was not to prove sympathetic to county school officials.

The Conservative Club was as good as its word. It backed candidates for each of the six school board seats in the 1958 election. The group were quickly dubbed the " 'sound education' candidates." All six urged a stress on the "fundamentals," and five of the six urged economy or "watchful" use of the tax dollar. The most unequivocal statement on economy came from Wylie Barrow, the member of both the board and the Parents League whom we have already met. He put his position bluntly: "The 'per pupil' cost to educate children in Montgomery County has risen sharply . . . the time has come for some leveling off. . . . I do not believe that dollars are necessarily the key to a good education."[24]

For the enlightenment of voters, the Montgomery County Council of PTA's prepared a detailed record of votes on selected split decisions made by the board. The two incumbent " 'sound education' " board members had been consistent in their votes on school money matters. They had consistently voted together, and usually without further support, on such matters as these: in favor of old building standards in elementary school construction, since the new standards would increase costs by 5 per cent; against increased salaries for teachers completing thirty hours of work beyond the Master's Degree; in favor of reducing scheduled salary increases for administrative personnel; against the expansion of elementary school libraries; and in favor of cutting "instructional-service" budget provisions by nearly 30 per cent.[25]

In the 1958 election, the "sound education" contingent was trounced: none of the group's six candidates was elected. Not to be outdone, four of the six would-be officeholders turned up several months later on the executive committee of a brand-new organization in Montgomery County: a "Council for Better Schools." One of the four was the former board member, also of the Parents League. Another had been a vice president of the old Parents League.

The announced purpose of the new organization was " 'to try to improve the quality of education . . . through . . . advocating that public schools concentrate more of their time, effort and money on intellectual development'. . ."[26] The educational fundamentalist position rings in the president's claim that "it seems eminently sensible to try some of the 'old fashioned' methods again."[27] But this is not really the emphasis which has come to be primarily associated with the Council. Local papers were soon referring to "the economy-minded Council for Better Education" as a group that "has repeatedly urged reductions in School Board budgets and tighter controls over its spending."[28] Two Council officials even brought suit to assure that the county manager retain the right to cut school board budget requests. The Council had backed many of the specific reductions made by the manager. Once again, there is nothing inherently evil about urging economy, even in schools, but it does make the "Better Education" label ambiguous.

The Council for Better Schools (or Better Education—it is called both) announced that it would nominate a full slate of candidates for the three school board seats at stake in the 1960 election. Again, voters turned down the educational fundamentalist position. But it is not likely that Montgomery County has heard the last of the Council for Better Education.

Meanwhile, the Conservative Club has not been wholly inactive either. Though the Council for Better Education has clearly raised the louder voice, the Conservatives occasionally have taken the lead—in protesting, for example, the donation of the county's obsolete textbooks to a program distributing them overseas.[29] Despite the 1958 reversal, the Conservative Club president had announced that the *next* school board election, in 1960, would be a prime concern of the organization. Local papers do not report whether CBE candidates received the official endorsement of the Conservative Club, but apparently the club did not find it necessary to name its own set of candidates.

Several things suggest that the Conservative Club is not done. Were the group's interests confined solely to education, its first school board election *might* have provided a real dampener to Club enthusiasm and activities. But its many interests not immediately related to education may provide the mortar to keep the organization together—and perhaps enable it to return to school issues. An editorial—glumly launched with the comment "Something like the Conservative Club was bound to happen"—suggests further why groups such as this one may tend gradually to enlist community cooperation:

> There are several reasons why the chip-on-the-shoulder organization was bound to spring up. There has been—and is—parental unrest. This has been brought on by many factors. The Conservative Club can be counted upon to seek out this unrest wherever it can find it and feed hungrily upon it. Wherever there is parental doubt and uncertainty, the Conservative Club will exploit it. Many parents with real grievances against the school system will flock to its banner. Others with imagined grievances (they're not teaching school now the way they did when I was a kid) will join up, too. Some who would tear down rather than build up are already active in the group.[30]

This suggests that the Conservative Club may tend to gather support for its stand on the schools from disparate, disgruntled elements. Why a "political action group" might seek earnestly to do just this is suggested again and again by the House Lobbying Activities Committee:

> Direct lobbying is increasingly giving way to more subtle and tangential methods of influence. The major emphasis in lobbying today is the effort to build and sustain public opinion, for the pressure groups have realized that public opinion in a democracy is the bedrock of legislative policy.
>
> Many pressure groups recognize the importance of educational institutions as molders of public opinion, and a particular effort is made to reach and to utilize these institutions to the fullest extent. . . .
>
> . . . These groups have long since recognized that lobbying of the traditional variety is not enough to insure lasting legislative success. As a consequence, they have entered upon a far-reaching and infinitely ambitious struggle to control public opinion. The effort to reach this opinion in the bud through dictation of . . . [education] is . . . one aspect of this struggle.[31]

The long life of the Parents League for Curriculum Improvement bears witness to the dogged and lively survival of education fundamentalism in the county. The League lasted at least ten years, was known to have joined forces with the Conservative Club on at least one occasion, and at present may lie restlessly dormant, ready to renew its battle.

The experience of the Montgomery County school system in its battle over educational fundamentalism is far from unique. Concerted demands for a return to the "fundamentals"—almost always accompanied by protests over school costs—have been heard in New York, Virginia, Indiana, Michigan, Ohio, Oregon, and California.

In a New York community such a fundamentalist group was successful in its campaign to defeat a much needed school bond issue. In an Ohio suburb a citizens' group known variously as the "Basic Education Committee," the "Basic Education Group," and the "Citizens Council for Basic Education" managed to elect two of its four candidates for school board membership. (Although, where the Council campaigned vigorously, "their candidates made a poorer showing than in precincts where little or no campaigning in their behalf was conducted.")[32] One of the two candidates elected promptly disassociated himself from the "basic education" program. The second very shortly became involved in such activities as harassing the administration, impugning the motives of the superintendent, denouncing the curriculum and the absence of standards, and releasing unfounded statements to local papers prior to board meetings.[33]

In the Far West, a division of community opinion over a school budget proposal led to the formation of two rival citizens' groups in one town. Both groups adopted names indicating interest in good schools; one group campaigned in favor of the budget proposal; the other led the fight against it. As the opposition group gained strength, it began to question the schools' aims, and denounce the curriculum. As a result, an "evaluation committee" representing both groups began to study the local schools.

The introduction of extraneous literature, however, may have somewhat impaired the committee's objectivity. A number of residents began receiving materials from a national organization that according to its own policies, could not partake in a local struggle. But its influence is apparent in the evaluation committee's final report:

> Public concern for their schools has developed and grown since about the time of World War II. . . . We began to hear of "bonehead" courses for college freshmen. . . . The scholar was no longer acclaimed. He abdicated to the "socially adjusted." Promotion was in order with or without defined standards of achievement. A high school diploma became a certificate of attendance, not a badge of accomplishment. New courses in high schools were instigated. . . . Costs and demands seemed to be growing faster than some people felt were justified. It became increasingly difficult for many to understand and approve all this or to maintain faith in their school system.[34]

More specifically, the committee found:

> . . . the District is failing to provide its students with a sound and rigorous training in the fundamental disciplines, and . . . basic subjects are being neglected in favor of a conglomeration of "enriched" electives and activities.
>
> . . .the District, for a long time, has been embarked on a program of "progressive" education including an emphasis on "life adjustment." . . . the blame, if any is due . . . must be laid at the doorway of the teacher training institutions . . . the Committee is opposed to all such theories of education and opposed to its continuance. The Committee is pleased

to note a shift away from the pragmatism and intellectual dishonesty of those theories.

. . . there is insufficient drill in arithmetic fundamentals and spelling while penmanship standards seem to be missing entirely . . . there must be a good basis upon which to build and the only way to provide that basis is by drill, and drill, and drill. . . .*

Perhaps of equal significance are a few other findings of a somewhat different nature:

. . . it is the opinion of the Committee that more money or less money has very little to do with the quality of product turned out by any given educational system.

. . . the reason, or at least a reason, for . . . per pupil cost is . . . the pupil-teacher ratio . . . serious consideration should be given . . . to increasing the pupil per teacher ratio. . . .

. . . Classrooms, equipment and materials used for classes other than basic are almost always considerably more expensive than the classrooms, equipment and materials used for the basic subjects.

The highly specific recommendations of the evaluation committee included a full reorganization of the grading system—complete with suggestions as to curriculum, methods, and administrative procedures to be followed at each level, a "tightening" of discipline in the schools, and an abolition of the state's teacher tenure law.

Thus, Montgomery County has not been alone in experiencing a recent revival of educational fundamentalism—nor has the "basic education-lower costs" combination been unique.

* This, despite the fact that two pages earlier there appears, "The Committee believes that it cannot, as a group of laymen criticize the methods used in teaching. . . ."

THE SECOND WAVE

6. Aiders and Abettors

A reminder is in order: since the purpose of this book is not to answer but to analyze criticism, the following is in no sense a rebuttal to specific charges. This bears repeating simply because these critics have deplored the introduction of so-called "extraneous" issues, demanding that attention focus exclusively upon the content of their complaints. They tend to dismiss as irrelevant any investigation of people who bring the complaints, or of the logic they employ. Yet it is the premise of this book, which we hope makes its own proof, that the critics themselves, the nature of their charges, and the methods they use are highly pertinent considerations.

The dominant spokesman for the Second Wave of criticism is the Council for Basic Education. Its theme is somewhat different from those already discussed. For example, one does not typically learn from these people that schools and educators are subversive, nor do they generally promote censorship or bans on controversial topics in classrooms. The motif of current charges is that schools are anti-intellectual, not that they lack patriotism. But although in general this group has ignored the patriotic theme and has even neglected John Dewey (except for phrasemaking purposes, as in "Dewey-eyed notion"), there are still certain similarities of the Council for Basic Education to the organizations associated with the First Wave of criticism.

Dewey himself may be largely overlooked, but the label "progressive education" is not. In fact, prime targets of CBE plaints and barbs have been practices associated with progressive education—such practices as the participation of students in the planning of their work, and various attempts at learning by direct observation and "doing." The familiar assertion that public schools just aren't teaching anything also echoes an old refrain.

CBE, like the First Wave organizations, seeks to influence public policy through the molding of public opinion, so it too is a pressure group. CBE assumes that the public needs "educating" toward a particular point of view, and apparently also assumes a rather pervasive ignorance on the part of our citizenry. Paradoxically it urges that citizens exercise their rights and assert control over public schools —and immediately thereafter it accounts for the unenlightened majority who will not respond in the "right" way—CBE's way:

> . . . the time when . . . [progressive education] was most alive was precisely the time when today's young parents and teachers were themselves going through school. Small wonder, if some of these find the expanded program acceptable. With what more meaningful curriculum are they in a position to compare it, unassisted?

The way in which CBE brings its message to the public is also familiar. Considerable and highly successful use is made of the national press. The need to work at the local level is exhorted. There are even similarities in techniques of criticizing and in weapons used. Unfortunately, the techniques show the First Wave's tendency toward overgeneralization, a lack of evidence for claims, and a failure to admit what is demonstrably true. The weapon used with much skill is ridicule.

We are not trying to lay out a set of tournament rules for fair play, but a few quotes from the CBE monthly *Bulletin* make it easy to see why many schoolmen think of CBE as an "anti" group rather than as a potential source of help and improvement:

> Until we abandon this fetish . . . ["false professionalism"] . . . our elementary schools will continue to be centers for half-baked experimentation conducted by half-educated teachers.

> [From the regular feature, "Trivia of the Month"] How to get Mother and Dad—and probably the universe—straightened out in

> half an hour a week: Youngsters in the elementary grades at Iowa State Teachers College Laboratory School devote this period of time to classroom discussions that range, according to the teacher, "over things that are common to all families and all people." Examples: 'Why doesn't mother treat me as well as little brother?' . . . 'Why does teacher have it in for me?' 'Why can't Johnny read, write or spell?' Oops, sorry—that last question was asked by somebody else.
>
> . . . By law or by custom many state universities welcome all graduates of public schools within their state. For such a university suddenly to set up entrance requirements just *might* reveal unpleasant facts about the state system of public instruction or certain schools within it. . . .[1]

These quotations suggest one reason why so many educators question the good faith of CBE, but there are other reasons too. One is CBE's readiness to guffaw at weaknesses while failing to propose feasible alternatives. For example, CBE, in a lengthy review, describes a book as "a devastating analysis of the weird world of psycho- and sociometric testing," and sums up with ". . . this book overflows with evidence that psychometry is about as pure and reliable as, let us say, astrology. . . ."[2]

Assume that the CBE position is accurate. Assume that the entire science of testing is a very sloppy one. What does CBE suggest as substitutes for all the tests they condemn? If, as the *Bulletin* book review points out, we cannot get a stable indication of intelligence from an IQ test, on what basis are students to be grouped in classes—a practice the Council repeatedly urges? No alternative is proposed (unless the reference to astrology is intended as such). But an organization sincerely dedicated to the realization of the "ideal of democratic education"[3] would seem to have some obligation to improve on what it finds deplorable.

The research specialist, as well as the teacher and administrator, has been a favorite butt of Council humor, and one might wonder why an organization primarily concerned with "basic education" should wander so far afield. There is a great strategic advantage involved. By dismissing educational research as a branch of science fiction, its findings can be wholly discounted. Thus when the educationist seeks to reply factually to CBE charges, his facts may be dismissed casually and effortlessly—with no more trouble than it takes to encase the word *research* or *study* in quotation marks.

There are at least three additional types of pronouncement accounting for the educator's reluctance to accept CBE's formal professions of good faith. The first of these has to do with what is attributed to the educationist in general. A great many would indignantly deny allegiance to such practices and beliefs as these:

> . . . it is undisputably true that interest and ability do have an effect on learning and must be taken into account. . . . But, *with typical disregard for true scientific method, the educationist recognizes no limits within which this idea may be valid. Instead he immediately advances the dogma that there is no learning without a prior interest.*
>
> . . . Your modern educator says not only that the school must deal with every side of the child's life but he often insists that *all sides are of equal importance*. . . .
>
> Derived from the teachings of the early progressives, *this dogma* [of "freedom"] *implies that discipline,* both in the sense of control of conduct and as the process of directed training, *is somehow harmful* to the youthful. *Many educators seem to feel that the only alternative to the methods of Mr. Squeers is a completely permissive classroom atmosphere*. . . .
>
> Many educators, perhaps a majority, feel that psychological and sociological research has established enough "truths" about the nature of the child and the learning process to provide *infallible* guides to method and even content in the education of the very young. . . .
>
> . . . the important element in professional preparation for teaching and administration is *not knowledge of what is taught* but knowledge of how to teach and knowledge of the child. . . . *The advocates of this dogma . . . now dominate the public schools*. . . . [Italics are ours.][4]

There just isn't enough salve in an occasional pacifier to the effect that there are exceptions. This is equivalent to hearing that one is not a horse thief although the rest of the family surely are.

Another CBE practice which has spelled warning to the educationist has been the organization's frequent suggestion that the *schoolman* lacks good faith and sincerity. This impugning of motives has come about largely since the responsibility for Russia's Sputnik was laid none too gently at the door of American public schools. It has taken the form of accusing educationists of bandwagon-hopping—without conviction. This is quite curious: here is an organization which has been attempting for several years to win "converts" to a position it claims to hold in the national interest. Yet when it sees evidence that it has no monopoly on this position, it greets alleged "converts" in this way, in several issues of the *Bulletin*:

> Among American educators there is much lip service to the conception of purpose and the curriculum we have outlined. We might add that in the face of increasing public approval of this viewpoint about purpose, there is on the part of the educators a certain amount of bandwagon-jumping. . . .
>
> Everyone is welcome, of course [on "this bandwagon for quality"]. We only hope that nobody is along just for the ride.
>
> . . . we are, as we have suggested before in these pages, somewhat skeptical when well-known devotees of Life Adjustment education suddenly blossom forth as advocates of tougher courses and tightened discipline. . . .
>
> There *has* been more talk than action since Sputnik—and some professional educators have managed Herculean feats of band-wagon jumping that should serve them in good stead come the next Olympics. We are even ready to admit that some of the "toughened up" courses in the basic subjects, devised by administrators to meet what they consider merely passing parental pressure, may have less substance than shadow. . . .
>
> This belief in and plea for cooperation seems to be based on the conviction that since the Sputniks—and now Lunik—we are *all* believers in basic education and that the statements of some of the leading schoolmen, declaring their fidelity to the cause, are to be taken at face value.

A final explanation for the hostility of some educationists can be found in CBE's claim to an *exclusive* concern with *quality* in education. To people who have spent their lives on just this problem, it must come as a distinct surprise to learn in CBE *Bulletins* that "in the last year or so, many . . . educational organizations and many prominent educators . . . have . . . discovered the intellect and have been protesting their devotion to its nurture." Further, it is only since the Sputnik that educationists "have come to feel that the need for quality in education is pressing and widespread. . . ." Moreover, should there be educationists audacious enough to profess an interest in quality *antedating* Sputnik hysteria, the *Bulletin* has an explanation:

"In the general soul-searching which followed that event, many of these organizations not only jumped on the bandwagon but were not adverse to posing as the original designers of the chassis."

In the course of pointing out why the educationist may hold CBE suspect, we have noted some of its protests. (Additional CBE criticisms appear in our tables of questionnaire replies.) But what is CBE *for?* There are several ways of finding out. One is the official CBE "Statement of Purposes." Another way is to adopt a pattern the Council itself has suggested: a statement of beliefs compiled by the analyst rather than by the group analyzed.[5] Our summation, based on a perusal of the Council's *Bulletin,* would read like this:

1. We're not for overlooking "individual differences"—but that doesn't mean you can't teach all kids the same thing.
2. We're not against paying something for schools—but let's not leave the house money until we're sure the menus planned are what we've ordered.
3. We're not opposed to kids *understanding* what they read—but it will all come clear when they know the alphabet.
4. We're not for installing European education over here—but that's where they know what education's really about.
5. We're not against taxes for schools—but if you'd sit those kids down at desks all day (where they belong) think of what we'd save on lunchrooms!
6. We're not uninterested in education for everybody—but let's face it: the gifted are the pay dirt.
7. We're not opposed to paying for good education—but money has nothing to do with good education.
8. We're not against "research"—but until it arrives at ultimate truth, we're not letting it confuse us.

Admittedly, the CBE's own "Statement of Purpose" shares few resemblances to our summation. The summation is based on an analysis of what the *Bulletin* has said, not on the formal affirmations of the organization. Here is the official version in full:

The Council for Basic Education was established in the belief that the purpose of education is the harmonious development of the mind, the will, and the conscience of each individual so that he may use to the full his intrinsic powers and shoulder the responsibilities of good citizenship. The Council believes in the principle of universal education and in the tax-supported public school system. It insists that only by the maintenance of high academic standards can the ideal of democratic education be realized—the ideal of offering to all the children of all the people of the United States not merely an opportunity to attend school, but the privilege of receiving there the soundest education that is afforded any place in the world.

The Council initiates and supports measures to ensure:

(1) That all students, excepting only those few whose intellectual equipment is clearly too limited, receive adequate instruction in the basic intellectual disciplines, especially English, mathematics, science, history, and foreign languages;

(2) That the fullest possible opportunity is afforded to students of high ability to reach mature levels of achievement without waste of time;

(3) That clear standards of actual accomplishment are used to measure each student's progress and to govern promotion to higher levels of the educational system;

(4) That teachers are thoroughly educated in the subjects they teach and in current developments therein;

(5) That vocational training is offered in due subordination to the school's fundamental purpose of intellectual discipline;

(6) That school administrators are encouraged and supported in resisting pressures to divert school time to activities of minor educational significance, to curricula overemphasizing social adjustment at the expense of intellectual discipline, and to programs that call upon the school to assume responsibilities properly belonging to the home, to religious bodies, and to other agencies.[6]

We have already dealt at length with the Council for Basic Education, and in far more detail than we gave organizations aiding and abetting First Wave critics. The reason for this imbalance is that the importance of some of the previously discussed groups is mainly historical. Their influence—hence their threat to schools—seems markedly less today than five years ago. But the CBE is very much alive right now. So if this book is to help in dealing with current criticism, even further detail is warranted. One such "detail" is an evaluation of the Council on the basis of our criteria for valid criticism. Violations of the rules of evidence do not per se invalidate all of CBE's claims; nor do they confute the Council's purposes. But the number and diversity of these violations do spell out a message of great practical import. They suggest what kind of charges we are likely to hear from an organization prompted or inspired by the Council in any given community—or from a speaker, approved by the

Council, invited to address a local group. Here are some samples of the Council's violation of our six rules of evidence:

- First rule: One is not likely to arrive at facts by over-generalizing.

  . . . [mathematicians] *usually agree* that traditional high school *math is a mess,* that *many teachers of it are mathematically incompetent,* and that *95% of the textbooks are inadequate* (being written, it seems, by almost anybody but mathematicians). . . .

  . . . the authors [of *Reading: Chaos and Cure*] are to be commended for bringing to print again what *every* upper-elementary teacher knows, what *every* high-school teacher deplores, what sends *every* teacher of college English into fits of helpless weeping: the fact that after generations of public education *the majority* of Americans are at best only semiliterate. . . .

- Second rule: Those concerned with arriving at truth do not distort evidence:

  The opening statement [of a state education department syllabus] *is a frank admission that standards are to be abandoned:* "A major purpose of the change in the state English requirement is to free the twelfth grade from any uniform examination requirement and thus to afford each school and teacher freedom to provide whatever sort of program students need as their culminating high school experience in the subject."

- Third rule: Those interested in establishing fact follow the rules of logical inference:

  . . . the young child . . . has a knack for rapid observation and memorization that diminishes with increasing age. *That is the reason* why *logically organized subject matter,* involving *drill and memory work,* is a *time-tested method* for inculcating in the young those symbols and facts which must be part of the natural furnishing of the mind before it can solve *any* problems.

- Fourth rule: Those concerned with establishing the facts of a situation use evidence to do so—rather than emotion, humor, appeals to authority in the face of counterevidence, or appeals to irrelevant authority.

  Of the four lively factions [involved in the reading controversy], the first presents us (in fat and nearly unreadable volumes) with a formidable body of "scientific" research that accounts for the present status of reading instruction in our schools. It is defended in militant, even shrill tones by apologists who are confronted with the fact that

> their system is producing a staggering percentage of retarded readers and non-readers and national reading "norms" that are deplorable.
>
> The reading controversy centers in one issue: shall we *begin* by teaching words as meaningful wholes or as symbols of sounds? The educationist experts, almost to a man, insist on the first approach. . . . The scientific linguistics scholars, the humanities professors, and a vast number of interested laymen would challenge . . . [this approach]. [Italics are ours.][7]

Having examined CBE foibles and antagonisms, let us take a look at the organization itself. The Council for Basic Education was incorporated in the District of Columbia on July 3, 1956, "by a group of individuals who have been active in urging, through writings and speeches, an increased emphasis in the public school upon the fundamental intellectual disciplines. . . ."[8] History Professor Arthur Bestor of the University of Illinois is generally credited with organizing the Council. Many also credit him with having launched the educational fundamentalism campaign nationally. There are, however, at least two other contenders for this distinction: romance languages Professor Harold Clapp of Grinnell College and botanist Harry Fuller of the University of Illinois. Regardless of how the idea began, the three men apparently divided the honors amicably: Professor Bestor served as the Council's first president; Professor Clapp became its first executive secretary; and Professor Fuller was the first chairman of the board.

The structure of CBE makes it unlikely that any insurgent group will ever wrest the reins by mere vote. Policy for the organization is made not by its members assembled but by its Senate. This body consists of four "Groups": the "Founding Group," which numbers ten members who hold office "until their resignation or death"; the "Officers and Directors" Group, who total nine; "Group III," consisting of no more than nine representatives of organizations affiliated with the Council; and "Group IV," a maximum of nine people elected by the membership at large. The two major tasks of the Senate are to elect officers and to determine policy—which includes adopting and amending bylaws. (Apparently members are not always informed of the Senate's activities. The full report to members after one annual Senate convocation, for instance, contained only this: "After the scheduled business of the meeting was accomplished, there was extended discussion of matters relating to general policy. . . .")[9] There is a standard complement of officers—a president, vice president, and treasurer—and these, plus six others, serve as CBE's directors. All the directors are elected by the Senate. Although the Senate is the policy-making body, the board of directors is the "legally responsible body"[10] of the Council.

CBE offers both individual and organizational memberships. At the end of its first six months of operation, there were 158 individual members; two years later, in 1958, membership was reported at 1,400. In 1959 it totaled 1,465.[11] The CBE *Bulletin* reports that among a "sample" consisting of the first 500 membership applications for 1957, there were 109 "educationists" (teachers and administrators), 175 higher education people, and 216 " 'laymen.' "

From the start, the Council has made provision for organizational memberships. Both the acceptable types of organization and the means by which such groups might become associated with CBE were spelled out in the original bylaws:

> Any learned society (or federation of such societies) concerned with the scholarly and scientific fields that are ordinarily represented in the public school curriculum, professional society, society concerned with the improvement of teaching in the various academic fields, or general organization that has manifested a continuous interest in education may, if it desires to associate itself in the work of the Council, nominate a representative. Such representative shall be elected to membership in the Council in the manner prescribed . . . for the election of individual members.

Since the representatives of up to nine of these associated groups comprise "Group III" of the CBE Senate, it is obvious that Council affiliates are offered some share in the determination of policy. As of 1958, these affiliates numbered ten: American Association of Teachers of Italian, American Classical League, American Geographical Society, Botanical Society of America, Classical Association of the Middle West and South, Classical Association of New England, Engineering Manpower Commission, Men Teachers Club of Chicago, Scientific Manpower Commission, and South Atlantic Modern Language Association. Of these, eight appear to have been affiliated with CBE from the start, with two joining later.

The organizational memberships provision gives rise to several questions of significance. First, according to the bylaws, any "society concerned with the improvement of teaching in the various academic fields, or general organization that has manifested a continuous interest in education . . ." is eligible to join CBE. If these criteria actually do govern the acceptance or rejection of petitioners, then *any* organization which has criticized schools is eligible. Thus, all those discussed in Chapter IV are eligible, as well as virtually all which replied to our questionnaire. The current affiliates are predominantly learned societies, but the bylaws may introduce difficulties for CBE at some future date—and, depending on the decision adopted, for schoolmen as well.

A question of equal import is the matter of *local* affiliates. With American educational decisions being made in local districts, the existence of CBE units within these districts could be of considerable significance—as events in Montgomery County clearly show. The wording of the bylaws statement on Council affiliates does not rule out local groups, but Council staff members denied that local groups are eligible for formal association, and at least one disclaimer has been publicly stated: ". . . there are no chapters or local branches of CBE. . . ."[12] Some of the problems posed by the question of local affiliates were discussed in the report of CBE's first executive secretary:

> . . . How far can CBE move in at the grass roots, and yet avoid entanglement in local, emotional feuds? We could make dreadful mistakes by rushing in swinging; yet to hold back, and play the judicious role will often look—to people that we ought to be helping—like coldness or simple poltroonery. Moreover, it is at the local level that the most effective work for our cause might be done; American education is essentially a grass-roots enterprise, not a Federal one. Yet to date we have felt obliged to forego the impetus that community chapters or regional branches of CBE might give to the movement.
>
> Perhaps some day we can find a formula by which we can enjoy the advantages of grass-roots organization without the grave disadvantages of a situation in which we would be held responsible for what was said and done in our name by persons over whom we could not claim any meaningful authority. . . .
>
> Our relationship with individual communities will continue to be on an *ad hoc* basis and a matter for as much tact as can be mustered, but useful policies can be created cumulatively. . . .

This report seemed to suggest that the question had not then been settled. But if official membership is not now extended to local organizations, several specific types of aid have clearly been offered. Among other services the Council provides to local groups, it sends material to specific individuals at the request of others to whom, apparently, it will assure anonymity.[13] On at least one occasion, the Council has prepared statements for local newspapers.[14]

It also maintains a list of speakers sharing CBE views, and from this list speakers are recommended to local groups. We have already mentioned that Mortimer Smith, then CBE executive secretary (now "Executive Director"), spoke before the Montgomery County Conservative Club. We asked a CBE staff member—the assistant to the secretary—whether Professor Willmoore Kendall, who also addressed the Conservative Club, had represented the Council. His answer was that the CBE keeps a list of speakers whose names are supplied to organizations seeking speakers.

Another local service initially advertised by the Council was the evaluation of specific school systems. Plans stated in both CBE's incorporation certificate and its first "descriptive leaflet" included arranging "school surveys . . . by properly qualified specialists. . . ." The surveys were to be undertaken at the request of "school boards or other legally responsible bodies." The executive secretary reported, however, that as of October, 1957, there had been "no takers." Perhaps it was this evident lack of enthusiasm which led to the deletion of the offer from revised descriptions of the CBE program.

At least one more service CBE has offered sympathizers in local communities is that of an employment bureau. As early as March, 1957, a *Bulletin* announced that while CBE was "not in a position to set up a full scale employment agency," the organization "would, however, like to be of use informally along this line. . . ." The offer has been repeated several times since, in more fully developed form: "If any superintendent, principal or school board of our persuasion is searching for congenial company the Council is willing to act as an informal (and of course, unpaid) broker." And, "We will be glad to place on file any names which are sent in and will do our best to help the right persons to come together."

CBE's national activities have been easier to trace than their local ones. In its first "descriptive leaflet," CBE stated that it would attempt the following: a news bulletin; sponsoring and/or encouraging investigations of teacher certification, curricula, examinations, and school legislation; proposals to improve curricula, and teacher preparation and certification; coordinating the educational activities of "scholarly and scientific" groups; urging that "the scholarly world" be represented in considerations of school policy; arranging school surveys; providing "good offices . . . to bring about cooperation between school authorities and learned societies . . ."; and arranging of educational conferences.

Apparently, not all the plans received attention. The *Bulletin* began to appear monthly immediately after CBE was formed. Some of the features fairly regularly included are reviews of publications and descriptions of "Programs in Practice"—some of which are lauded and others of which are described under the heading "Trivia of the Month."

Three or four attempts at improving the general educational situation have been under way. One seems to have grown from rather humble and informal beginnings. A May, 1957, *Bulletin* item—"Arithmetic Anyone?"—asked, "Can anyone contribute or lend to CBE any interesting arithmetic textbooks of an earlier era or from good school systems abroad? We would like to embark on a little comparative study." Six months later, CBE's associate secretary reported that a comparative study of European and American textbooks in elementary arithmetic was under way. The purpose was to help settle the question of whether European mathematics teaching is superior to that available in this country, and to "point to improvements where they are needed."[15]

Another CBE textbook study well worth watching seeks to evaluate social studies texts. The choice of a director for the study may prove costly to the Council's carefully cultivated nonpartisan image, for his rightist preoccupations are known. Dr. Jerzy Hauptman has contributed to the conservative journal *Modern Age*. He also brings to CBE's staff his experience gleaned in a textbook evaluation effort under the leadership of rightist spokesman Russell Kirk.[16]

Perhaps the most extensive CBE effort undertaken to date is a Basic Curriculum Study that culminated in a volume entitled *The Case for Basic Education*. The initial announcement described the aim of this project as "the production of a handbook for laymen, school boards, teachers, and administrators defining academic standards in each of the basic subjects. . . ."[17] More comprehensively, the undertaking arose from the need for "an authoritative statement, emanating from the learned world, that would explain the importance of the basic subjects and set forth what knowledge and understanding a student ought to be equipped with at the end of twelve years of public schooling."[18] The list of basic subjects stated in the original announcement was later lengthened to include these twelve: American history, European history, political science, English composition, literature, classical languages, modern languages, geography, mathematics, biology, chemistry, and physics.

The volume itself represents sixteen contributors' ideas of just what constitutes "basic education" in as many fields, plus an opening chapter by Clifton Fadiman and a finale by a school board member with nine years' service to his credit. We are told that the work is not intended as a curriculum guide or syllabus and that it includes no attention to such matters as sequence or "whether a given subject should be offered as one course or several." Although there are actually quite a number of comments to these points, CBE apparently plans to devote a separate book to such problems.

The Case for Basic Education makes clear from the start that the authors are concerned solely with "the student who is variously called 'bright,' 'capable,' 'able,' 'serious,' or simply 'good.'" This preoccupation becomes evident time and again throughout the work—in such fundamental fashion, for example, as to serve as a criterion for electives recommended in the book: "Art and music are most often chosen by good students and so are included here. . . ." (The other two electives thought appropriate for high school students are speech and philosophy.)

The book is but Phase I of a three-part project. Phase II will be concerned with the means of attaining goals, and Phase III will apparently offer a program for preparing people to teach under the circumstances described in Phases I and II.*

* Interestingly, Phases II and III will lead the Council into a realm they have deplored as unworthy of investigation: the bewildering world of pedagogy. CBE's position—sometimes tacit, sometimes explicit—has been that *teaching* is no problem; having mastered a field, a man can teach it. By even entertaining thoughts of a volume devoted to curriculum planning and course guides (Phase II)—and another to teacher preparation (Phase III)—CBE has reversed itself! The plan suggests the fascinating prospect of rival camps of "educationists."

One feature emphasized in the planning for Phase I bears repeating:

> The Council wishes to stress two points about the first phase of the Study: (1) It is not being conducted by "curriculum specialists," but by subject matter specialists and scholars; and (2) although each participant will benefit by discussion with and criticism from his colleagues (and a certain unity of viewpoint may therefore be expected), the completed document will not be a committee, or group, report but will represent the seasoned opinions of individual specialists in the various subject areas.[19]

Chapters vary in approach, concern, and merit—as might be expected to follow from CBE's general condemnation of committee work. It is interesting to note, however, that the foreword states "acknowledgment is . . . made to all those, and their number is great, who helped in the construction of the book. . . ." And author Ray Billington, of the chapter on American history, apparently did not operate according to CBE's lone wolf policy. He expresses appreciation to a list of thirty-four individuals.

Many of the recommendations advanced in *The Case for Basic Education* have long been supported warmly and widely by high school teachers, and there is more than one vigorous condemnation of alleged practices one would have to search long and hard to find. Amid a number of suggestions both good and bad, one finds such paradoxes as a lively denunciation of the lumping together of "social studies"—followed by the geographer's insistence that geography stress "the vast and complex *economic and political interrelations* between parts of the earth's surface"; and the historian's insistence that "particularly in high school, it should be *integrated* history . . . it should deal with economic, social, political, and cultural developments. . . ." (Italics are ours.) But integrated "social studies" are out.

According to the *Bulletin*, "several projected research studies" have also been considered. Although none is named in the report, several have been mentioned elsewhere. In announcing the Council's basic curriculum study, the *Bulletin* mentioned a study "to determine what proportion of the general student population can actually handle a rigorous program of studies, including foreign languages and advanced mathematics," and noted that CBE directors feel such a study to be important and "one which has not, to their knowledge, been undertaken before." A second project mentioned frequently is the development of "a national system of academic achievement examinations for students. . . ." CBE has long deplored the dearth of tests that reliably measure the "quality" of educational achievement. This project would evidently solve the problem, and would be followed by a "system of examinations" to reveal teachers' competence in the subjects they teach.

* * *

Throughout this book we have assumed that three sets of factors are important in determining what an organization stands for: what it says it stands for; what it does—its statements and activities in the course of carrying out its program—and its relationships to other organizations and individuals active in the same or related fields. We have now examined CBE in the light of the first two factors. Before leaving it, we need to give some attention to the third. We must look at some individuals and organizations endorsed by CBE, and inquire carefully into one type with which CBE seems to have much in common.

We are not ascribing guilt by association. In fact, CBE would doubtless feel—and with justification—that no guilt follows from these names. Among those who stand in well enough with CBE to merit more than one *Bulletin* mention are Hyman Rickover, Paul Woodring, John Keats, Clifton Fadiman, the late Dorothy Thompson, and the latter-day Sloan Wilson.

CBE has given Admiral Rickover's addresses on education the rare epithet "wise." To clinch the affinity, his stature was assured when the *Bulletin* noted "the fact that the name of Admiral Hyman Rickover is mud among many American educators. . . ." Enthusiasm for the educational psychologist Woodring is more restrained—on the ground that "while there is much to be said for being middle-of-the-road, bumping along the road-bed between the tracks isn't the most efficient means of locomotion." But the *Bulletin* does review a Woodring book favorably, with the conclusion that "it is almost always on the side of the angels—CBE's side, of course."[20] Several of John Keats's works have been recommended to readers of the *Bulletin*, and it is said that for the uninitiated his *Schools Without Scholars* "may well be the ideal book for clarifying the issues."

There have been plaudits for several other professional publicists, as well as for Keats. Clifton Fadiman has been congratulated on two grounds—his defense of formalism with respect to the English language, and his spotting of " 'the current mess in education.' "[21] The recent Sloan Wilson—converted from the days of his early articles—earned laurels with a feature on the costs of school construction.[22] But the object of virtually unbounded CBE admiration was Dorothy Thompson, "enlightened critic of American education." Her work was cited so often—as consisting of "cogent pleas for worthy programs of education," and as revealing "wisdom and common sense in the wisest and most sensible series of education articles that we know"—that an apology was printed: "We trust our frequent mention of Miss Thompson is not getting tiresome but . . ."

A somewhat different kind of relationship may be shared by CBE and certain periodicals. Several national magazines seem to have contributed to the Council's cause, but, as we have stated before, this may either reflect editorial sympathy or commitment, or may show only what is judged likely to sell magazines. At any rate, a decisive CBE sympathy for the *Reader's Digest* has matured. The January, 1959, *Bulletin* mourned with the *Digest* "one of the elementary facts of life—namely, that those who criticize public education, no matter how honestly, are apt to be 'misrepresented and maligned' by national organizations." The "victimizing" of the *Digest* occurred, not after its initial question-begging article, "Do School Pupils Need Costly Palaces?"* but a year later—after the publication of two barbed articles in a single issue: "Must Schools Be Palaces?" and "The Mess in Education."[23]

These condolences lead us to CBE's views on school costs. The *Digest's* position seems clear. It denied any but a "constructive" policy with respect to public education.[24] After charging that the articles had provoked "an immediate outcry from the National School Boards Association and allied bureaucracies," the editors align themselves with "the public interest in these days of onerous taxation," and conclude —after a fascinating bit of fancy footwork—that those criticizing the articles are thereby "putting themselves on record as advocating unchecked extravagance with the taxpayers' money."

Lower taxes and government economy are not exactly new interests

* Once more: "When did you stop beating your wife?"

for the *Reader's Digest*. The magazine has reprinted at least three articles of the Foundation for Economic Education, an organization to be considered at length in the next chapter.[25] The FEE president told the House Lobbying Committee that "there are quite a number of members of the senior staff of *Reader's Digest* who by request are on our mailing list." Indeed, one of these senior staff members requested that the *Digest* get previews of all FEE materials, in order to reprint them before other publications might do so. And a *Digest* officer wrote of the magazine's responsibility for educating the public, "for their own good and for the good of the country, to an understanding of sound economics."[26]

What has this to do with the Council for Basic Education? Since CBE has been on the receiving end of criticism from educationists, any sympathies for the *Reader's Digest* conceivably might reveal only an instance of "fellow feeling." But there is evidence that the sympathy involved may extend beyond condolences, and to views shared by the two organizations.

The stand of the *Digest*'s editors on school costs may be inferred from the titles of two of the articles we have cited—"Do School Pupils Need Costly Palaces?" and "Must Schools Be Palaces?"—particularly when these are considered in the light of the magazine's interest in "sound economics" and in the program of the Foundation for Economic Education. The position of the Council for Basic Education on school costs is a bit more elusive. There is nothing on school costs and financing in CBE's Statement of Purpose. The report of the first executive secretary seems to warn against taking a stand on the subject. Dr. Clapp cautioned Council members, ". . . we would dissipate our possible effectiveness to the vanishing point, and become quickly discredited in circles where we need allies, if we were to take a stand on certain large questions that we have avoided. . . ." Among the questions he specifically mentioned was that of federal aid to public schools.

The official stand, however, has not constrained the CBE *Bulletin* to skirt the issue. Even during Professor Clapp's term of office, when he edited the *Bulletin*, there were a number of statements suggesting that we might desirably spend less than we now allot to public education. In no case do these references consist of out-and-out recommendations that school funds be reduced. The Council simply says repeatedly that there is little or no relationship between the quality of education and the money spent on it. Apparently to "prove" the point, two issues of the *Bulletin* contained articles maintaining that a state which "ranks among the top states in financial support of education . . . is also a leader . . . in . . . educational nonsense."[27] The "proof" involves a painful logical error—a startling emanation from "the learned world": The Council apparently perceives no difference between what constitutes a *necessary* condition and what amounts to a *sufficient* condition. Although many educationists believe money to be necessary to quality education, to our knowledge there have been none so brash as to suggest that it is *all* that is needed.

Bulletin titles alone suggest CBE sentiments on the subject of school costs. One subtly inquires, "Can Good Education Be Bought?" while another asserts "Money Is Not the Root of All Improvement." An article on school construction is expressively titled "Build Thee More Stately Mansions." These and other articles—sometimes with totally unrelated general themes—include such italicized statements as:

> . . . *the correlation between cost and academic achievement is practically zero!* . . .
>
> *The average child of today ought to be as thoroughly educated as the exceptional child of 1900, because he is spending much more time in school and receiving far more costly instruction.**[28]

CBE seems to have departed from Clapp's warning against the federal aid issue. *Bulletin* articles have dealt directly with the subject. One consists largely of quoted testimony before a House Committee, and contains no comment. The effect of the paragraphs quoted, however, is to show that federal government scholarships are unnecessary in getting the talented to college, and would probably have the effect of discouraging private and state scholarships.[29] The distance of such a theme from CBE's official "sound education" purposes seems to render this article totally irrelevant. In another article touching on federal aid, CBE briefly discussed the 1958 National Defense Education Act ("a hotchpotch"). Also noted was the NEA president's

* We cannot refrain from solving all the world's ills by pursuing this argument to its conclusion. If we are really serious about current problems, let's put all children into year-round, full-time schools—which we shall finance with the whole of the gross national product—and produce thereby a full generation of Einsteins.

statement that the Act was gratifying but—in terms of actual needs—" 'a drop in the bucket.' " In typical bulletinese, CBE comments, "Some drop! Some bucket!"

Whether or not the Council has formally opposed federal aid to schools, other federal-aid opponents believe they have found a staunch ally in CBE. The basis of this belief, as reported by one such group, is not inconsiderable:

> Mortimer Smith, Executive Secretary of the Council for Basic Education, has aligned the authority of his respected organization against the Federal aid proponents. In a letter to the *Washington Post*, January 8 [1958], Smith said that "my fear is that this mountain of Federal cash they seek will only strengthen and perpetuate the 'soft' theory of education which they have imposed on the schools for 30 or more years. . . . I suggest that before we Americans plug too hard for Federal money, we ask ourselves if we are satisfied with the *status quo* in education and want to buy more of the same."[30]

We must admit that this quotation contains an element that should be recognized and conceded: however devious we may judge its exploitation, there is a certain logical tie between CBE's apparent position on money for schools and other portions of the Council program. CBE opposes subjects it thinks are "non-essential." It also expresses opposition to certain teaching media such as educational television. If we were to strip the curriculum of all content not deemed "basic" by CBE, and eliminate instructional media it abhors, public schools *would* cost less. Therefore it is possible that CBE arguments and asides on extravagant educational spending reflect no more than a means of accomplishing announced and central purposes. But this is a possibility we strongly doubt. First, statements like those we have quoted suggest a stronger, less incidental role for the theme of economy. Second, CBE's intelligent officials *must* be aware of the threat to any and all kinds of public education—their version or some other—currently posed by interests primarily concerned with lowering taxes. The Council must realize that continued harping on the money theme plays directly into the hands of such interests—yet the refrain continues. And third, we believe that CBE concern with spending may extend beyond a logical relationship to Council purposes, on the grounds to be explored in our next chapter.

Economy was a prominent part of the First Wave of criticism, and there are many who believe that desires to reduce school costs motivated and largely carried the First Wave. We have now seen that these interests are a part of the Second Wave too. The "costly palaces" magazine articles serve to limit *local* spending, while efforts to oppose federal funds for schools are also widespread. The United States Chamber of Commerce distributes editorials opposing federal aid.[31] In Washington a group representing no less than thirty-seven state taxpayers' organizations has fired at federal aid proposals.[32] When efforts to block national funds are combined with local attempts to curb spending, the effects on schools can be far-reaching indeed.

Let us take a close look at one of the newer organizations opposing the allegedly exorbitant costs of public schools—the Institute for Social Science Research. We have already seen how complex the interstructure of critical groups can be. So it is with the Institute for Social Science Research. Established in 1956, the institute shared offices for almost two years with the American Enterprise Association.[33] Although no formal relationship between the two groups has been publicly acknowledged, Felix Morley, chairman of the ISSR's board of trustees also serves as a member of AEA's advisory board. And ISSR's staff director, Roger Freeman, was reported at one time to be serving simultaneously in the same executive capacity for AEA.

Thus, to understand the Institute for Social Science Research, we must also examine the American Enterprise Association. AEA has been described as a "lobbying organization" which "on the surface . . . has the lofty goal of educating members of Congress regarding legislation on a nonpartisan basis."[34] An analysis of the organization's leadership reveals names linked to other organizations we have mentioned and shall mention later. One member of the board of trustees, for example—Robert Lund—has also served in a similar capacity for the Committee for Constitutional Government's Fighters for Freedom, and is a past president of America's Future. Two members of the AEA advisory board—Henry Hazlitt and Leo Wolman—wrote for the Foundation for Economic Education, to be discussed in the next chapter. Another AEA advisory board member, Felix Morley, is a member of a new project of America's Future—a project to be discussed in Chapter VIII. It is the guidance of such personnel that must have led the columnist quoted above to conclude, "One look at the conservative if not reactionary gentlemen behind the Enterprise Association gives away the real goal."

The AEA program consists largely of allegedly factual analyses of bills pending before Congress, and more detailed factual studies on "National Economic Problems." Not infrequently, however, the studies produce conclusions and specific legislative recommendations found warranted by the investigators. For example, in 1955 the AEA published *Federal Aid to Education—Boon or Bane?* by Roger A. Freeman. According to an advertisement, Freeman arrives at a very definite answer to the title question: "States and localities are . . . in a better position to finance education than the federal government." This publication has not been the sole manifestation of AEA's interest in education. In 1958 there appeared *National Aid to Higher Education*—devoted to pointing out that such aid is unnecessary.[35]

Early in 1958, while AEA worked to defeat national aid to higher education, the Institute for Social Science Research was doing the same for national aid to public schools. The latter investigation was published a month after that of AEA. Under the authorship of Roger A. Freeman, ISSR's vice president, the book—*School Needs in the Decade Ahead*—proved tremendously controversial. There have been so many statistical analyses of Mr. Freeman's study that we hardly need to examine his figures and inferences here.[36] Suffice it to say that the quarrels have centered largely on Mr. Freeman's present and projected school enrollment figures, and present and projected school costs figures—and that the effect of his findings has been to show that education is getting a generous share of the national wealth, and neither now nor later merits more.

One of the largely overlooked aspects of Freeman's book may portend the gravest long-range danger to public education. Mr. Freeman —whose training admittedly is confined to economics, and whose organization is patently identifiable with the conservative politico-economic orientation—by no means confines himself to economics in his book. *School Needs in the Decade Ahead* makes some highly specific observations on what is wrong with American education. Among these are:

A considerable body of opinion holds that American schools have gone too far in retaining, and advancing to higher grades, youths who profit little by staying in school and hinder the education of their classmates. . . . Numerous suggestions have been made, particularly in the past two or three years, that such youngsters ought to be eliminated from the classrooms. . . .

If methods are adopted for a fuller and more effective utilization of teachers and school facilities, if television, films and other technological methods of widening the range of good teachers and saving manpower are adopted, if the schools concentrate on subject-matter teaching and eliminate frills, the quality of school education will be lifted but school funds will not need to rise much. . . .

If the schools will concentrate on subject-matter teaching—as the public schools did until a quarter of a century ago, and as some American public and nonpublic schools as well as schools outside the United States still do—costs will need to rise only moderately beyond the rate of increase in pupil enrollment.[37]

These are hardly issues in economic theory. For our purposes, Freeman's comments mean this: We have noted and documented the links tying political and economic conservatism to attacks on schools, as these seemed to operate in the First Wave of contemporary educational criticism. Now, in a study produced by part of the Second Wave we find the same kinship. Moreover, here the links are even more firmly and visibly forged. *School Needs in the Decade Ahead* adds up to several vital messages. Mr. Freeman—and the ISSR—are openly saying, "Why pour money down the drain of public schools, when they are not so good anyway?" And, "If we could substitute *our* brand of education, it would not only be better; it would be cheaper."

The affinity of the conservative mind for Mr. Freeman's economic-political-educational ideas has also been clear. One journal, decidedly conservative, has hailed the book as "the most valuable arsenal in the fight against Federal aid to education."[38] From the Capitol floor, Congressman Ralph Gwinn (former researcher for the Committee for Constitutional Government, and We, The People! president) delivered a eulogistic oration on *School Needs in the Decade Ahead*. In denying that Freeman takes a "cash-register view of education,"[39] Mr. Gwinn commented:

Mr. Freeman's strongest emphasis in this book is upon the imperative need for better education. . . .

. . . Mr. Freeman proposes higher standards of curriculum, promotion, and graduation in the schools and a more efficient and effective use of the available human and physical resources. . . .[40]

The Council for Basic Education also commented on the book, labeling its review "Recommended Reading." After citing Freeman's figures and views—which, according to CBE, explains why "many educators are willing to vote it the-book-we-would-most-like-to-see-flop"—the Council concludes in a more solemn vein:

We at CBE are not financial experts or statisticians and do not feel competent to pass on all the details of Mr. Freeman's argument. We feel, however, that the book is worth the serious attention of all those who are troubled by the enormous problem of cost in maintaining our public school system. . . .[41]

Granted, this represents a *qualified* endorsement, but we have seen that CBE is independently committed to many of Mr. Freeman's diagnoses and prescriptions. With this in mind, it is interesting to note that the organization which stood the cost of ISSR's *School Needs in the Decade Ahead* also assumed the financial burden of CBE's basic curriculum study. Furthermore, this organization—the Relm Foundation—not only *paid* for both, but announced the two as "companion" studies.[42] The significance that may attach to the question of CBE finances is the topic of our next chapter.

We have traveled a long road in examining national organizations associated with the Second Wave of educational criticism. What does the future seem to hold for them, and for the others we have looked into? Is the intensified criticism we have witnessed since the close of World War II likely to continue?

There are few signs of abatement. There is no diminution of space devoted to articles critical of schools; in fact, the reverse may be true. There also seems to be an increasing tendency for mass circulation periodicals to carry such articles. Critics working diligently for years have now laid an extensive foundation; it seems highly possible that the national academic attack on education will soon be followed by local campaigns. The seeds have been sown and carefully tended in the national press and it is not improbable that the fruit will be borne in individual school systems within the next few years.

As we have seen, worry over school finance is chronic. It has been an integral part of both waves of criticism—first being voiced along with complaints that schools are teaching the wrong social-political-economic "facts," and more recently tied to criticisms charging anti-intellectualism. The flexibility and adaptability of the "cash register" approach seems to augur a long and healthy life for this theme—certainly as long as state and federal spending continue to require large sums of tax support.

What chances are there for truly mediating the existing differences? Is cooperation possible among schoolmen and those critics with whom this chapter dealt? The official statements of belief of the Council for Basic Education constitute a position whose legitimacy cannot be questioned. And it is a position apparently shared by a number of intellectual leaders in our society. Equally significant is the fact that CBE's educational views are *also* shared by a large number of the educationists they scorn. It is our firm belief that had the Council pursued its program in a more temperate fashion, its membership, for better or worse, would now include an infinitely greater number of teachers and administrators. The lack of restraint makes for a gloomy forecast.

Since men can only come to the conference table bringing their resentments—generated by charges that they are ignorant or malicious—cooperation among schoolmen and these critics seems impossible. The differences dividing the academicians and the educationists are not *solely* personal conflicts by any means—there are also wide chasms of belief between many of those in the two groups. But until the struggle is confined to a battle of ideas and not of men, there seems little hope that the ideological differences can be jointly examined—much less composed.

THE SECOND WAVE

7. *Who Pays?*

Assuming that one measure of an organization's position is its relationships with other groups sharing similar interests, we have explored some of CBE's kinships as well as its activities. There remains to be examined, however, one more important kind of relationship. Obviously, the Council's projects cost money. Just as obviously, membership dues could hardly finance such an ambitious program. Thus a consideration of CBE cannot be complete without a look into the source of the organization's funds.

According to the Council's first "descriptive leaflet," initial requests for support were directed to only one source of help—the William Volker Fund. This foundation agreed to underwrite the program for a three-year period, with a grant totaling $114,000. The Council hoped to become self-supporting by the end of the three years, but this hope soon dimmed. Apparently CBE quickly outran its estimates. The *Bulletin* reported that additional grants totaling close to $15,000 were obtained for operating expenses early in 1957. And at the second annual meeting, the Council treasurer reported that the original sponsor would continue support through 1959—"with a grant for general operating expenses in the amount of $100,000. . . ." Altogether, published CBE figures suggest that grants provided or promised by the original donor add up to about a quarter of a million dollars.[1]

CBE's reluctance to reveal its source of support aroused considerable suspicion. Toward the end of the first year of operation, however, the Council explained its silence: ". . . with anyone . . . interested, we have freely discussed the identity of our sponsoring foundation; out of deference to the wishes of its founder—a man who disapproved mixing personal publicity with charity—we have requested only that the name not be printed. . . ." This practice of the Volker Fund has been explained as the founder's devout belief that " 'alms should be made in secret.' "[2]

The scope of Volker Fund interests is broad: "aged, children, democracy and citizenship, economics, education, government and public administration, handicapped, health and medicine, humanities, international matters, libraries, religion (all faiths), social sciences, social welfare."[3] Since the establishment of the fund in 1932, economics and education have received considerable emphasis. Yet the very mention of "education" as an interest of the Volker Fund seems strange, since the fund's president apparently believes that public schools are "socialist institutions."[4] And there can be no doubt that the Volker Fund president is an enemy of anything even vaguely socialistic.

The Volker Fund's emphasis on economics is far more easily understood. Between 1946 and 1949 the fund made contributions totaling $170,000 to the Foundation for Economic Education.[5] It also gave what the chairman of a congressional committee called "a very large and a very high aggregate sum"[6] to the National Economic Council. The "sum" came to less than $33,000 between 1947 and 1950, but this was enough to make the Volker Fund one of NEC's best donors.[7]

There are several reasons why Volker Fund generosity is important to our immediate interest, the Council for Basic Education. First, it is unlikely that the foundation doles out funds at cross-purposes. Thus, since Volker Fund money has gone to the Foundation for Economic Education, the National Economic Council, *and* to the Council for Basic Education, we may assume that there is no conflict among the purposes of these groups—or at any rate, that Volker Fund officials perceive no conflict in their programs.

Another, even more direct reason why various Volker Fund grants concern us is that this kind of generosity may bestow privilege of a most significant type. One of the conclusions reached by the House Lobbying Committee in the course of its lengthy investigations of two Volker Fund beneficiaries (plus other groups) is that "he who pays the piper . . . calls the tune."[8] Insofar as the statement applied to Volker Fund relationships with FEE and NEC—as the House Committee strongly suggests—it bears investigating in the case that concerns us: the Volker Fund and the Council for Basic Education.

There is also a reason why the Volker Fund itself may be of interest to us, even beyond its generous aid to the Council for Basic Education. As we have remarked, one can distinguish themes marking off two waves of postwar school criticism: the patriotic-political theme and the intellectualistic theme. Two Volker Fund beneficiaries—FEE and NEC—are associated with the first; a third beneficiary, CBE, is the prime spokesman for the second. This gives the Volker Fund a rather prominent role in both the First and Second waves of school criticism. More explicitly, if the Lobbying Committee's metaphor applies, the fund may have "called both tunes."

A direct and careful look at several Volker Fund beneficiaries thus seems in order. If such an examination immediately reveals ideas that are familiar to us—striking similarities to the views of those First Wave critics discussed in Chapter IV—the Lobbying Committee tells why:

> An analysis of five typical foundations, American Enterprise Association, National Economic Council, Committee for Constitutional Government, Foundation for Economic Education, and America's Future reveals that eight men have served as officers, directors, or trustees of at least two of the five organizations. These organizations, although technically separate, cannot help but be closely and practically linked through their overlapping personnel. . . .*[9]

What, then, are the interests of Volker Fund beneficiaries—the Foundation for Economic Education and the National Economic Council? The FEE has stated that it "takes no position on anything as an institution. . . ." and that it "does not make resolutions or pass resolutions."[10] If this is the case, it seems so only in a strictly formal sense—and only because full consensus makes voting a superfluous technicality. Although FEE's president continued to insist that his

* Note that one of the five organizations mentioned here—the American Enterprise Association—was discussed in the preceding chapter. Two others, the Committee for Constitutional Government and America's Future, were discussed in Chapter IV, and the other two of the five organizations mentioned are discussed in this chapter.

organization was educational, correspondence brought to light in congressional hearings tends to cast doubt on FEE's use of the term *educational*. For example, a college professor wrote to the organization, suggesting that it might make a real contribution by presenting *both* sides of all issues considered. He even pointed out that the strength of FEE convictions should make the group confident of its triumph in such a debate. The answers to this suggestion reveal FEE's conception of an "educational" organization: first, both sides are unnecessary and undesirable, because only the truth *ought* to be presented; and second, this sort of "objectivity" is appropriate only to indecision—that is, for use by those who have not decided what the truth is.[11]

The view that is thus equated with truth is stated in an FEE pamphlet:

> A minimum of restrictions against persons is—or rather was—the American ideal of government. In fact, the original American theory was that government should apply just enough coercion or force or restrictions against persons to prevent illiberal persons from trespassing on the liberty of others.
>
> Today, a rampage of governmental controls is being offered as a cure for every social ill. Individual liberty is being replaced by an alien concept of freedom. This so-called new freedom is nothing more than the idea of repressing the actions of individual persons by substituting the plans of rulers; only the rulers have freedom of choice under this concept.[12]

Some of the more specific positions taken by the foundation can be inferred from the titles it gives its publications: *High Prices; Liberty and Taxes; Profits and the Ability to Pay Wages; Planned Chaos; So You Believe in Rent Control;* and *Will Dollars Save the World?*

FEE stands foursquare against socialism. It forthrightly declares, "The Foundation for Economic Education makes no pretense of 'presenting both sides' of the socialist question. We of the staff are opposed to socialism. . . ."[13] But before commending the group, we should do well to ask, What *is* Socialism, according to FEE? There are indications that the group's definition includes public schools—that the very establishment of such schools constitutes "Socialism." Indeed, the organization's magazine, the *Freeman*, has contained such articles as "Education is a Private Responsibility" and "The Case for

Religious Schools,"[14] and these excerpts from a third item show the extent of the opposition:

> When citizens turn to any government for financial support, they must always remember that with such "aid" come "strings. . . ."
>
> The current conflict raging over racial integration is merely one more inevitable controversy created by the use of public funds in the field of education.
>
> Parents . . . have paid dearly. Reliance on government to "educate" their youngsters has meant relinquishing their freedom of choice and control of their personal spending in this field. . . .
>
> One specific step toward a solution of today's government school "problem" would be repeal of the state compulsory attendance requirements. . . .
>
> Experience with our government school system has raised serious doubts as to the suitability of force to serve the cause of true education. Therefore, why not consider removing government restraints on individual initiative in that field? If the most effective way to get the most and the best of anything and everything is to leave its production in the hands of private individuals, in a free market, why not try leaving the solution of today's school "problem" to the market? . . .[15]

The FEE president summed up his organization's position on education in a memorable statement. Asked "if he favored abolishing public schools, he replied, '. . . I would have no objection to public schools were they supported in the same way and were they as absent from State control as are churches, the Red Cross and similar institutions. . . .' "[16]—in other words, were they not *public* schools.

What has this to do with the Volker Fund, which has contributed so generously to the Council for Basic Education? The fund, remember, provided for the Foundation for Economic Education as well. Furthermore, the assistance offered FEE was not limited to financial aid. Harold Luhnow, who has been president of both the William Volker Fund and William Volker and Company, served as a member of the original FEE Board of Trustees.[17] He also attested to his interest in the foundation in other significant ways. Mr. Luhnow agreed, for example, to mail FEE materials to the 10,000 dealers associated with William Volker and Company.[18] According to FEE records, he distributed 62,000 copies of six FEE publications.[19] Collectively these publications served to oppose wage and rent controls, government spending, inflation, and foreign aid.

Still other forms of aid have been extended to the FEE program through the Volker Fund president. For example, when the foundation president Leonard Read visited Kansas City in 1947, Mr. Luhnow arranged a meeting of forty people whom Read addressed, outlining the FEE program—and incidentally stressing the fact that FEE lives by the contributions of sympathizers.[20] In return, the foundation seems to have performed a service for the Volker Fund in the "handling of details and disbursements" in connection with a conference held in Switzerland.[21]

Despite such close and extensive cooperation, Volker Fund enthusiasm for FEE eventually waned. The president of another organization soon to win the fund's favor—the National Economic Council—reported Mr. Luhnow's disappointment in the accomplishments of the then one-year-old FEE.[22] Tangible effects of the disappointment soon became evident: FEE, which had hopefully anticipated $200,000 from the Volker Fund, instead received a mere $170,000; and of this sum, $80,000 was reportedly a loan and not a gift.[23] Neither did the early purchases of materials live up to their promise. After enthusiastically distributing four FEE publications in five months, the Volker Fund did not place another order for almost a year—and the final purchase reported was not made for still another year. But the Volker Fund had not discontinued mass distribution of "educational" literature. It was merely buying from a new source—the National Economic Council.

Merwin K. Hart, the man who leads NEC, is a prominent figure in rightist movements, heading New York's oldest chapter of the John Birch Society. Nor is he unknown in education circles. About twenty years ago he became actively concerned over the costs of public education and its subversive influences. In 1940, to combat the menace of alleged Communist-Socialist teachings, he formed the American Parents' Council on Education.[24] Although this organization appears to have been largely inactive and short-lived,[25] Hart seems to have carried on its interests in his role as president of the National Economic Council. NEC is somewhat more extreme than the Foundation for Economic Education, and it is far more plain-spoken—though a certain community of interest is clear. NEC has flatly opposed federal aid to education as Socialism.[26] As a federal lobbying group, it takes a stand on various other legislative proposals also. Here are some of the provisions of the National Economic Council has said it would like to see:

Removal of present Supreme Court and barring of its Justices from holding judicial office
Limiting of Government's taxing power through constitutional amendment
A ceiling on income tax levies
Aid to Spain
Taxation of cooperatives[27]

On the other hand, the Council consistently has opposed such things as:

Federal aid to education
Further immigration
Public housing
United States participation in UN
FEPC, anti-lynching bill, and other civil-rights measures
Rent Control
Marshall Plan
United States support for an independent Israel
Social Security
Farm-price support
Point 4 program
Reciprocal Trade Agreements Act
TVA
Atomic Energy Act
World Federation resolution
Militant Zionism
Anti-trust suits against A.&P., Du Pont

Several items on the NEC opposition list suggest anti-Semitism. Hart himself has been described as a "professional anti-Semite,"[28] and indeed, his writings would tend to substantiate this charge. His unique likening of the activities of Jewish groups to Hitler's tactics is a case in point.[29] But because Hart has repeatedly denied anti-Semitism on his own or the Council's part, his own words might prove useful means for assessing his denials. The following appeared in a single recent issue of the NEC's semimonthly *Letter*:

. . . the founding of Palestine was the price paid the Zionists for their bringing America into World War I. . . . Had it not been for the Zionists, America would undoubtedly never have got into that War. Probably there would have been no World War II. Soviet Russia might never have existed. There probably would be no world communism. . . .

. . . If there were six million Jews within reach of Hitler, which number is widely questioned, and if they have all disappeared, where are they?

Is it not likely that many of these six million, claimed to have been killed by Hitler and Eichmann, are right here in the United States and are now joining in the agitation for more and more support for the State of Israel—even if the American Republic goes down?

. . . most of the American press has been trying Eichmann in various columns. . . . Nearly every piece printed mentions the "six million Jews." The publicity has been well-nigh nauseating to Americans who are deeply concerned with the communist and economic threat to their own country.[30]

If the above lists and quotations show NEC's stand, they do not do full justice to the posture with which these positions are maintained. A list of a few titles from the *Economic Council Letter* shows this, and a few more NEC viewpoints as well: "Communist Infiltration Has Produced Modern Republicanism"; " 'Immigrationists' Conspire to Destroy America"; "The Red Hand in New York Schools"; "Government by Usurpation"; "Why They Teach Socialism"; "Mental Health—A Marxist Weapon."[31]

As we have already noted, the total Volker Fund contribution to NEC was considerably smaller, in the late forties, than the funds supplied the Foundation for Economic Education. Furthermore, approximately a third of the $33,000 that went to NEC represented large-scale purchases. But perhaps this represents the greater tribute. For the Volker Fund saw fit to distribute about 200,000 pieces of NEC literature.[32] Between 1947 and 1949, NEC records show that 10,000 to 12,000 copies each of sixteen titles were delivered to Mr. Luhnow who apparently continued the monthly mailings to William Volker and Company dealers.

The first Volker order for Council materials was for the semimonthly NEC newsletter, and for a book-review publication distributed by the council. The newsletter began with a biblical quotation in which Samuel warns of the dangers of kings. The reader begins to get the point when he reads "Now Samuel . . . was what we would call a statesman. Mix up George Washington, Thomas Jefferson, Abraham Lincoln, Herbert Hoover, and say Harry S. [*sic*] Byrd, and you would probably have something very like Samuel."[33] This *Economic Council Letter*—of which Volker's Mr. Luhnow ordered 10,000 copies—also contains a denunciation of federal aid to education on double-barreled grounds: "The socialistic teachings in our schools and colleges today would be multiplied several times." And, besides, "If this Congress should yield to the bureaucrats and leftwingers who are the core of the demand for 'federal aid to education,' . . . it would soon yield to the whole Communistic-Socialistic program."[34] The monthly book review purchased simultaneously had an even stronger religious motif, and reveals why an economic council has such a great deal to say on theology: the theory of natural, God-given law is explicated in the finest eighteenth century tradition, with laws governing man's relationships (specifically, economic and political) as surely and invariably as other laws of nature rule the physical world.[35]

Other NEC literature purchased in quantity by the Volker Fund includes:

1. A lively polemic against socialized medicine, which points out that "behind the demand for political medicine" lie "American Communists."
2. Arguments to the effect that the 1948 presidential election actually was not a mandate for the Communistic government-spending programs proposed by the victor.
3. A monthly book review devoted to a defense of capitalism (revealing "the real McCoy, the genuine stuff, the low-down, the cold hard facts") and to a daring exposé to the effect that "Communists have infiltrated the YWCA."
4. An exposé of world government proposals, concluding, "If we Americans don't like our republican form of government, and believe a government by the yellow and brown and black races (controlled by Soviet Russia) would be superior to ours, we can let plans for 'world government' go right ahead."
5. A book review revealing the North Atlantic Pact as "the next-to-last step of a plan to demolish the American Constitution. . . ."
6. A complaint that the National Association of Manufacturers is not sufficiently devoted to protecting the interests of capital and private enterprise![36]

In addition to distributing these periodicals, the Volker Fund obtained from NEC, and circulated, several works of British authors. The titles of two—"Governed to Death" and "British Socialism Is

Destroying British Freedom"[37]—attest to the messages conveyed. Mr. Luhnow was also instrumental in bringing the author of the second piece—Cecil Palmer—to this country for a lecture tour arranged by NEC.[38]

What link connects such an extreme set of views as those of the NEC with the Volker Fund—or, one step further removed, with the Council for Basic Education? Well, the Volker Fund has openly endorsed NEC views through generous gifts and by disseminating NEC literature. As we have seen, NEC leadership has some rather decisive views about public schools: there have been objections to costs and charges of subversion. The Volker Fund has also expressed tangible approval of the Council for Basic Education—an organization ostensibly devoted to improving education. When one adds to this the view of Volker Fund President Luhnow that public schools per se constitute Socialism, what are we to conclude? Can it be that the Volker Fund sees the National Economic Council and the Council for Basic Education as complementary efforts? Or is it more plausible to assume that the right hand is supposed to be building what the left seems intent on destroying?

Before leaving the several interests of the Volker Fund, there is another vigorous critic of public education whom the fund has reportedly aided. NEC's President Hart noted the following, after a conference with Mr. Luhnow: "He [Luhnow] urged me to get in touch with George Benson to whom they are contributing heavily and of whose program they think very well."[39] The "George Benson" referred to seems to be President George Stuart Benson of Harding College, an educational critic of some reknown, and the producer of a now defunct radio program called "Land of the Free."

The radio series was just one part of a "National Education Program" carried out at Harding. Other features include a weekly column prepared by Benson, a monthly newsletter, an annual conference assembling industrial and business representatives, and a cartoon series designed to promote a system of unfettered free enterprise. One product bringing recent fame to Harding and the National Education Program is "Communism on the Map." It is the distribution of this filmstrip which Founder Robert Welch lists as the major accomplishment of the John Birch Society. The recent charge that the whole

National Education Program is a "front" organization for the Birch Society is obviously inaccurate, since the Program long predates the Birch group,[40] but the areas of mutual concern and assistance are undeniably extensive.

A Benson sympathizer labels him an "Arkansas Crusader," and explains his quasi-political career this way: When Benson first went to Harding in 1936, he discovered "the startling fact that the difficulties which beset Harding College were only local symptoms of a nationwide moral, social and economic breakdown."[41] A less sympathetic observer who describes the program apparently devised to cure this moral-social-economic crisis aptly names his analysis "Whooping It Up for Adam Smith." According to this interpreter, the National Education Program is "designed to prove that free enterprise is the only true religion. . . ."[42] A former instructor at Harding explains the extent to which a more traditional type of theology is also involved in Dr. Benson's thinking. His statement may reveal, too, how Benson obtained a million dollars for the National Education Program:

> "Until recently Harding loudly championed religious fundamentalism. An appeal to sectarianism will move but a limited number. The objects of spite need but be changed to attract a larger number. Dr. Benson's method is simplicity itself: all his outcries follow the same pattern, whether he is fulminating against other denominations or against members of political parties, as he finds it profitable to do today. He has a new object to attack, but he uses the old methods commingled with camp-meeting histrionics. Hard-boiled business men succumb to emotional appeals when cleverly made. Benson's lingo is tailored to appeal to the high-class trade."[43]

Dr. Benson's interests seem to center mainly on the economic but he also apparently shares other commitments of the extreme right. A case in point was his leadership role in "For America"—an organization devoted to opposing alleged " 'super-internationalism and internationalism.' "[44] With this general persuasion in mind, one can more easily comprehend Benson's unbridled opposition to federal aid for education. Otherwise it is somewhat startling to find a college president with the avocation of testifying against aid for schools. His opposition is particularly marked in one of the several statements he has submitted to the House Committee on Education:

> The taxpayers' association in a State which is 47th in per capita income—$512—and which is 46th in value of school property per pupil in attendance—$116—and which is 47th in per capita expenditure per student enrolled in the public schools—$34.18—believes that Federal aid to education is neither necessary nor desirable.[45]

The statement is not incomprehensible when one notes that Dr. Benson wears two hats. He is not a college president only; he is also chairman of the executive committee of the Arkansas Public Expenditure Council.

The twin bases on which Benson has repeatedly opposed federal aid are:

> 1) "The argument that the States cannot afford an adequate educational program is absurd. . . ."
> 2) Federal aid will mean federal control, and should this come to pass . . . "it is my very firm conviction that within a generation our children will have been educated to seek Federal control of our industries, of agriculture, and of our social welfare, thus making America a totalitarian state."[46]

Some of Dr. Benson's other views on education, which include criticisms of school textbooks and curricula, are shown in his reply to our questionnaire.

Having seen some of the specific programs which—in addition to that of the Council for Basic Education—have received Volker Fund support, let us return now to the question of CBE finances. There have been other donors: in 1959, when the original grant from the Volker Foundation expired, CBE gratefully acknowledged donations from three other foundations—the Maytag Foundation, the Old Dominion Foundation, and the Marquette Charitable Organization.[47] The first two seem to be fairly standard grantors of funds for educational purposes. Among the beneficiaries of Old Dominion, for example, have been Virginia's Council of Higher Education, Rutgers University, the Association of American Colleges, and St. John's College.

The Marquette Charitable Organization seems to be a foundation of a slightly different character. The organization was established by the same Regnery family that administers the ultraconservative Henry Regnery Publishing Company. This is the firm which makes possible the dissemination of the views of many of the educational critics mentioned elsewhere in this book—for example, William F. Buckley, Jr., Russell Kirk, Medford Evans, Charles Tansill, Felix Morley, Mortimer Smith, Anthony Bouscaren, and William McGovern.

Still another CBE benefactor is the Relm Foundation of Ann Arbor, Michigan, which granted "up to $34,000" for CBE's curriculum study—the study that produced *The Case for Basic Education.* This foundation was established in 1950 by Harry B. Earhart, "to provide grants for educational, religious and charitable purposes."[48] Mr. Earhart had taken an interest in education and was a personal contributor to the National Economic Council. NEC President Hart further credits Earhart with a suggestion which has probably returned many times the value of Earhart's financial contributions. Because the idea has apparently been used to finance the activities of many school critics, it is worth explaining. NEC was unable to obtain the tax-exempt status of an educational organization, and since donors therefore could not deduct their contributions, NEC realized that an attractive feature was lacking. Earhart is credited with solving the problem: for non-deductible gifts made directly to NEC, he substituted *purchases* of NEC materials earmarked as gifts to institutions which *do* have deductibility status.[49] Thus Mr. Earhart made $4,500 available to NEC through the purchase of 450 subscriptions to the *Economic Council Letter* as gifts for colleges, libraries, and/or churches.[50]

Mr. Earhart was even more generous with the Foundation for Economic Education—which did enjoy the tax-deductibility status. His personal gifts to FEE in 1947–1948 totaled $16,000, and the "Earhart Foundation" in 1947 and 1949 contributed a total of $45,000 to FEE.[51]

One of the two founders of the Relm Foundation is reported to have agreed with Mr. Luhnow of the Volker Fund, that public schools are socialist institutions.[52] And at least two recent Relm grants suggest some unfriendliness toward public education: At approximately the same time the Relm Foundation committed itself to the support of CBE's basic curriculum study, it provided funds to a Texas church, for the "development of church-supported primary and secondary education."[53] The second grant—described as facilitating a "companion study" to CBE's curriculum project—was made to the

Institute for Social Science Research, for the study which culminated in the controversial *School Needs in the Decade Ahead*.

The Council for Basic Education has not been successful in all its bids for funds. A major foundation, for example, turned down the chance to finance a study called "Johnny Can't Write, Either"[54]—perhaps because the project's title implies that the would-be researchers answered the question prior to launching the investigation. In fact, things must have indeed been gloomy at CBE for a while, since the executive secretary devoted a fourth of a year to full-time fund-raising.[55] New membership categories were established to help meet the financial problem, and now dues range from $3.50 for an "Educational Membership" to $1,000 for a "Patron Membership." Through one new category—the Corporation Membership—the Council offers an "opportunity for business organizations to make a significant contribution to basic education . . . without direct involvement on the local level. . . ."[56] The offer appears to promise home-town anonymity to prospective contributors. It follows a statement of CBE's tax status and the resulting tax deductibility for contributors.

8. *Operation Textbook*

While those critics we have dubbed the "Second Wave" have busily usurped the limelight, the First Wave has been far from dormant. A highly significant development in current educational criticism has recently come from a First Wave organization—America's Future. The development, a newly established "Textbook Evaluation Committee," can hardly be called a *resurgence* of activity on the part of America's Future. For though AF, like other First Wave critics, has been out of the news for several years, this does not mean they have relaxed their efforts or abandoned their cause.

The typical complaint of the Second Wave critic has been an alleged anti-intellectualism on the part of schools. As a group, the academicians bringing the charge are not so convinced as were earlier critics that a traitor lurks in the bosom of every educationist and textbook author. As a result there has been a lull in the earlier demands for teacher investigation and textbook censorship. The last national-scale textbook "evaluation" effort expired in 1953. Now, the America's Future Textbook Evaluation Committee, militantly tagged "Operation Textbook," bids fair to fill the gap.

The new group of evaluators is an important development for several reasons. The resources potentially at its disposal suggest that it may be in a position to carve an influential place for itself. Recall the sharing of funds and facilities disclosed by the Lobbying Committee among the old America's Future, the Committee for Constitutional Government, Fighters for Freedom, Features for America, and the Constitution and Free Enterprise Foundation. Equally important, in terms of the strength the Textbook Evaluation Committee may wield, is the fact that it seeks to fuse the First and Second waves of educational criticism: the members of the committee are academicians.

Of the thirteen original members, all except the executive secretary had been college professors. Eleven are currently active or retired academicians, and the other two are publicists known primarily for their concerns about the world's evil conspiracies. (Of these last two, the career of one has been devoted to exposing subversion in religious and political circles, while the other directed a prominent search for subversion in school textbooks.) The selection of committee members was obviously designed to capitalize on the prominence and popularity now enjoyed by the liberal arts critic of public education. The specific views of every one of these academicians also suggests that the project bringing them together represents a merging of the two types of educational criticism. This fusion of forces could ultimately produce far more serious and widespread effects than earlier attempts at censorship.

Operation Textbook is important not only in terms of its potential effects but also because of its single-mindedness. One looks in vain for varied politico-economic orientations on the America's Future Textbook Evaluation Committee. Now, if the *writing* of textbooks is not and should not be a strictly subjective enterprise—a point repeatedly stressed by the patriots of the right—it is an odd coincidence that all those chosen to *evaluate* them represent a single approach to the world's problems.

The plans of the committee have been carefully set down in a prospectus designed to attract financial contributions. The motive purportedly giving rise to the project stems from "innumerable" inquiries addressed to America's Future for information on textbooks. With complete incredulity, AF says, "Difficult as it is to believe, *there is not a single agency in the United States to which we could refer these correspondents. . . .*"[1] And compounding the deplorable nature of this state of affairs:

. . . it is through the textbooks used in the schools, particularly in the field of the so-called "social sciences" that the progressivist revolutionaries have done their most damaging work in the past quarter of a century. But so slyly and slickly has the collectivist-internationalist philosophy been inserted into the books, and the meaning of the American form of government and its free enterprise economy cried down, that it is difficult, if not impossible, for the average parent or school board member any longer to tell what is a good textbook and what is not. And they have nowhere to turn for an objective opinion of the books. . . .[2]

As a result of this situation, the Textbook Evaluation Committee has dual purposes: first, to provide an "objective" evaluation of any social science textbook to anyone interested, and second—in somewhat ominous terms—"To acquaint textbook publishers . . . and the textbook purchasing committees in the schools . . . with the existence of an agency which is evaluating the product in which they deal."

The committee was to begin with high school textbooks. In its first year of operation it expected to evaluate 250 of 300 high school social science textbooks in existence. When all 300 had been subjected to rigorous analysis, AF thought it would simply be a question ". . . of keeping up-to-date by evaluating new texts as they appear. . . ." But a progress report of the committee's accomplishments as of June, 1960, suggests that the task was more difficult than anticipated. After about a year's efforts, 50 reviews had been completed, 22 more were in process, and an additional 50 were under assignment to committee evaluators.[3]

Actually, the reviews issued by the committee to date seem generally less vitriolic than those of the earlier major attempt at textbook evaluation—or censorship. That effort, which took the form of a quarterly review called the *Educational Reviewer*, was typically irate. To judge from references and comparisons, however, its work is not being ignored by the new Operation Textbook staff. America's Future evaluators refer to the "notable" earlier criticism of the *Educational Reviewer*, and one Operation Textbook committee member suggests that he is merely taking up where the *Reviewer* left off.[4] Despite the fact that the AF evaluators find the books they review far more acceptable then the *Educational Reviewer* found earlier editions of the same works, a persistent and well-remembered echo sounds through Operation Textbook reviews:

American Problems Today, a textbook for high schools, is a skillfully done work of socialist propaganda. The book is bound to have a damaging impact on youthful minds. . . .

> The author does not discuss the many weaknesses of the United Nations and its dismal failure to settle in a satisfactory manner the Communist action in Korea. . . . his textbook is a fervid plea for Americans to forget their glorious past and their outstanding achievements. . . . Our ancient heritage and everything that has been characteristically-American *[sic]* will be tossed into an international melting pot from which will come some new coin of dubious value. . . . The slogan "We will bankrupt America to bankroll the world" is the curtain line of the drama of the United Nations. . . .
>
> . . . Undoubtedly the writer tried to be impartial, but the overall impression is that he is hostile to the profit motive, to large enterprise, to the use of credit, and, on the whole, to the free enterprise system.
>
> . . . union power is a monopoly power supported by government, . . . union leaders intend to control all industry, and . . . they are determined to prevent our government from restraining them.[5]

Mixing gloom and sunshine, an America's Future progress report suggests, "While far too many of the texts reviewed have proved most revealing of the mind-conditioning—even brainwashing—so prevalent among our youth, it has been a pleasant experience . . . to have discovered at least a few texts which can be recommended. . . ."[6] It should hardly be surprising that one of the recommended books is the product of a member of the committee.

Although the social sciences are, at least "for the time being" the committee's primary concern, there have also been reviews on textbooks in mathematics, literature, journalism, and guidance.[7] The reason for such quick branching out is evident in the review of an English text. The reviewer finds that "The authors, quite evidently, are suffering from the usual 'liberal' hypnosis. Their general attitude toward language is a bit too loose, too pragmatic; they tend to be relativists and to ignore absolute standards. . . ."[8]

Each book considered gets two evaluations—a "full, detailed, professional . . . 1500 to 2000" word analysis, and a 500-word condensation. According to the prospectus, the full analyses are provided to school people on request, but the condensations are widely distributed to "active lists" of educators, board members, PTA's, *plus* publications, "officers of patriotic organizations, and other leaders of public opinion." The total mailing list numbers 318,000—the greater portion of which was to be bought at a cost of $4,360! Other features of the committee's program were also expected to run high: The estimated budget requirements for the first year's operation totaled $109,668!

The prospectus lists 29 criteria by which each text is evaluated, among them:

> Does it [the text under consideration] reflect an understanding and appreciation of American sovereignty and the reason for preserving it? Or does it attempt to instill in the student the idea of "world-mindedness," or world citizenship and world government, under which personal liberty and American sovereignty will be curtailed or lost?

Even with those criteria where no such bias appears, there are other problems. They are stated in such a way that one would do well to ask about the criteria for the criteria. How, for example, would one apply this measure of adequacy: "How does the textbook treat socialism, communism and capitalism and related subjects under each system?" As a means of facilitating "objective evaluation," the question leaves much to be desired. For if one believes that the proper treatment of socialism and communism is to exclude them, *his* objective evaluation of the book would be quite different from that of the individual who believes that excoriation of both is proper treatment.

Some clue to the criteria for the criteria is found in the examples cited in the guide to be used by evaluators. Here are two:

> Most modern American civics texts give a great deal of attention to "civil liberties" such as freedom of religion, speech and press. Is sufficient or equal attention given to other rights, such as the right to acquire and hold property, the right to work, the right to engage in free enterprise, the right of a free society to protect itself against subversion, etc.?
>
> One social science textbook, in discussing American labor, carries cartoons selected from the public press showing labor as downtrodden and exploited. There are no cartoons illustrating exploitation of labor by unscrupulous labor leaders or racketeering unions.[9]

As we have seen, the criteria by which Operation Textbook personnel evaluate textbooks are not stated with much precision and clarity. Thus, in each book review, the subjective element must loom large. For this reason, the ideas and experiences of the evaluators may provide a better basis for predicting the future work of the committee than the criteria officially employed in judging a textbook.

The thirteen original members of the committee were introduced in the project prospectus developed by America's Future. They have also been introduced by other organizations. For example, the Minute Women of the U.S.A.—a highly sympathetic group—greeted the committee exultantly and may have been the first to bestow on it the label "Operation Textbook." Claiming that the effort "is certainly deserving of support," and endorsing it as an endeavor to "rid high school textbooks of misleading propaganda—in a proper and constructive manner . . ." the Minute Women possessively introduced committee personnel in this way:

> Neil Carothers, Medford Evans, A. H. Hobbs, Willmoore Kendall, Russell Kirk, Ella Lonn, Marie Madden, J. B. Matthews, William M. McGovern, Felix Morley, E. Merrill Root, and Charles Callan Tansill. And to top it all the Executive Secretary is none other than our own Lucille Cardin Crain.[10]

An economist and formerly dean of Lehigh's College of Business Administration, Dean Emeritus Neil Carothers has written several books on money. His approach to economics can be discovered in a series of newspaper articles prepared in the dark year of 1933. It was the purpose of the series—reprinted in book form, as *Experimenting with Our Money*[11]—to point out the danger of several steps then under way to restore the nation's economy. Although it might seem unfair to judge Dr. Carothers from the superior height of thirty years' hindsight, actually it is not. For if economic laws are as fixed and immutable as he would have us believe, then they would be as applicable in 2033 as they were in 1933.

In the spring of 1933, Dr. Carothers wrote: "All history shows that a depression . . . contains the seeds of its own recovery, and that it must work out its own cure in its own time. . . ." On the brighter side, "There are harbingers of better times on every hand." Because of these, "it would be grim tragedy to have this certain recovery jeopardized by the adoption of some will-o'-the-wisp currency policy. . . ."[12]

The particular "will-o'-the-wisp" in Dr. Carothers' mind was inflation. Here are his grounds for opposing it: First, "it is an arbitrary and unnecessary interference with a recovery already begun." Second, it is "the device of a government unwilling to pay its debts but quite willing to dishonor its promises. . . ." Third, all wage earners are injured by inflation—except ". . . workers in a position to coerce their employers. . . . These are the aristocrats of labor . . . the same groups that . . . extorted wages so high in the boom period that they contributed to the collapse in 1929. . . ." And finally, inflation launches a direct attack on the nation's morals: "It is one of the commonplaces of history that . . . peoples are led by inflation into an era of dissipation and 'jazz'. . . ."[13]

Now, with the possible exception of the *coup de grâce,* these ideas represent a respectable, if dwindling, school of economics: the classical, laissez-faire liberalism of the eighteenth and nineteenth centuries. It is possible, of course, that some of Dr. Carothers' social, economic, and political ideas have changed in the nearly thirty years that have passed since *Experimenting with Our Money* appeared. Risking the error of logical circularity, however, we may speculate that his very appointment to Operation Textbook offers evidence that there have been no definitive changes in Dr. Carothers' thinking.

Whatever his competence as an economist, Dr. Carothers probably refers many of the problems involved in reviewing high school textbooks to colleagues who have some acquaintance with schools. For he replied to our questionnaire inquiry by saying he could not make knowledgeable replies to any of the questions asked. Under these circumstances his reticence does him credit as a scholar, but it also raises the question of what his contribution to textbook evaluation will be.

A second member of Operation Textbook, Medford Evans, testifies to a greater familiarity with the current ills of public education. His questionnaire reply indicates that he has personally investigated nine of the eleven areas listed. As our table of replies reveals, he finds schools wanting with respect to each area, save that of money; and the complaint here is that we are spending too much on public education. Dr. Evans is an ex-member of the Social Sciences Department of Louisiana's Northwestern State College. He left the position early in 1960, reportedly "a victim of conformist pressures."[14]

Professor Evans's name is well known to conservative circles. He has written extensively for rightist publications, and serves as a contributing editor of the John Birch Society's *American Opinion.* As a former employee of the Atomic Energy Commission, he has written a book and several articles on the subject. He is listed as a "contributor" to the magazine *National Review,* and is apparently that periodical's expert on nuclear and missile warfare. In this capacity he devoted one interesting piece to his grave doubts about the real existence of Russia's first two sputniks.[15] In other articles as well, Dr. Evans has shown a willingness to traffic in the spectacular, calling one of his contributions "Why I Am an Anti-Intellectual." Not an ultra-bizarre title, perhaps, but a type rarely encountered over the signature of a college professor. The promise of the title is fulfilled in the very first sentence: "I am an anti-intellectual because intellectuals, as the term is now used, are treacherous and stupid. . . ." In addition, they are: fickle, cynical, self-indulgent, cowardly, dishonorable, authoritarian, dogmatic, and obscurant.[16] Professor Evans states eleven points characterizing the "intellectual" group from which he disassociates himself. Just *why* he places himself outside the group is revealed with clarity, if not logic:

> Gallup polls show . . . that, on issues involving our national sovereignty, college graduates . . . tend to vote for a weak policy far more often than do citizens with only elementary-school training. High school graduates are in between. Thus the trend of intellectual training in the United States is toward the liquidation of the sovereignty of the United States.

Another of Dr. Evans's article bears as a sort of subtitle—which we hope he did not write—the statement that he is "easily the world's greatest authority on the subject of Dr. Oppenheimer."[17] This expertise presumably arose from Dr. Evans's service with the Atomic Energy Commission, an experience that seems to have left him with the impression that in almost any capacity Dr. Oppenheimer is a dire threat to America's security. Dr. Evans even made a trip to Cambridge in order to protest Oppenheimer's appointment as Harvard's William James Lecturer in philosophy.

Professor Evans was aided in the debate by another of his colleagues-to-be on the America's Future Textbook Evaluation Committee: Willmoore Kendall, a Yale professor of political science. At a moment in history when scholars throughout the world urge interdisciplinary effort—warning that compartmentalization may obstruct our use of knowledge—Professor Kendall took the bewildering position that Oppenheimer's appointment would " 'further . . . blur the line between science and philosophy—for the leftist intellectual never tires of proclaiming that we live in a scientific age.' "[18]

Dr. Kendall is a specialist in psychological warfare and a former Army Intelligence officer. He is a member of the American Political Science Association, the American Academy of Political and Social Science, and the American Association of Rhodes Scholars. In 1953–1954 he held a research grant from the Henry Regnery Foundation for a study of American political ideals. He has also been sponsored by another group we have mentioned, the William Volker Foundation, which apparently backed a lecture series on democratic theory delivered by Professor Kendall.

Dr. Kendall is also on the staff of *National Review*, serving as an editor. In this capacity we may assume that he subscribes to the statement of beliefs printed in the early issues of that periodical:

> . . . the nation's leading opinion-makers for the most part share the Liberal point of view, trying indefatigably to inculcate it in their readers' minds, and to that end employ the techniques of propaganda;
>
> . . . we may properly speak of them as a huge *propaganda* machine, engaged in a major, sustained assault upon the sanity, and upon the prudence and the morality of the American people—its sanity, because the political reality of which they speak is a dream world that nowhere exists, its prudence and morality because their values and goals are in sharpest conflict with the goals and values appropriate to the American tradition;
>
> . . . NATIONAL REVIEW must keep a watchful eye on the day-to-day operations of the Liberal propaganda machine. . . .[19]

Within this framework—which has aptly been called "the Conspiracy Theory of politics"[20]—Professor Kendall stated the premises of his own column, "The Liberal Line." This feature gracing the pages of *National Review* for several years was written to explain political events, which are not otherwise comprehensible because of the efficiency of the "Liberal propaganda machine." According to Dr. Kendall:

> . . . the Liberal intellectuals . . . possess a moral and intellectual smugness the like of which the world has never before seen;

. . . together, they constitute a mutual admiration society that acts enough like a machine to justify our treating it, for purposes of analysis, *as* a machine.[21]

Dr. Kendall's academic career began with a brilliant doctoral dissertation—a reinterpretation of John Locke which provoked much discussion and favorable comment among political scientists. A number of the interpretations he has since advanced hardly seem to have come from the same pen. His editor-in-chief, William F. Buckley, Jr., suggests that in recent years Professor Kendall has had difficulties with fellow political scientists, as well as with various colleagues at Yale and with that university's student body. (This set of circumstances, incidentally, puts Mr. Buckley in the otherwise incongruous position of endorsing tenure for the teaching profession.)[22]

That Professor Kendall thinks little of contemporary public education does not, of course, reflect on his scholarship. The universals he seems willing to apply in this regard, however, do tend to suggest scholarly aberration. Remember that Professor Kendall is the speaker who climaxed his address to the Montgomery County Conservative Club with the statement, " 'I am skeptical . . . of any report that any public school system is much good.' " That the comment was not a spurious, inadvertent one, generated by the heat of the moment, is clear in other statements—from an earlier article of the professor's, for instance, entitled "Why Johnny Can't Do Nothing."[23] Amid the wisdom of this article, there is a sentence that reveals several facets of Dr. Kendall's prose and peeves. In discussing the centennial history of the National Education Association, he advises the reader that the volume "belongs on your bookshelf beside that other book in which stupid crimes and criminal stupidities are related as deeds to be proud of, namely: Rousseau's *Confessions*."[24]

Dr. Russell Kirk, another appointee to the Textbook Evaluation Committee, shares several things in common with Dr. Kendall. He too is a student of political theory, and a featured columnist in *National Review*. In addition, he edits his own magazine, *Modern Age: A Conservative Review*, and has produced a number of books—for example, *The Conservative Mind, The Intelligent Woman's Guide to Conservatism,* and *A Program for Conservatives*. The titles seem accurately to reflect Dr. Kirk's interests and preoccupations. One title that might prove misleading, however, is *Academic Freedom.* While it is true that Dr. Kirk does not here argue—as he elsewhere seems to—that it is a mistake "to tolerate persons who never would tolerate us,"[25] his discussion differs sharply from most. We find among other things, that "religious conviction remains an indispensable support to academic freedom, and that an aggressive secularism . . . is a menace to the academy's liberal functioning. . . ."[26]

Dr. Kirk's writings are extremely varied, but they are consistent and obviously reflect the same cast of mind. For example, Dr. Kirk only *appears* to wander away from his interest in political theory when he discusses pornography. For to his mind, the links between "political and moral intransigency" are exposed by the fact that a Chicago bookshop specializing in picture of "naked ladies" *also* sells Communist literature.[27]

Professor Kirk is currently a research professor of political science at Long Island University's C. W. Post College. He has also been serving on the staff of the New School for Social Research. And to those who might be struck by the incongruity of the association, Professor Kirk wrote that this institution has "probably the highest degree of academic freedom to be found in the United States."[28] For several years, Dr. Kirk taught at Michigan State University, but he sadly reports that at that institution, "it pays to be a Liberal." The fact that (according to Kirk) "one conservative professor after another has been nudged off the campus" may explain his own departure and account for the charges he flings so bitterly at Michigan's two state institutions of higher learning—for example, "The distinguished scholars on the faculty . . . [at Michigan State] may be numbered on the fingers of one hand," and Kirk's references to the two schools as "this carnival and this matrimonial bureau."[29]

In appraising the acts of others professionally involved in educating, Kirk is a severe critic with high standards:

> . . . the lectures at most places [colleges and universities], are . . . cribbed from superficial textbooks.
>
> . . . I suggest that one of these days you peek into a school library of 1958—the one in your town. Possibly it still is a good library—just possibly. But the odds are against it.

Is higher education in America fit for human beings?

> Let us not deceive ourselves: the educationists who set our school norms are resolved not to allow us any "subject-matter" standards; "plant," "enriching experiences," and "varied curricula" (by which they mean fun and games) are the "significant" aspects of education in the eyes of these gentry. . . .[30]

For other features of Professor Kirk's wholesale criticism of public education, see his reply to our questionnaire.

Dr. Kirk has provided us with a gracious introduction to still another member of the America's Future Textbook Evaluation Committee: to "Professor William Montgomery McGovern, one of the wittiest, best-informed, and most interesting people in the Academy. . . ."[31] At present, Dr. McGovern is a retired member of "the Academy," with the title "Professor Emeritus" from Northwestern University. He, too, is a political scientist.

Dr. McGovern seems to have done less writing than some of his colleagues in the new textbook venture. He is, however, co-author of a book whose theme should now be wholly familiar: Its title is *Radicals and Conservatives*.[32] From the start, the authors clear the way for identifying themselves with the "liberal" position! They accomplish this in the simplest way possible: semantic preemption. They merely define "Liberalism" in terms which jibe with their own position—rather than accepting the definition the rest of the country associates with this word.*

But the case is not yet won. The argument-by-definition continues with the division of "liberals" into two camps—radicals and conservatives. Here, again, the authors manage to lose uninitiated readers in the maze. They do so not only by obscure definitions subsuming otherwise opposed points of view under a single genre. They also set up unique and unfamiliar antitheses: radicals and conservatives. For most of us, the political antithesis of *radical* is *reactionary*—not conservative. The purpose of the new set of polarities soon becomes clear: most of us are sufficiently imbued with the ideal of modera-

* In fairness, we should note here that the definition of liberalism offered in *Radicals and Conservatives* is the one that *was* used in the eighteenth and nineteenth centuries. For most Americans, however, the meaning of the term has changed. To avoid the semantic confusion resulting from arbitrary, counter-to-usage definition introduced by this insistence on the *classical* definition, many contemporary conservatives have more straightforwardly applied the label *Libertarianism* to their position.

tion that to oppose a *moderate* position with an extreme and intemperate one is virtually to deny the reader the privilege of choosing sides. In this way the choice is made for him, and it is as wise and commendable as the obvious choice in the good-and-evil contest. For the book introduces a radical as "one who admits of no compromise,"[33] but the case for the other side—the conservative—is munificently stated in this way:

> The conservatives have always claimed to be great admirers of reason, but they have rejected all political schemes based solely upon abstract reason without reference to concrete experience and the accumulated wisdom of many generations. They have insisted that any one generation of men can progress only if it is willing and able to profit from the mistakes and successes of past generations and to make use of the stored-up practical wisdom of its ancestors. For this reason they insist that a society can be progressive only if it conserves its traditions.[34]

Sure enough, before the first chapter is done, we find the authors making the only decent choice: ". . . more often than not it is the conservatives rather than the radicals whom we find getting the best of the argument." More precisely, the selection they make—after carefully rendering it an indistinguishable position—is "conservative liberalism."[35]

Semantic gymnastics have not been the only media for the expression of Professor McGovern's conservatism. He reportedly has served on the board of directors of the Abraham Lincoln National Republican Club—a name misleading in its suggestion of official or ideological kinship with even the more conservative elements of the twentieth century Republican party. (A potential relationship is suggested in that the group "hopes . . . eventually to recapture the Republican Party for conservatism.")[36]

Reflecting a bit more of the moderation his book seems to urge, Dr. McGovern served with the Republican Educational Foundation and was a sponsor of a 1956 "Knowland for President" committee. He also found time to write a foreword to the late senator's book, *McCarthyism—The Fight for America.* But not all of Professor McGovern's activities have been so circumspect. At Northwestern, he served as faculty sponsor for the university's "Students for America" chapter. A student member reports that "many colleges . . . have refused to recognize chapters due to the nature of the group," and that the organization has "incurred the wrath of the so-called 'liberals' and left-wing faculty members. . . ."[37] Another interpreter, however, has said that the organization was refused official sanction on one campus on the grounds that it was a "Kindergarten Ku Klux Klan."[38]

A summary policy statement of Students for America is found—of all places—in an advertisement in one of the publications of Mrs. Kitty Jones.[39] In two parallel columns, the ad's sponsors state "What We're For" and "What We're Against." On the positive side there is "The Constitution, Religious Principles, Free Enterprise, Strong Foreign Policy, Economy." On the negative: "Socialistic Expansion, Appeasement, Immorality in Government, Subversive Elements, Waste in Government." The extent of Professor McGovern's commitment to these principles is not known. But even if we cannot assume McGovern's SFA sponsorship to imply commitment, there seems sufficient evidence in his book to place the professor well to the right of political center.

Our next retired member of "the Academy" is, if anything, a less restrained devotee of the right than those previously discussed. E. Merrill Root, his publisher tells us, is a Phi Beta Kappa, and until recently a professor of English at Indiana's Earlham College. Dr. Root's formal training and earlier literary efforts were largely confined to poetry, but he seems to have become diverted. In 1955 appeared Professor Root's exposé, *Collectivism on the Campus*. In late 1958 came *Brainwashing in the High Schools*.[40]

This latter entry in the library of sensational exposés is devoted largely to an analysis of eleven textbooks widely used in secondary schools across the nation. Dr. Root explains his fears this way: We are losing the Cold War. Why? Without wasting any time on possible dead ends, Root leads us quickly to the heart of the matter: The Cold War is a struggle for men's belief and allegiance. "Since it has to do with a vacuum in the *mind*, we can only attribute it to the educational system that has taken upon itself the training of our youth."[41] Q.E.D. But either Professor Root's efforts do not measure up to the enormity of the problem, or else he believes that the "educational system" consists only of the American history textbook. For his investigation is confined solely to the "brainwashing" accomplished by the history text.

Professor Root's quarrel with these books rests on their "social" view of history; their exaltation of "the common man"; their claim that the United States has indulged in "imperialistic" ventures; their emphasis on the nation as a "democracy" rather than on "the American form of constitutional republican government"; their critical evaluation of free enterprise; and their receptivity to a "world superstate." These sins are said to characterize ten of the eleven books Professor Root undertakes to analyze—and even the eleventh does not receive a completely clean bill of health. His examination leads Root to the fastidious conclusion, "What American schools need is a thorough housecleaning." And the only way to achieve this is through a "genuine American revolution" in which schools would refuse to use these textbooks. Meanwhile, to pave the way for glorious rebellion, teachers should "*mercilessly criticize*" the books.[42]

Needless to add, Root's efforts have aroused the wrath of what he doubtless thinks of as the "left-wing liberals." But this group has expressed its ire in a factual and highly convincing indictment. Professor Root seems to have been a bit careless with his facts—and the high school whose list of eleven texts he claims to have started out with has compiled a list of sample misstatements. To cite just one example, Dr. Root lauds the alert citizens of this community who, in 1952, "demanded a book that did not so grossly follow the leftist line as did the others in use."[43] But the textbook in question—the one in eleven partially exonerated by Root—was not even *published* until two years later. At that time it was adopted according to the school's usual procedure, unaccompanied by ultimatum or incident.[44]

Dr. Root's "facts" have not been the only point of criticism. Several of his reviewers have remarked upon his unique criterion of determining textbook bias: comparing the number of lines devoted to various topics in the *index*. Others have suggested that Professor Root's goal is not the elimination of "brainwashing" at all; rather, that it is the substitution of different content in the alleged indoctrination process. One reviewer concludes that what Root has done is to raise "his own historical interpretations, his prejudices and his predilections to the plane of ultimate truth"—while another assesses the particular direction of these bents: "Where Root stands, there is no further room to the right and everything else looks left."[45]

Dr. Root's less controversial literary efforts are more obscure than his sallies into the sensational. Many are difficult to find, but in order that readers not entirely forego the experience of Dr. Root's prose, here is a segment from a rather effusive book review. The passage tends to suggest that Dr. Root's commitment to the last century is not only in what he thinks but in how he says it as well:

> Campbell's greatest poetry, which will live when our bards of shreds and patches are rags in the wind, came early. He was a South African, warmed by fiercer suns, splendidly savage with the land of elephant and leopard. There was in him that central fire that keeps earth's heart still a star: out of that star-fire his poems leaped like elemental jets of lava. . . .[46]

Dr. Root is a lecturer as well as an author. In 1953 he addressed the first Congress of Freedom assembly, telling members of the group (which is a coalition comparable to We, The People!) that there were a thousand "out-and-out Communists" in American colleges. Even more alarming were the " 'much larger number of dupes and fellow travelers.' " As a criterion for selecting a college for one's offspring, Dr. Root proposed an interview with each institution's president—the major purpose of which would be to ascertain whether "at least 50 per cent of the faculty be zealously for the American system."[47]

Dr. Root has also served on the National Advisory Board of We, The People!, and is a member of the "National Board of Fellows" of the Freedom School. (See the tables of our questionnaire replies for its director's views of public education, and those of We, The People!) He is on a rather mysterious "Citizens' Foreign Relations Committee"—mysterious because, since no one is authorized to speak for the group, its views must remain unknown![48] Recent events may shed some light: the Foreign Relations Committee is reported to have grown out of an organization called the "Committee of Endorsers." It may be that this is the now renowned "Committee of Indorsers" of the John Birch Society. Also suggestive of some such tie between the old "Citizens' Foreign Relations Committee" and the Birch Society is the fact that one Birch front group has been named (or misnamed) "Foreign Aid Committee." In any event, Operation Textbook evaluator Merrill Root is a member of the Citizens' Foreign Relations Committee and the currently constituted Committee of Indorsers of the John Birch Society.[49]

The first literary eruption of Root's search for subversion in education was *Collectivism on the Campus*, which is devoted largely to a series of case studies. One chapter, entitled "Who Are the Fellow Travelers?" gives attention to several well-known scientists and scholars. Chapter 10 is called "Ignorance in High Places." The high places turn out to be university presidencies—and the "ignorance" discussed includes that of Hutchins, Eisenhower, and Wriston. One helpful contribution the book makes is to shed some light on one of Professor Root's colleagues on the America's Future Textbook Evaluation Committee. In Root's chapter on "Ordeal by 'Liberalism,'" A. H. Hobbs is one of three professors who has presumably undergone the "ordeal."

Professor Hobbs teaches sociology at the University of Pennsylvania's Wharton School. Why Dr. Hobbs entered the field, and why he remains in it, pose twin enigmas. At least two of his three books are given over entirely to rather vindictive indictments of the discipline. His purpose seems nothing less than to expose the gigantic hoax perpetrated by those who work in sociology. Of the two books expressing this theme, the first published was *The Claims of Sociology: A Critique of Textbooks*.[50] In the words of Dr. Root—who may have used this book as a model for his own subsequent textbook investigation—"Professor Hobbs takes 83 leading textbooks in sociology, used in high schools and colleges. . . . He discovers that in varying degrees, they are all slanted toward collectivism. . . ."[51] Root is not the only "right reason" disciple to spot this as the dominating theme of Dr. Hobbs's investigation. Others lauding the book have also testified to its presence.[52] The "collectivism" label is not used by Hobbs himself. As he states it, his purpose is "to demonstrate that the claims contained in sociology texts constitute a biased presentation . . . not justified on the basis of scientific data, nor on the basis of scientific method."[53]

Hobbs does, however, admit to some bias—"Skepticism regarding the scientific validity and the practical applicability of much of the material which is presented as 'sociological knowledge.'" But he hastens to add that this does not invalidate his conclusions, since "other investigators, *with a similar critical approach*, would arrive at similar conclusions."[54] We certainly take no exception to this last statement—indeed, it is unassailable.

One serious weakness of the book is that Professor Hobbs's shattering conclusions are totally unaccompanied by documentation. The only evidence given for such statements as "Thirty-nine texts offer alternatives to the present economic system" is an occasional illustrative quote. He explains the oversight this way: "The temptation to include a list of the citations was resisted by the feeling that their inclusion would be more nearly an exercise in pedantic pretentiousness than a demonstration of scholarship. . . ."[55]

Dr. Hobbs's second book, *Social Problems and Scientism,*[56] provides different reasons for the same conclusion—that sociology's claims are fraudulent and unworthy of attention. One or two themes merely suggested in the first volume, however, are more forthrightly stated in the second. While the first book "established" the fact of bias among sociologists, the second one points out their specific prejudices. Dr. Hobbs reports the correlation he finds between a faith in science and a general tendency to leftist belief. Although his purpose is ostensibly to raise the standards of social science from their current level of "scientism" to the acceptable level of "science," valid grounds for questioning Dr. Hobbs are found in just one of several terminal warnings he gives his readers: "Do not reject findings because they are scientific, but do not feel compelled to accept them on this basis alone, particularly if they affect your life or the society. . . ."[57]

Apparently Hobbs's singular contributions and his unique approach to improving his chosen field have been received as mixed blessings. His professional story, as told by Dr. Root, is one of little recognition and less reward. Hobbs reports having been told that he would never receive a promotion; indeed, he cites instances of promotions for younger men with less seniority. In the words of Root, "Professor Hobbs . . . traced his trouble to the fact that he was a philosophic conservative. . . ." To this Hobbs adds a plaintive and wondering, " 'I cannot prove that I was so treated because I was a "conservative." Yet, what other motivation could there have been?' "[58]

Without venturing a reply, we shall move on to another member of the Textbook Evaluation Committee—and another for whom Professor Root has at least an oblique word of approval. One of the bases of Root's criticism of current high school textbooks is their omission of the research of Professor Charles Callan Tansill. Dr. Tansill is the author of several multivolumed works; but the title to which Dr. Root has reference is *Back Door to War*—a "critical" study of events leading to our participation in World War II.[59]

Little is known of Dr. Tansill's views on public education, although he became a member of the board of governors of Allen Zoll's new Federation of Conservatives—a group taking a vigorous stand against alleged subversion in public schools. To our knowledge Dr. Tansill has not expressed himself directly on the current status of American schools, and he did not reply to the questionnaire inquiry we addressed to him. What he might have to say about integration as one feature of contemporary public education, however, is clear: Dr. Tansill has very pronounced views about Negroes.

Until 1955 Dr. Tansill had taught in the Washington, D.C., area for a number of years. In 1936 or 1937, after an outspoken defense of Hitler and the Nazi regime, he left American University. The reasons for his departure have been variously reported.[60] After this professional reversal, Tansill taught at Washington's Georgetown University for several years. At the end of this time, his employment was again terminated following heated controversy.

The strife which preceded Dr. Tansill's departure from Georgetown began with an address he made to a local chapter of the Defenders of State Sovereignty and Individual Liberties. (See the table of questionnaire replies for its criticisms of public education.) The university, whose Jesuit administration makes it an unlikely choice for charges of subversive "leftism," did not object to Tansill's reported membership in this unique "Defender" organization. Nor did the university's protest stem from Tansill's recommendation that "Virginia muster its state militia, if necessary, to prevent enforcement of the Supreme Court [school integration] decision." The university's vigorous exception was to such ideas as " 'The Negro is a moron,' "[61] and "No Negro . . . [has] ever made any contribution whatever to any civilization anywhere—unless he had white blood,"[62] and to the attacks on Jews and Italians that Tansill managed also to weave in.[63]

Dr. Tansill issued a wan defense. When Georgetown's president disavowed Tansill's racial views, the professor countered with the claim that all his derogatory remarks were quoted, and " 'I am not responsible for the reading of a series of quotations.' "[64] (President Bunn's response: " 'That reply is absurd.' ") Manifestly, it *is* an uncommon point of view. One wonders whether Dr. Tansill is applying it impartially in his work on Operation Textbook—for example, to textbook authors quoting the long list of those whom Dr. Tansill does not admire.

Dr. Tansill has aroused a number of controversies. The topic of one of these suggests that he may have much to talk over with another member of the America's Future Textbook Evaluation Committee, historian Dr. Ella Lonn. The ruckus in question—minor in comparison with some of Dr. Tansill's involvements—was occasioned by his theory that Abraham Lincoln deviously contrived to "trick" the South into the war.[65]

Dr. Lonn's several books on The War Between the States are noteworthy for their scholarship. All reflect meticulous thoroughness and, to cite just one, *Salt as a Factor in the Confederacy*[66] makes a unique contribution. But in assessing what she contributes to high school textbook evaluation, other features of Dr. Lonn's career may be more central. For many years a history teacher at Baltimore's Goucher College, Professor Emeritus Lonn has also been active in a number of organizations. Many of these have taken a strong position on national and international affairs, and some have also concerned themselves with public education. These organizations provide some clue as to what Dr. Lonn may wish to insert into or eliminate from the reading of high school students.

Dr. Lonn has been an official of Operation America's National Assembly Committee. In the organization's words, its purpose was to serve "those individuals of the Right, who wish to remain masters of their own lives, and masters of their government, rather than to live as a subordinated mass under a Government that is their master."[67] At a 1952 meeting called by Operation America to assess the need for coordinating like-minded groups, Dr. Lonn was on the six-member committee that drafted proposals subsequently adopted by Operation America. (Another of the six: Lucille Cardin Crain, first executive secretary of Operation Textbook.) Among the committee's recommendations was a two-pronged Constitutional amendment barring the federal government from business ventures, and banning any foreign agreement conflicting with federal or state laws. They also urged opposition to " 'World Government' " and " 'the theory of progressive income tax.' "[68] Several months later, with the hope of realizing these proposals, Operation America spawned a new organization: the Congress of Freedom, one of today's four major rightist coalitions, and the group to which Dr. Root gave his estimate of one thousand Communist professors.

Dr. Lonn has also been an active member of another of the nation's coalitions of rightist groups. She has served on the National Advisory Board of We, The People! and has been a vice president of the organization. She has taken an active part in the Minute Women organization of Maryland, and in fact it appears that it was as a representative of this group that she served as an Operation America official, and requested Operation America to hold the previously mentioned conference, in the summer of 1952. The purpose of the conference was to map rightist strategy for the presidential campaign then under way. The Minute Women were dissatisfied with the candidates and platforms of both parties.[69]

The Minute Women of the U.S.A., Inc., is a national organization founded in 1949. Its controlling purpose has been to bring together " 'a group of kindred souls dedicated to the preservation of the United States as a free, independent Republic.' "[70] Although its national chairman stated in reply to our questionnaire inquiry that the *national* has no specific program in education, it is reported that members take a pledge, on joining, " 'to demand the removal of supporters of Socialism and Communism in . . . our educational system, and demand the teaching of our American heritage in our schools and colleges. . . .' "[71] The national chairman did say that local chapters of the Minute Women have concerned themselves with education. One of these, the Houston chapter, is generally credited with an attack on an assistant superintendent in that city. The attack apparently began with a determination to "make an example of somebody," and with the information that a group to which the unfortunate administrator had belonged once recommended books of two allegedly Communist authors.[72]

One more affiliation of Dr. Ella Lonn sheds further light on her political and economic beliefs, and suggests a particular answer to the question of what textbooks ought to be. In October of 1952, the *Educational Reviewer* welcomed her "with the greatest pleasure" to the periodical's consulting staff.[73] Dr. Lonn apparently subscribed to the general policies of the *Reviewer* (which will be discussed later), since it seems to have been the task of the three-member consulting staff to check and approve the reviews submitted.[74] In this position, Dr. Lonn doubtless met another member of the Textbook Evaluation Committee, Marie R. Madden.

Dr. Madden, who retired in 1954, was for many years a New York City high school teacher. Prior to this time, she was a professor of Spanish history and political theory at Fordham University. *Political Theory and Law in Medieval Spain* which is apparently her only book, was published in 1930 when Dr. Madden was at Fordham. In a foreword by the chairman of her department, it is stated that the book should serve to counteract current tendencies in political theory—especially the tendency " 'to separate morals from law' "—and to arrive at postulates inductively instead of assuming them to be " 'logical deductions from great moral or religious principles. . . .' "[75] Whatever this book may suggest for Dr. Madden's approach to political theory and practice, there is direct evidence of her approach to textbook evaluation.

Among Dr. Madden's reviews for the *Educational Reviewer* were several on a pamphlet series published by the National Education Association. Although one of these pamphlets dealt with representative government, and the other with the American business system, Dr. Madden's analyses of them give considerable attention to Marxism and modern Communism as well. She provides her readers with information about the connections of the authors—for example, one "is identified with the New School for Social Research. . . . This institution is a center for the advocacy of 'change,' the 'new social order,' and collectivism." The reviewer further finds that the authors' "line of reasoning, their manner of treatment and their general style of writing follow closely what is known as Marxian dialectics . . ." and that there is, "in the authors' thought . . . the idea of the uselessness and eventual disappearance of the state. . . ."[76]

The pamphlet dealing with representative government fares no better. According to Dr. Madden's review, it suggests "that we need a complete change in our form of government, a change to a government which in theory will be socialist, in form centralized. . . ." Dr. Madden's hostility to change of almost any kind seems implicit in her conclusion: She has difficulty in reconciling the author's belief in teaching American government, with his belief that any changes might desirably be made in it.[77]

The eleventh member of the Textbook Evaluation Committee is Felix Morley. Like several of his co-workers on Operation Textbook, Dr. Morley is a student of political science. Economics has also been an area of special concern to this former president of Pennsylvania's Haverford College. Since leaving Haverford in 1945, Dr. Morley has been primarily involved with writing and editing. For five years he was editor and publisher of the conservative weekly *Human Events,* for which several of his America's Future colleagues have also written. Later, Dr. Morley was the Washington correspondent for the financial publication *Barron's Weekly.*

Many of Dr. Morley's ideas have become widely known through his feature in the Chamber of Commerce magazine *Nation's Business.* A prominent position is assigned his column, "The State of the Nation," which is said to discuss "trends." In reading the columns, one cannot help noticing that the number of trends Dr. Morley finds significant is rapidly and steadily narrowing. In earlier years his commentaries—which are largely confined to trends he finds unfavorable—dealt with such diverse topics as centralization and federal power, school integration, and foreign policy. An overwhelming proportion of his more recent assessments of "the state of the nation" deal with money or with the ills of public education. Significantly, the two concerns often appear in the same article.

The amount of money spent on public schools is a recurring theme in Dr. Morley's columns. In one issue he argues that we pay teachers too much, in terms of (1) the secure, unharassed, short-working-hour conditions of their employment, and (2) the salaries paid instructors in small colleges.[78] More recently he has managed to contort the question of federal aid into a direct attack on "the fundamental principle of a federal republic," and to interpret the issue as a test of whether Congress is really committed to democracy.[79] Like many of those objecting to the amount of money spent on schools, Dr. Morley finds a large number of shortcomings in current education. But his questionnaire reply reveals that he not only feels that schools are doing things they should not be doing—and a poor job of what they should be doing—he also believes that they are godless and un-American. Few of his articles stress this important aspect of Dr. Morley's views on public schools. Most of his negative comments pertain to inefficiency and "frills."

Comparatively, there are few suggestions for remedying the situation—unless there be one in the title "Quality or Quantity? Our High Schools Must Choose."[80] But the lamentations are many. In one article Dr. Morley mourns "the triumph of the theory that public education should be entertaining rather than disciplinary."[81] In others, we find examples of the wishing-will-make-it-so approach to school criticism:

For a long time there has been rather more than a suspicion that the basis of public education in this country, once unquestionably firm, is decoratively painted but rotted underneath.

Fortunately, Americans are increasingly coming to realize that the central problem of the public schools is . . . an easy-going, noncompetitive, "life adjustment" curriculum. . . .[82]

In both the last articles quoted, there are plugs for the work of Roger Freeman and the Institute for Social Science Research, which published its director's controversial prediction of *School Needs in the Decade Ahead,* and of whose board of trustees Dr. Morley is president.

Leaving Dr. Morley, we come to one of the most colorful figures in Operation Textbook. The militancy of the label is particularly apt in introducing the member who has been called "Mr. Anti-Communist": J. B. Matthews.[83] That part of Dr. Matthews's extraordinary career which first led him into the limelight began with his work for Congressman Martin Dies' House Un-American Activities Committee. More recently, Matthews was employed by Senator McCarthy's subcommittee investigating Communist influence. His statement that " 'The largest single group supporting the Communist apparatus in the United States today is composed of Protestant clergymen' " led to Matthews' resignation as McCarthy's executive staff director.[84] Currently he serves as an associate editor of the John Birch Society's *American Opinion,* and among other activities he has

. . . lent his name to a subtle kind of anti-Semitism; . . . co-authored with Allen Zoll, the notorious pamphlet, "How Red Is The National Council of Churches?" . . . helped prepare the document *Red-Ucators at Harvard.* . . .[85]

But if Dr. Matthews's present extremism has been a professional liability in recent years, it has proved no more so than did his *liberal* views in earlier years. His incongruous career began with a role that could never have foretold his later interests. He began as a missionary to Java, and when that career ended because of his sympathy for the natives and their growing nationalism, Dr. Matthews turned to teaching in religious schools. In three of them his liberal views worked to his disadvantage, leading eventually to his departure from each institution. Dr. Matthews then formally embraced Socialism. "He says that he never actually joined the Communist party, but . . . that he was the most faithful and publicized of its fellow travelers."[86] The ideological reversal occurred following a change in Dr. Matthews's fortunes. He became an executive of a growing and successful corporation. When in this capacity he was confronted with a strike, he viewed his employees as "mutineers" and himself "the victim of a Communist plot."[87] It was soon after the strike ruined his organization that he became the chief investigator for the House Un-American Activities Committee.

Dr. Matthews has dropped from the public eye, but at every opportunity he continues to charge that American Protestantism is shot through with Communism, and he reportedly still maintains "the largest card file of Communists and communist front members in the U.S."[88] Doubtless this file is handy as Dr. Matthews comes to evaluate high school textbooks. His appointment to the Evaluation Committee seems clearly to assume that evil conspiracies are afoot in American education. For one of the few consistencies in Dr. Matthews's thinking has been his conviction of sinister forces duping the public through secret and devious means. When he belonged to the extreme left he wrote a book charging that the people and their churches were being victimized by such infamous schemers as J. Pierpont Morgan and Andrew Mellon.[89] After his conversion to the right, the source of evil changed: it is now the Communists who threaten the people and their churches—and their schools as well.

The final member of the original America's Future Textbook Evaluation Committee was the project's executive secretary, Mrs. Lucille Cardin Crain. Like Dr. Matthews's work, Mrs. Crain's has brought her considerable fame, and like him too, she has dedicated herself to seeking and exposing subversion. But while Dr. Matthews's search drew him into the churches and the political arena, Mrs. Crain has sniffed out subversion in the nation's schools and textbooks. In 1949 she was chosen to edit the *Educational Reviewer,* a quarterly established to examine textbooks "from the point of view of their attachment to the principles of 'personal liberty and economic liberty,' and their freedom from 'concealed theories of collectivism.' "[90]

The *Reviewer* was sponsored and published by the Conference of American Small Business Organizations. During the period in which the periodical was issued, the sponsoring organization claimed to represent about 3,000 members—individuals, business concerns, and trade associations. CASBO further claimed to express " 'the deliberated opinion of delegates from organizations representing over 260 different lines of industry in 48 States, representing an affiliated membership of over 600,000 small business concerns. . . .' "[91] Despite these impressive figures, however, the House Lobbying Activities Committee expressed grave doubts about the extent to which CASBO was committed to the interests of small business. One basis for this skepticism was the breadth of the organization's solicitations—leading the congressional committee to conclude that "CASBO has made devious and sometimes successful efforts to secure big-business support for its activities."

Be that as it may, there can be little doubt of CASBO's dedication in the matter of textbook evaluation. The first issue of the quarterly, in the summer of 1949, makes very clear the reason for its existence: " 'The Educational Reviewer grew out of the concerns of Americans . . . who . . . became aware of the propaganda for collectivist doctrines their sons and daughters were absorbing in their schools. . . .' "[92] The project developed from a CASBO resolution to appoint " 'a committee on un-American activities. . . .' " This genesis suggests that the new periodical began by assuming the answer to the very question it might instead have *asked.* One bemused analyzer found that out of eighteen reviews listed by the *Educational Reviewer* in a single index, only four books received even mild enthusiasm.[93] One group that "reviewed" the *Reviewer* offers this explanation for the alarming textbook situation thus revealed: In their zeal to discover subversion, reviewers failed to portray the books accurately. There were instances of quoting out of context and even of blatant misquoting.[94]

Mrs. Crain, the *Reviewer*'s editor, did not limit herself to the printed word. In Omaha, for instance, she—along with Dr. Root—spoke before the first Congress of Freedom. While Root addressed himself to collectivism in colleges, Mrs. Crain impartially told the audience of its permeation of " 'private and parochial schools as well as public schools.' "[95] Earlier the same year she had told a Chicago audience that "all levels of education from kindergarten to adult, especially teacher education, are set up to promote world government, loss of liberty, and loss of sovereignty."[96]

A somewhat negative approach seems to pervade the pages of the *Educational Reviewer* as well its editor's various addresses. While it is not difficult to discern what the lady is against, there are few statements indicating what she is for. The amusing report of an interview granted by Mrs. Crain would suggest that, as of mid-1951, she had not made up her mind on this question:

> When I asked Mrs. Crain what she thought the proper aims of education should be, she seemed to be pushed . . . far out to sea. . . . After remaining silent for a spell Mrs. Crain, moved by a sudden inspiration, said brightly, "I like our little slogan on the *Educational Reviewer*." (This reads: "In the light of truth, objectivity and established American ideals, to examine the publications used in instructing American youth.") There seemed little point in pressing that subject further.[97]

Mrs. Crain's many activities facilitate a clearer picture of her position on political and economic questions. With Dr. Lonn, she served on the Executive Committee of Operation America's National Assembly Committee—apparently serving in this capacity as the representative of the *Reviewer*. The two also served together on the six-member committee that drafted the Operation America action proposals we have already cited. They have further been associated as members of the National Advisory Board of We, The People!. In addition, Mrs. Crain is a member of the John Birch Society's Committee of Indorsers.[98]

We have now met the thirteen original members of the America's Future Textbook Evaluation Committee. But since the launching of Operation Textbook, the personnel has expanded. In the unrestrained prose of the parent organization, "several new and distinguished members have been added to the already exemplary Textbook

Evaluation Committee." No mention is made of deletions from the "exemplary" group, but a June, 1960, list of "the full committee as of this date" omits without fanfare the name of Lucille Cardin Crain.[99]

The new Operation Textbook secretary is George A. Membrez, Jr., a social studies teacher in Stillwater, Minnesota. America's Future reported only that "Mr. Membrez is a teacher, school-board member, and educational consultant to the vice-president of a large industrial corporation."[100] He has reportedly been active in America's Future, sharing the organization's conviction of Communist penetration in public education, and has written articles for the *America's Future Weekly*. Locally, Mr. Membrez is credited with bringing the Council for Basic Education's Arthur Bestor and James Koerner into Stillwater several years ago. In 1958 he introduced the CBE officials at meetings in Minnesota.[101]

Another addition to the Textbook Evaluation Committee is Hans F. Sennholz, chairman of the Economics Department at Grove City College. Although he seems to have been less directly concerned with public education than have some of his committee colleagues, his ideological kinship with the group is fairly clear. If they had not met before, Professor Sennholz probably became acquainted with his America's Future colleagues under the auspices of the Foundation for Economic Education. Dr. Sennholz has been a frequent contributor to the FEE magazine, the *Freeman,* billed as "A Monthly for Libertarians" and more explicitly as "educational champion of private property, the free market, the profit and loss system, and limited government." Both Russell Kirk and Merrill Root have also written for the *Freeman;* in fact, a single issue has contained articles by three of the current Operation Textbook reviewers. To top it off, Professor Sennholz is the third of this textbook group to serve as an editor of the John Birch Society's *American Opinion.*

Dr. Sennholz is an economist with a viewpoint difficult to duplicate among contemporary scholars. He judges any government antitrust activity as Marxian, claiming that "in an unhampered market economy a monopoly affords no cause for alarm. . . ." He even opposes such government intervention as the protective tariff, the issuance of patents, and the fact that "they [the government] own and operate the whole postal industry. . . ."[102] And, to round out our view of Dr. Sennholz' position, we cite the following miscellaneous judgments:

> The Welfare State . . . seeks to solve the [slum] problem through housing projects that breed new slums. Thus government housing is slowly substituted for privately owned homes, and socialism advances another step. . . .
>
> In a market economy there can be no exploitation of labor. . . .
>
> [The European Economic Community is] a delaying action by the planners in Europe [instigated thusly:] When the disastrous effects of national economic planning become apparent to everyone, planners seek solace and hope in international planning. . . .[103]

The final person who has been named to serve on Operation Textbook is Anthony T. Bouscaren. Like Dr. Sennholz, Bouscaren is comparatively young, is a college professor, and enjoys a similar approach to national problems.

Dr. Bouscaren is a professor of political science at Le Moyne College. His statements are generally more temperate than those of some of his colleagues on the America's Future committee. Although he has long been associated with the political right, one gets the impression that Professor Bouscaren is not so anxious to repeal the twentieth century as are many others. This mild departure has surely been noted by his America's Future colleagues, but whatever irregularities there may be are clearly not sufficient to ostracize Bouscaren. We find that he has been a frequent contributor to such publications as *National Review, National Republic,* and *Human Events,* and has often addressed the political right. He has, for example, participated frequently as a speaker at Congress of Freedom meetings.

One cannot help wondering whether Professor Bouscaren has at times been an unwitting contributor to weak causes. Recently, for example, he prepared an article for the magazine *The Cross and The Flag.* It was a persuasive story, urging a legitimate course of action: greater security checks for aliens admitted to the United States.[104] But it is mildly surprising to find a professor of political science writing for Gerald L. K. Smith's magazine—and permitting his article to be backed up by a Smith piece entitled "An Introduction to the International Jew."

Communism is Dr. Bouscaren's area of specialization. He is the author of several books, the most recent of which is *A Guide to Anti-Communist Action.*[105] America's Future paid tribute to author and work this way: "The author . . . is a rarity among the 'liberal' conformists of the campus—a college professor who is thoroughly anti-communist. But his book is not written for his 'intellectual' confreres (though God knows they need to read it), [*sic*] but for the everyday citizen with the uneasy feeling that the battle between American freedom and communist slavery is going by default. . . ."[106]

Apparently a favorite topic of Professor Bouscaren's is what he calls a "double standard" on the part of liberals: he finds that they denounce Naziism but are reluctant to come out as strongly against Communism. Internationally, "the UN operates to safeguard the prestige of the USSR, while making it impossible for anti-communism to get a hearing. . . ."[107] One wonders if Professor Bouscaren is really serious about the solution he has elsewhere suggested: "The basic dilemma with which we are confronted is this: Can the United States afford in the future to take the first blow before attacking?"[108] Whatever the solution may be, it is obvious that Dr. Bouscaren does not think it will come from schools: "unless and until social science teaching cleans house, . . . education is *not* the answer to communism."[109] It is evidently this house-cleaning task which is occupying Dr. Bouscaren as a member of Operation Textbook.

This detailed consideration of the people who are evaluating high school textbooks under the sponsorship of America's Future makes plain several characteristics of the group as a whole. First, it is beyond all question that this is a highly conservative assemblage. The political and economic attitude the members share is that of Classical Liberalism with its controlling distrust of government, and its belief that both individuals and societies are better off with an absolute minimum of interference. Through their affiliation with various patriot organizations, more than half the members of the Textbook Evaluation Committee also reveal a very narrowly construed patriotism—a love of country that is expressed by an unmitigated veneration of its early history and leaders, by a desire to keep the country aloof from the problems and concerns of the rest of the world, and by attempts to limit severely those who might become citizens through immigration.

As individuals, these people also seem to share a number of other things. One of these is age. Six of the committee members are retired —one having passed eighty. We have also seen that many members of the committee knew one another before they were brought together by America's Future. Mrs. Crain had worked with Dr. Lonn and Dr. Madden on the *Educational Reviewer* and had shared the speaker's platform with Dr. Root. He, in turn, has praised the work of Professors Hobbs and Tansill. Professor Kirk has spoken admiringly of Professor McGovern. Doctors Morley and Evans could hardly have escaped knowing each other when both worked for *Human Events*, and the *National Review* undoubtedly brought together Doctors Evans, Kirk, Kendall, Bouscaren, Matthews, and Root. And of course, there is the ubiquitous John Birch Society, in which four of the reviewers serve as leaders.

The question that concerns us is the purpose to which these friends and acquaintances have been reunited: that of examining textbooks. It is to be hoped that one's political and economic commitments do not always and entirely dominate one's approach to textbook writing and evaluation. Two factors may, however, often dictate an intrusion of personal commitments. One of these is the intensity of the commitment. The writings and activities we have explored point up political and economic commitments that are very intense indeed. A second factor that might preclude objectivity on the part of committee members is the specific beliefs to which they are committed. If, for example, members of this committee believe that only *some* viewpoints in a controversy are entitled to be heard—if they oppose listening to the full and accurate presentations of all viewpoints—this is a belief or commitment that will greatly influence the kind of textbook evaluating they do.

The nature of forthcoming reviews seems evident—implicit not only in the thinking of committee personnel but also in the nature of the organization sponsoring the project. What might be the results for public education? One possible effect could well be a serious attempt at textbook censorship. So obvious did this aim appear in the earlier "evaluating" by the *Educational Reviewer* that the House Lobbying Activities Committee likened it to the frantic book burnings of Nazi Germany. As was the case with the *Reviewer*, there will undoubtedly be people accepting and acting on the conclusions of the

America's Future committee without having examined the evidence.

The names and titles of Operation Textbook personnel will doubtless provide false assurance to the uninitiated. After all, outside "the Academy" itself, how many groups can boast a full complement of doctor's degrees, with each member a college professor? That the Textbook Evaluation Committee represents a resurgence of the First Wave of contemporary educational criticism, or a merging of patriotic and intellectual themes—with college educators lined up against public schools on both counts—seems clear. What is also obvious is that the group's danger potential is great enough so that we simply cannot afford to overlook it.

9. *Results, Reaction, and Reply*

Events accompanying and following concerted attacks on schools have been as diverse as critics' purposes. Where there has been a particular focus of attack—a specific curriculum area, activity, or textbook—the aftermath has sometimes been the elimination of whatever single feature has given critics offense. But more often, as the instigators have gathered sympathizers, they have also enlarged their demands, so that, instead of a single fault, critics have found a "general mess" in the schools. Frequently, in such cases, the superintendent and his top appointees have been held responsible for the undesirable state of affairs. Occasionally, with less logic, a subordinate administrative official or even a classroom teacher has been selected as the fount of all evil; and sometimes this individual has been dismissed accordingly. Such outcomes are only the most dramatic and widely publicized results of intense criticism. Attacks on education have produced various other effects as well.

There are many events at local, state, and national levels which seem closely tied to the concentrated educational criticism of recent years. Of the three, the relationship of national events to attacks on education is the most difficult to establish. Asking whether the national events caused the criticism or vice-versa leads only to the chicken-or-egg controversy. It is even possible, of course, that some other cause created both. But regardless of which initially shapes which, it is reasonable to suppose that once generated, attacks on schools may have decided effects on national concerns. For example, whether or not the claims of subversion in education occurred as a result of broader and more general subversion claims, the critics who sounded the theme may have influenced national legislators.

The climax of the First Wave of educational criticism occurred during the same year that set a record for congressional investigations of subversion in education. With the opening of the Eighty-third Congress in 1953, no fewer than four committees claimed the right to look into Communist influence in education. The Velde House Un-American Activities Committee and the Jenner Senate Internal Security Subcommittee inquired into the beliefs and backgrounds of college educators. During the same year, the Cox Committee investigated educational foundations. Perhaps because of disappointment over the clearance given the foundations, a reinvestigation was carried out the following year by the Reece Committee. The peak of the congressional search for subversive influences in education had passed by 1954—possibly due to such exposés as the Reece Committee's finding that a papal encyclical was a typical Communist statement.[1] Whether or not the First Wave educational critics can claim much credit for the activities of these committees, the two expounders of the subversion theme shared the same period of popularity.

During this period, comparable events were taking place at the state level. Here there seems a closer tie to the charges of local critics claiming subversion in state-supported schools. In a number of states, special loyalty oaths for teachers and professors were one of the most outstanding results. Another outcome was an effort to censor textbooks used in state-supported schools. The high point in this connection seems to have been reached in Alabama, with a law providing that the publishers of every book *certify* whether the authors were or had been Communists, "pro-Communist, pro-Marxian Socialist, or . . . [members of] any group . . . considered subversive by any committee of Congress or by the Attorney General."[2] Furthermore, the publisher's certification had to extend also to any authors *mentioned* in the books purchased. Alabama's Polytechnic Institute merely commented that the required investigation of the 28,000,000 authors thus implicated in its library would cost more than a million dollars.

The flow of federal and state funds to the schools seems also to have been affected by criticism. While here again it is impossible to say that the criticism has led directly to curtailment of financial aid to schools, it is reasonable to assume that much of the extreme and wholesale criticism we have examined might well incline legislators to allot scarce funds elsewhere. Particularly might this result from the efforts of those critics who maintain that the ills of public education bear little relation to finances and that additional funds will not remedy the situation.

Critics would be delighted to take credit for state-level developments affecting the preparation of teachers. In several states there have been movements to reduce the professional education requirements for certification—and one state came close to abolishing *all* unique preparation generally given future teachers.[3] Perhaps even more significant is the fact that in such moves, recommendations of members of the teaching profession have been assigned little weight in the decisions. When these developments in certification are considered alongside certain trends at several state universities—removing all teacher preparation decisions from the college of education and placing them in the hands of all-university committees—things indeed seem to be moving in the direction of critics' demands. If such developments cannot be traced directly to the contemporary attacks of academicians, they clearly accord with a pet claim of this group: teaching (outside the university, of course) involves no unique competence.

On the local level, it has perhaps been only natural that some of the most widely publicized effects of attacks on schools have been those involving the dismissal of a school employee. The educator's interest in such an event is obvious; but for the public as well, the situation offers enough drama to stimulate a great deal of interest. For example, the forced resignation of Willard Goslin as Superintendent of Pasadena schools had enough appeal to warrant prominent attention in the national press.[4]

At least two careful investigations found Dr. Goslin's dismissal to result largely from the demands of a comparatively small but very vocal group of critics.[5] Dr. Goslin had received a warm welcome as the new superintendent. The end of the honeymoon period began with the defeat of a tax proposal to provide educational funds. The organization which had spearheaded the campaign to defeat the tax went on to denounce as leftist and educationally unsound the "Progressive Education" Goslin was alleged to represent. And despite the strong, though unorganized, support the superintendent seems to have had, the board asked for his resignation.

Another case where a dismissal seems to have been a direct outgrowth of intense educational criticism is that of Deputy Superintendent of Houston Schools George W. Ebey. Here the school attack had begun long before the victim arrived in the city. In 1949 a textbook that allegedly "tended to undermine the American way of life"[6] was banned. Violent protests had opposed speaking appearances in the city by prominent national figures who were locally alleged to be subversive. Two of these speakers seem to have been objectionable on the grounds that they had been Rhodes Scholars, and hence were obviously "agents in England's effort to rule the world"![7] There were also attacks on the United Nations and UNESCO, accompanied by demands to eliminate both from classroom consideration.

This was the morass into which Dr. Ebey stepped. He lasted one year. Following public charges that he had "Communist leanings" (brought largely by an attorney who consistently refused to identify his clients), the board voted not to reemploy Dr. Ebey—despite a commercial investigating concern's failure to find any evidence of disloyalty.

The Ebey case seems far more ominous than Goslin's departure from Pasadena. Despite untruths and what appears to be a sore absence of justice, the Goslin case at least involved events transpiring while he was on the scene. In the case of Ebey, however, the restlessness and dissension that eventually led to his dismissal had long preceded him in Houston. The conclusions of the NEA Defense Commission committee that investigated the Houston affair suggest that the unfortunate deputy superintendent may have been a victim of wholly extraneous forces—a "test case" for warring *political* factions.

Not all attacks on schools reach such a dramatic and pronounced climax. But even in more typical cases where school personnel are not threatened to such an extent, intense assaults have widespread ramifications among school employees. The Tenafly superintendent reported severe undermining of teachers' morale during the Jones-Cartwright attack. Similar unrest in Montgomery County has seemed to go hand in hand with increased activity on the part of chronic critics. A survey conducted by the NEA Defense Commission substantiates such effects of attacks on schools: various morale problems, and numerous resignations by teachers as well as by administrators.[8]

Because of the teacher's central role, it is sometimes difficult to separate the effects of attacks on teachers from the effects on education itself. But it is unmistakable that the attacks have had decided effects on the way teachers teach. The survey just cited revealed that during 1953, 13 per cent of the high school teachers replying felt they had been "subject to increased pressures against freedom to learn." A reluctance to deal with controversial issues—even in connection with approved or required content—has been noted many times.[9] Perhaps even more insidious is the erosion of the educator's willingness to act on his professional judgment in the face of potential controversy. In one community, for example, an art teacher who had been given the task of choosing the paintings for a new school building completely omitted the work of Picasso, which he admired and introduced to his classes. The teacher explained that since Picasso's beliefs had been questioned, perhaps the exhibition of his work would provoke trouble.

In another incident, a "family living" unit which included content on human reproduction had once been a part of the high school home economics program. Owing to a combination of circumstances, the unit was shortened and transferred to a social studies course. It soon disappeared altogether. When asked why it had been dropped, no teacher commented on the unit's lack of value or observed that there was no need for it. The replies were all to the effect that because "sex education" had been the target of an attack (which incidentally had been roundly defeated in its early stages), perhaps the school would be better off without it.

The important issue in these two incidents is not their immediate content. An excellent case might be made for omitting both Picasso and sex education from the American high school. What does seem highly significant is the basis on which the two decisions were reached. Teachers avoided taking a professional stand, choosing instead that course of action least likely to offend anyone.* How many times have such incidents occurred? How many educators have acted similarly when the content involved was far from trivial? There are instances

* Despite the comparative triviality of both these incidents—as compared, for instance, with the question of whether the UN and Communism ought similarly to be omitted—a case assigning them crucial significance can easily be built: Either there is appropriate educational value in Picasso and sex eduction—in which case they have a place in schools—or there is not, in which event neither belongs there. If it is decided that sex education has the appropriate educational value, omitting it on some *other* grounds constitutes a breach of professional ethics.

in which entire courses have been completely overhauled or abolished after criticisms. Changes in methods of teaching have similarly resulted,[10] and book censorship efforts have been carried out even more assiduously when locally inspired than at the state level. In an Oklahoma town, for example, a committee found several books to "favor Socialism" or to use " 'improper language' "—and with dispatch "the condemned books were accordingly burned."[11]

Indirect effects on the educational program can be as severe as direct ones. The curtailment of funds to carry on education obviously affects the quality of schools. In the same manner that wholesale denunciations of the public schools may have influenced *legislators* to allot available funds elsewhere, tax-burdened citizens may be similarly influenced. (It is worth noting, however, that the typical pattern of the development of extreme criticism seems to be the reverse of this. More often, the economy demands *precede*, rather than follow, an attack on schools. In fact, these demands may actually constitute the first phase of an attack.)

Another kind of indirect result of educational criticism, and one that is often overlooked, is the amount of effort required to deal with an attack. This effort means not only the schoolman's time—hence taxpayers' money—but it also necessitates the sacrifice of other responsibilities and concerns. The hours devoted to refuting charges made by illegitimate critics come at a high cost to the community and its schools. We referred earlier to the expert memorandum prepared by one school superintendent during an investigation, requested by the Board, of Kitty Jones's charges against the Iowa Tests. It is clear that in the course of preparing this memorandum, the superintendent wrote a series of letters, exchanged numerous phone calls with his staff and others, and undertook a survey to discover which schools used the tests. Obviously, a reappraisal of a testing program can be a valuable enterprise, but the refutation of charges such as those brought by Mrs. Jones hardly constitutes such a reappraisal. And the hours devoted to this project represent dollars lost by the community.

Whatever affects teachers and the school program is also likely to affect pupils. What are the effects on youngsters attending schools that are under attack? Teachers report instances of student morale problems, but such language hardly suggests the conflicts to which a youngster may be subject: On the one hand his very presence in school implies society's belief that his teachers can give him something important; on the other, he learns at home or from his neighbors that these teachers are to be feared or despised. The charges brought against Robert Olivier, Mrs. Jones's collaborator on *Progressive Education is REDucation,* only suggests some of the incidents arising from such a situation. At Olivier's school, students reacted to the dissension with overt disobedience to teachers and administrators, "booing" members of the faculty, and " 'rebellious and riotous' " behavior.[12]

One part of the attack on Houston schools consisted of the efforts of a local radio announcer to build what he called a " '*Watchdog* organization.' " Members would consist of " 'informers in all schools and in all classes' "—expressly including kindergarten—" 'to report on what is being taught.' "[13] Although this particular idea may have been sufficiently distasteful and absurd to discredit it, youngsters are far from untouched by the climate in which such a proposal circulates. One of the surveys we have cited disclosed the reluctance of students and teachers to express unpopular views, or even to talk about a number of major issues.[14] Another investigation showed the effects of a climate of suspicion on one type of student—the future teacher: ". . . a substantial minority . . . have a fear of association with people who are socialistic, a fear of speaking on controversial issues, and a wariness about . . . extracurricular organizations. . . ."[15]

The events which affect teachers and students are bound to reverberate also within the community at large. We mentioned earlier how Kitty Jones's attack on Tenafly schools very specifically affected at least one other institution—her church. An editor in neighboring Englewood wrote that the behavior of her colleague Mr. Cartwright was ". . . creating fear, distrust, and racial and religious unrest."[16] And according to journalist John Bainbridge, the attack on Pasadena schools had so rent the city that "in considerable measure social groups . . . have realigned on the basis of the school problem."[17]

How have educators reacted to attacks on schools? How have they sought to meet them? Insofar as history can provide guides for dealing with the future, it may be helpful to examine some of the ways in which the profession has reacted to the extreme educational criticism that has followed World War II.

It was in the late fall of 1950 that educators became fully aware of the gravity of the attacks under way on the schools of many communities. The forced resignation of Willard Goslin from the Pasadena superintendency apparently proved the eye-opening incident for American schoolmen. Prior to this, their inclination seems to have been simply to ignore unfair criticism as unworthy of reply—except of course in those communities where a full-scale attack finally developed. Counting on a public awareness and support which were all too often nonexistent, many schoolmen simply refused to answer charges that were patently unjust. In some cases this policy may have stemmed from the faulty assumption that the public could not be taken in; but in others it was apparently based on the view that replying to critics was not strategic. Many held that a rebuttal would do no more than give even further publicity to the charges.

Ignoring the attacks might have been a successful technique under certain circumstances. But as we have seen repeatedly, many of the attacks of the late forties were highly organized and nationally instigated. Under such conditions, with the time and money which organizations with full-time personnel were willing to devote, the prohibitive cost of the "ignore 'em" policy became obvious. As educators saw their schools and colleagues victimized, it grew increasingly plain that a more positive program was essential.

It would be unfair to claim that all this trouble had been brewing without any notice whatsoever on the part of the profession. Several events of the early forties suggest at least isolated instances of awareness. In 1941, for example, the NEA had established its National Commission for the Defense of Democracy Through Education, noting "Various organizations have become active . . . attempting to create a distrust of the efficiency of the public schools and of the loyalty of the teaching profession. This must be met. . . ."[18] In 1949 this Commission held a conference to consider the attacks on education, and simliar conferences were convened in 1950 and 1951. Criticisms of many school systems had begun to differ in kind, amount, and intensity, from the varieties of complaint which are virtually a part of the American education scene. And in different parts of the country—in Missouri in 1947, in Colorado in 1949, in New York, Minnesota, and Oregon in 1950—local schoolmen were made painfully aware of the problem.

It took the ouster of Goslin from Pasadena, however, to force a national awareness. Even then no concerted approach was organized, but several kinds of response to criticism emerged. Educators persistently sought to refute the charges of their critics. Specific criticisms were met on an intellectual level, with calm, documented refutation. One example of this kind of answer is found in the reply of two education professors to Professor Bestor, "A Scholar's Documents."[19] In an extremely detailed, painstaking analysis, the authors patiently point out each flaw in the facts and arguments advanced by Bestor.

Still another kind of effort at unemotional refutation was the large number of research reports that began to appear in educational magazines. Acknowledged experts in specific subjects began to write articles presenting the evidence for particular methods or practices. The major purpose of these reports was obviously to equip the schoolman to reply in the event of local attack. Such reports also began to find their way into popular magazines—in greatly watered-down versions. To aid the educator in responding to such general charges as "The schools just aren't doing a good job, period," a number of "then-and-now" studies appeared, contrasting contemporary pupil achievement with the achievement of yesteryear's pupils. Write-ups of this kind of research were widely disseminated, and the NEA's Research Division even produced lists and summaries of such studies.

Possibly because of a lack of faith in the capacity of fact to persuade, a number of replies to the crtics were written in a satiric vein, matching the rapier approach of many of the critics.[20] An example of this sort of reply is William Clark Trow's "Academic Utopia? An Evaluation of *Educational Wastelands*"—a review of Bestor's book. A brief quotation from the introductory paragraphs of this article serves to illustrate the sort of reply Trow's ably represents:

> "The Retreat from Learning in Our Public Schools" appears as a kind of subtitle opposite the title page . . . and may be considered the theme of the book, which is largely made up of papers recently published in several different journals. It is to be regretted that the author in his haste to publish did not see fit to revise the manuscript more carefully, since many of the errors and misconceptions in the original articles reappear in the present volume. But this should perhaps be overlooked, since public education is outside the field of his special competence, and as the jacket blurb puts it, "He writes with a sense of urgency."[21]

Other educators replied to criticism with strenuous counterattacks on a fight-fire-with-fire basis. Because many of the critics—especially those of the academic, liberal arts orientation—employed ridicule in stating their accusations, some of the replies were stated in the same way. Many within the education profession condemned this willingness to do battle on such a snide level. Others pessimistically pointed out the impossibility of dealing effectively with this type of criticism on *any* level. Still another group maintained that replies phrased as sensationally as the criticisms might obtain a hearing for education's side of the story which would otherwise be impossible.

A second and far more frequent sort of counterattack was the impugning of the critic. This sort of reply ranged in intensity—from the mild form in the quote from Professor Trow above, to an angry and general defamation of the critic's character.

It began to appear strange that educators—who were constantly urging critics to deal with issues and not with personalities—were themselves employing the denounced techniques. But when the background of some of the critics became known, many felt that the exposés had been legitimate. A good case was made for the *ad hominem* argument. The examination of a man's competence in a given area seemed a valid basis for judging what he had to say. In contradiction to the apparent belief of many citizens that education is a field in which "all men are equal" in competence, it was thought relevant to inquire into the particular claims to competence which many criticisms seemed to assume.

The critic who took the most vicious blows dealt by the counterattack was Allen Zoll. The prominent affixing to his signature of one supposed symbol of competence—"Allen Zoll, Ph.D."—led to an investigation of Mr. Zoll's academic background. Writing in 1951, journalist Arthur Morse reported that Zoll's doctorate had been conferred by a one-man citadel of higher learning—the faculty consisting of a D. Scott Swain, who also served as the institution's "Archbishop Primate." Morse was unable to determine the date when Zoll had obtained his degree (the college having been "sold" prior to 1951); but he did note that Archbishop Primate Swain had once blanketly conferred doctorates on an entire audience, in a moment of alcohol-inspired generosity.[22]

Others went on to defame Zoll blatantly, with relentless attempts to show him a scoundrel. He was accused of anti-Semitism, duplicity in covertly representing both sides in a picketing incident, and contributing extensively to Fascist groups.[23] Educators felt strongly that such a personal history was of direct relevance in evaluating a man's claims that " 'Progressive' Education Is Subverting America" and " 'Progressive' Education Promotes Socialism."[24]

Alongside this vigorous counterattack an entirely different sort of response to criticism began to grow: increased attention to the schools' public relations. The Pasadena incident had suggested that poor communication with the public was at least partially responsible for the existence of a group willing to be led by instigators. In 1950 the NEA admitted the National School Public Relations Association as a department. One of its pamphlets soon outsold all the NEA's several hundred publications.

Many eagerly grasped the notion of successful school public relations programs as a potential panacea. The major, almost exclusive emphasis of these early efforts was on getting the word to the public—telling the community what its schools were doing and how and why they were doing it. But soon, some began to protest this blind adoption of industry's programs. Professor George Axtelle, for example, stressed the need for an entirely different approach: ". . . I am convinced that conventional approaches to public relations will fail utterly. The whole conception of public relations prevailing in private enterprise is quite inappropriate to the task. . . ."[25] It soon occurred to many that this emphasis on standard one-way communication methods was inadequate. The very existence of criticism suggested that a clearly defined procedure must be established whereby citizens could express their reactions to the information reaching them. Some means had to be provided for the public to register approval or disapproval and to express its wishes.

This realization led to efforts at improving the quality of school public relations programs, and introduced a phenomenon new to most schools. This was the development of various means to obtain wider community participation in the schools' program. One such means was the provision of educational programs for adults and teen-agers not currently enrolled in school. Through such programs participants were to gain a firsthand acquaintance with what schools were doing, and how. Another means to obtaining participation was the establishment of various types of parent and citizen committees. As a result, citizen advisory groups now function in many communities. A somewhat different approach, and one that perhaps offers considerably more promise than either of the above, is the attempt to secure community participation and support through action research. The reasons for this approach make up a large part of our last chapter.

When, in 1952, the nature of the critics began to change—if not always the nature of their criticisms—education's response had to change correspondingly. The onslaught now was coming primarily from the liberal arts contingent, and in some respects entirely different *means* of reply had to be adopted.[26] In the first place, the submergence of several of the key organizations initiating the attacks of the earlier period meant that the most vindictive aspects of the counterattack might no longer be applicable.[27] While to some it still remained relevant to question the competence of the liberal arts professor in recommending pedagogical methods, few questions were raised about the competence of these men in their own fields. Furthermore, while some educators have questioned the liberal arts critic's desire to be helpful, many of their colleagues would vouch for his sincerity. And a number of "educationists" have stanchly and consistently agreed that there is much to be said for the viewpoint of the liberal arts critic.

Since 1955 there has been an increase in the number and urgency of articles warning that all criticisms and complaints not be dismissed as "attacks."[28] Despite the continuing tendency of some, first to distinguish between the sincerely constructive and the hostile critic—and then to deal only with the former—there is an increasing number of pleas that we listen to all criticism. Many point to the risk involved in the purely defensive reaction: the danger of overlooking potentially helpful ideas.

Currently, schoolmen perceive a recurrence of the late-forties type of attack, and many see the current liberal arts onslaught as equally dangerous. There has been no significant decrease in the space devoted to attacks in professional magazines, and at professional meetings a good deal of time is still devoted to their consideration.

The emphasis on public relations has persisted, emerging as a means of *preventing* attacks rather than as a method of reply. As a part of these programs, sometimes as a basis for them, there have been a number of studies of what a community thinks of its schools—whether local citizens approve what the schools are trying to do, and whether they feel these things are being carried out successfully.

Another type of study growing out of critical literature of the current period is the compilation of various criticisms and answers. Several such volumes of representative complaints and replies have been prepared. These anthologies have no doubt been useful in circulating the charges and the rebuttals, but they have not been enough. Equally useful, we believe, is an analysis of the criticisms as a whole. What has caused them?

10. *What Are the Causes?*

It goes without saying that educational critics and charges may be born out of a sorely deficient school system, possibly in some instances a corrupt or malintentioned one. In such cases, loudly voiced grievances are both understandable and desirable. But it should long since have become obvious that it is not with such critics and criticism that we are here concerned. Our focus has been on criticism we have deemed "invalid" and on the critics we have chosen to call "illegitimate."

We have seen critics make "factual" claims which are patently inaccurate. We have seen accomplished scholars advance generalizations on grounds they themselves must recognize as indefensible. We have seen evidence of values clearly at odds with those to which we, as a nation, are officially committed. What has caused all this? Why do men persist in claims that have been shown false? What explains those value systems at such variance with our traditions? Whatever the reasons may be, it is unlikely that the early explanations of simple malevolence or neurosis provide adequate answers. Sheer numbers—the size of the group who are active school critics—immediately render such "simple" answers complex. For if the explanation is individual malevolence or aberration, we must then ask why these traits are so generously distributed among our citizens.

Educators, psychologists, and sociologists have all tried to account for the postwar epidemic of attacks on public education. In this chapter we shall look at three different types of explanation.

Many of the early explanations for the outburst of criticism following the Second World War were of an *individualistic* variety. The causes of the criticism were thought to reside within the critic himself. Some saw the critic as one who sought money or fame and chose school criticism as a means of attaining his personal ambitions. Others thought many critics were fanatics—and tended then to dismiss them on the grounds that few would heed a crank. Still others bored deeply into the personality structure of the critic—and located the source of his denunciations as a compulsion to strike out against something, his fears, or his authoritarian tendencies. As we shall see, each of these individualistic explanations seems to account for one or more prominent critics.

Opportunism was one of the first explanations offered to account for the intensified criticism, and Allen Zoll was the prime example. Interpreters showed him to have moved from one activity to another—each of which added to Mr. Zoll's personal fame, and presumably to his purse. Another stanch critic—John T. Flynn of America's Future—had even seemed to invite such an interpretation of his career. Years ago, Mr. Flynn wrote an article he called "To Get Rich Scare the Rich." Although at that time the columnist was a defender of schools, rather than an accuser, it is not surprising that his diagnosis has since been turned upon him:

> The art of getting rich consists largely in capitalizing the emotions, weaknesses, follies, fears of the rest of us. . . .
>
> One good field . . . is the schools. There the Bolsheviki are ceaseless [in the minds of the alarmed]. . . . Therefore what better racket than to save the schools from this monster. Therefore organize an agency. . . . Send out letters, bulletins, circulars, and pamphlets. . . . Then you can call on patriotic rich men to subscribe $100, $150 or maybe $1,000 to carry on the great work. . . .[1]

Yet even with a statement such as this, there is other evidence suggesting that opportunism does not constitute a wholly adequate explanation for the case of Zoll *or* Flynn. A single thread runs through most of the ways in which Mr. Zoll may have sought private gain: his support of Father Coughlin, his fascist-labeled "American Patriots, Inc.," his open opposition, on religious grounds, to the Supreme Court appointment of Felix Frankfurter, his National Council for American Education seeking to "'eradicate from our schools Marxism, Socialism, Communism' "[2]—all of these suggest a particular world view within whose framework Mr. Zoll sought to make his fortune.

Even in the more complicated case of Mr. Flynn—once an avid liberal, now an equally avid conservative—one can detect a certain perverse consistency: Mr. Flynn is a chronic worrier over the "sinister movement in our midst."[3] The nature of the sinister has changed, but not the theme. In 1936 it was "organized business"; today it is organized collectivism. Thus, even should we be correct in labeling both these educational critics "opportunists," it still may be asked why they have pursued this particular means to self-aggrandizement. Any problems these two have brought the schools do not result from either's desire for enhancement; the problems stem instead from the *form* their ambitions have taken. And if this be so, to say that opportunism explains attacks on schools is to deal with the question only obliquely.

A number of interpreters have applied the "opportunist" explanation to critics with "vested interests." Various groups grinding one ax or another have been called opportunist in their desire to realize tangible or ideological gains. There is obviously much to be said for this interpretation. It may well be, for example, that the scathing criticism of a tax association stems directly from members' interest in lower taxes. To view such groups as opportunistic calls our attention to the fact that things are not always as they may seem—and that some critics may well be circuitous if not plainly devious. It suggests, for example, that the motives of the group urging "objectivity" in textbooks may actually be the complete elimination of half the story —to assure that young readers will line themselves up on the "right" side.

But even so, to describe as mere opportunists all critics who represent vested interests is to obscure what may be the far bigger problem: Such a view fails to account for the many groups which sincerely identify the nation's interests with their own—after the famous model "What's good for General Motors is good for the country." It is not necessary to suspect such critics of ulterior opportunism in order to perceive them as a danger to public education. In fact, one of the major conclusions of this book is the threat posed by those critics who quite openly state their bases of criticism—usually in the form of a specific social-political-economic program.

A second very popular individualist interpretation of the critic simply questions his rationality. This is actually a type of devil theory that labels some of education's critics fanatic, maladjusted, or even demented. Regardless of the number of cases where the characterization may seem apt, this explanation of educational criticism has been a costly one. It has seemed to carry the erroneous corollary that if a given critic is a mental deviant, he can therefore be treated lightly.

Several years ago, for example, a writer discussed at length "The Curious Crusade of R. C. Hoiles." Mr. Hoiles was identified as "one of the country's foremost eccentrics," and an individual who "has the courage of his confusions."[4] An impressive amount of evidence is offered for these claims: for instance, Hoiles opposes public education flatly and in principle, on the grounds that it violates "the Ten Commandments, the Golden Rule and the Declaration of Independence."* As an illustration of the reasoning which underlies such stands, the first-named transgression exists because " 'those who advocate government schools covet the property of others . . . and . . . initiate . . . force to take property from dissenters . . . in violation of . . . the stealing commandment.' "[5]

Several of Mr. Hoiles's other ideas also serve to mark him as a man of unique conviction (for example, his objections to government-supported highways, post offices, police and armed forces, plus the American Bar and Medical associations, the National Association of Manufacturers, and the Young Women's Christian Association). But anyone concluding that on these grounds Mr. Hoiles may be dismissed as harmless does so at considerable risk. Here is a critic who is in an excellent position to influence public opinion. As of 1952, Robert Cyrus Hoiles owned a chain of ten newspapers. In addition, he is said to possess twenty million dollars. Hence, even should we make the dangerous assumption that his unorthodox ideas make Mr. Hoiles's editorials ineffective, he has *other* means of waging his battle against public education. Should he choose to do so, Mr. Hoiles could finance the programs of an impressive array of potentially influential critics of education.

The error in assuming that inordinate views will simply be dismissed

* We should note that Mr. Hoiles may since have undergone a change of heart. Although the author of the article quoted above cites evidence that can hardly be controverted (his subject's published statements), Mr. Hoiles's reply to our questionnaire does not seem to suggest such fundamental and thoroughgoing opposition to public schools as of now.

is brought home forcefully at meetings of educational critics. In an Illinois town an elderly woman obviously bordering on hysteria elicited grave nods of assent to her virtual ravings from a lecture platform. At another meeting, in Virginia, not a single member of the audience so much as smiled when a frenzied patriot "proved" the radicalism of educators by revealing that the NEA handbook does not include the Twenty-third Psalm! Many would think both speakers deranged. But whether or not that diagnosis is correct, these critics struck a responsive chord in their audiences. We can speculate, of course, on whether the audiences *also* shared in the aberration. But as long as there are audiences like this—and in one of our two examples, the group was a fair percentage of the local population—we cannot afford to dismiss critics just because they seem irrational.

Public opinion determines the fate of schools; and as long as any individual has the means to help shape public opinion, he poses a threat—no matter how unreasonable his views may appear. Thus, to explain school critics in terms of their emotional maladies lulls us into an unrealistic sense of security. Furthermore, to say that a particular individual criticizes the schools because he is odd suggests no feasible remedy whatsoever.

A related type of explanation for postwar school criticism sought to assess the *nature* of the emotional disturbances of school critics. One plausible theory has been of a "protest syndrome."[6] This view holds that there are personalities which are consistently drawn to protesting one or another aspect of the current scene. The object of the criticism might be political, social, or religious. It shifts from time to time, so that the individual protesting the number of communists in government today may be the school critic of tomorrow—perhaps protesting Communist infiltration of the schools, or bringing charges with new themes, such as "Schools mollycoddle youngsters." Whatever the protest of the moment, such an individual is seldom without some fervent complaint about one or more aspects of society.

The careers of many critics tend to support this explanation. A number of those involved in contemporary attacks on schools have indeed enthusiastically participated in other highly critical movements—protesting the existence of income taxes, internationalism, and even racial and religious groups. We have seen how Kitty Jones moved from a protest against Communism to a protest against schools. A number of anti-Negro and anti-Semitic organizations are also antischool groups. (See, for example, the questionnaire replies of Gerald L. K. Smith's Christian Nationalist Crusade, and the intensely anti-Jewish Keep America Committee.) It could even appear that a "free-floating" protestor might attach himself to whatever object of complaint is a "popular" target at the moment. This would explain the rash of complaints against the schools as a fad in which many exhibiting the protest syndrome made the same choice of target.

But this interpretation too has practical shortcomings. First, it tells us nothing about the kind of conditions (educational, social, cosmic) that are conducive to protests against schools. Second, it suggests nothing that school people can say or do in order to prevent or cope with school criticism. It leaves us only with the conclusion that some form of psychotherapy is the best hope and, unfortunately, this measure cannot ordinarily be prescribed by schoolmen.

Many observers have sought to explain school criticism at an even deeper level of the critic's personality. What, they have asked, *causes* the urge to protest? One very careful study showed relationships between certain personality traits and specific social and political views. The study in question related personality traits to such attitudes and beliefs as conservatism, anti-Semitism, and ethnocentrism.[7] And we have seen repeated evidence of these attitudes and beliefs in individuals vehemently critical of schools. Hence, if personality traits do make one receptive to the conservative dogma, perhaps they also create a similar disposition for hostility to public education.

It has also been suggested that frustrations produce the aggressiveness and hostility expressed in some educational criticism.[8] Others have claimed that these same frustrations produce a drive for power that can be indulged in the educational debate.[9] Such interpretations are extremely difficult to support in specific cases, since few of those advancing them have access to intimate knowledge of a given critic's life and experiences.

Still another individualistic explanation of educational criticism is general fear and anxiety on the part of the critic. This seems plausible in terms of the many educational critics we have identified as extremely conservative in politics. Many of these people see a world that has already moved away from what they believe it should be.

Events carrying them more and more rapidly away from what they think right and desirable could reasonably create fear and anxiety.

The single explanation perhaps most widely accepted as the reason for the postwar spurt of complaints against schools is "scapegoating." This phenomenon would reconcile some of the explanations already discussed since it, in turn, is seen to rise from such varied roots as deprivation, frustration, guilt, fear, anxiety, or desires for self-enhancement.[10] The fact that scapegoating is associated with periods of restlessness and tension lends support to the idea that this may indeed be what public education is undergoing. Various features of the schools make them an easy mark—their nation-wide accessibility, for example, and their comparative defenselessness. Further, even our traditional respect for education may have made it vulnerable. Since economic, political, and social ills have multiplied—despite the increasing universality of schooling—the failure of formal education to remake the world may have left schools the scapegoat for myriad disappointments. So this theory too is plausible, but it suffers from the same limitations of the other individualistic explanations of school criticism which we have examined. It too suggests no recourse, no remedy other than some form of psychotherapy.

Partly because of the limitations of these individualistic interpretations, an entirely different sort of explanation has been offered: a *sociological* account of educational criticism. Such an interpretation locates the cause of the problem not in the individual but in external circumstances or in social conditions. One such view is of educational criticism as a perennial or cyclic affair. Another claims that the trouble in the schools more or less accurately reflects the maladies of society.

As with the individualistic interpretations, it is not difficult to find evidence for the sociological explanations of contemporary educational criticism. Every public agency has always had its detractors, and from their beginning public schools have been no exception. According to one historian, ever since a statement of Harvard's Board of Trustees in 1650, some learned group has come forth every twenty years with a report to the effect that the quality of education is in rapid decline.[11] It is even possible to cite instances of today's complaints voiced fifty, a hundred, a hundred and fifty years ago. In fact, there is evidence that the "younger generation is going to the dogs" theme even reared itself in ancient Greece![12] The quotations supporting the argument that educational criticism is chronic are virtually without end. A few of them, from diverse periods in our history, read this way:

"Not more than half of the boys and girls attending the public schools between the ages of 12 and 16 know the names of our Presidents!"

Year: 1847

"The unhappy instructors [at Harvard] are confronted with immature thoughts set down in a crabbed and slovenly hand, miserably expressed and wretchedly spelled."

Year: 1894

"When we were mere boys, . . . boys had to do a little work in school. They were not coaxed; they were hammered. . . . In these more fortunate times, elementary education has become in many places a sort of vaudeville show. The child must be kept amused and learn what he pleases."

Year: 1902

"It is a common complaint among businessmen that young people seeking employment are not well grounded in the fundamentals."

Year: 1910

Never has there been so much criticism of education, and never has it been so savage. . . .[13]

Year: 1927

If any further evidence is needed of the past constancy—and perhaps the future durability—of educational criticism, it can be found in the conflicting demands of the critics. The repeated arising of many complaints stems from the fact that we in the United States have never agreed on the purpose of education—and most assuredly we do not now. One of the people quoted above, a college president, was pleading for a "liberal" education rather than a narrowly vocational one. The same battle still rages today, some thirty years later. Not even the catchwords are new: "Quackery in the Public Schools," the provocative title selected by modern critic, Albert Lynd, was first used in 1888.[14]

But if we assume denunciations of public education to be cyclic, what causes the turning of the wheel? At what periods can we predict that intense criticism is likely to occur, and why? And if we assume criticism to be either perennial or recurring, what specifically accounts for its popularity beginning in 1948? And how would this theory explain the fact that in 1952 the magazine articles dealing with educational criticism were sixteen times more numerous than those appearing ten years earlier?[15]

Another type of sociological explanation for the current attacks on schools offers answers to such questions. In general, this interpretation holds, the schools mirror the status of society. Conflicts within the society at large are thus reflected in education. Education is complicated and subject to criticism because we are not agreed on what society itself should be. Robert Oppenheimer suggests a full commitment to this view in stating that education is doing an adequate job of transmitting what we *do* have, but that "it cannot hand on what we do *not* have: a viable culture."[16]

One widespread version of this theory is that current educational criticism is merely one part of a reaction against the liberalism of the thirties. We saw a swing to conservatism in politics, and attempts to undo some of the changes of the New Deal. Certainly the domestic struggle against Communism has also occasioned a large part of the conservative trend. But as one observer noted, "Americans are reacting not only against communism, but from the effects of twenty years of change as profound as has occurred in any period in our history. . . ."[17]

It is perhaps not merely coincidental, as some would argue, that the subversion theme in educational criticism both flourished and waned almost simultaneously with McCarthyism.

Although much must be said for these attempts to explain contemporary attacks on schools in sociological terms, such interpretations share a major disadvantage with the individualistic explanations reviewed earlier. They do not suggest any means for dealing effectively with the problem of educational criticism. Both types of interpretation lead only to the pessimistic conclusion that educational criticism is simply in the nature of things—one to the conclusion that this is the way men (or some men) are, the other to the conclusion that this is the way the world is.

There has been still a third, popular explanation for the postwar assault on education. It includes a variety of specific interpretations, all sharing one important feature: each attempts to account for the attacks in terms of man's reason rather than in those of his emotional problems or the social conditions in which he finds himself.

One such *rationalistic* explanation is simply that the American people have not decided what they want their schools to be. Many hold the prime task of schooling to be the molding of citizens, or "the whole man." Others insist instead that the school's exclusive function is the development of man's intellectual powers. Inevitably, the educational programs following from these two conceptions would diverge. Compromise is all but impossible, and criticism has to stem from whichever faction is the loser. The academician flatly states that the psyches of its charges are not the school's affair—while an irate father publishes a bitter indictment for the unfeeling treatment accorded his son.[18] A vocal group demands the raising of academic standards at any cost—while newspaper editors score the college professor who failed 70 per cent of his students.[19] Some insist that schools transmit the culture uncritically and intact; others point out that to do so is to perpetuate wars, depressions—all our social evils—and that schools must help youth examine the national heritage critically. There is a continuous struggle between those who demand religious neutrality in public schools and those who scathingly call sectarian education godless.

Situations such as these lend credence to the view that ultimately it is the public which is responsible for much of the current criticism. It would seem that blame can hardly be assigned the educator for the public's failure to define the purposes of schooling. But there are many who place the responsibility for the criticism squarely with the schoolman.* The most frequent variety of this latter type of explanation is that schoolmen have failed in their relations with the public. Some have bluntly laid the blame to errors in human relations. Others have claimed that the educator has done a miserable job of presenting

* Of course, virtually all critics adhere to this view. Thus their explanation for the criticism would have to be that schools and those who staff them are guilty as charged. It may be wise here once again to say that this is quite probably the case with some complaints. But it is not these complaints with which we are concerned. The causes of criticism examined here are offered to account only for those criticisms where education is *not* guilty as charged.

education to the public—and, as one glib spokesman summed it up, "What the people in a democracy are not up on, they are likely to be down on."

It is probable that these interpretations accurately account for some situations. Indeed, concentrated efforts at public relations—which is the cure suggested by these explanations—were among the first positive reactions of educators to the outbreak of criticism. But the tendency to explain *all* the charges in terms of poor community relations waned somewhat during the latter stages of the First Wave of criticism—perhaps owing to the facts which became known about some critics. Then, with the coming of the Second Wave, the explanation was revived—possibly because the academician was a man of good will; hence he could only be attacking another man of good will out of some sort of communications failure. Indeed, one educator reported that "most of the disagreements . . . are the result of misunderstanding rather than of deep-seated disagreement. . . . In a few cases, emotional clashes of personality have been added. . . ."[20]

Such conclusions are not only at variance with the facts but are also hazardous. It seems utterly preposterous to think that mere "misunderstanding"—not deep-seated disagreement—divides the accusers from the defenders. And this seems equally true not only of First Wave critics, such as Allen Zoll, R. C. Hoiles, and Lucille Crain, but also of such Second Wave stalwarts as Arthur Bestor. There may well be instances of misinformation, but the tenacity with which this misinformation is embraced is *alone* sufficient to rule out the "misunderstanding" hypothesis. The danger of such interpretations lies in the course of action they imply. An erroneous diagnosis—comforting though it may be—dictates a useless or harmful prescription in a case where we can ill afford error.

Another explanation also suggesting that schoolmen must bear a part of the responsibility for attacks proclaims that educators have literally asked for the difficulties in which they find themselves. This interpretation, which seems to be gaining respect, is that the educator has invited the public to take far too *specific* an interest in education. This has come about by a kind of mismanagement, by educators, of the principle that ultimate educational decisions should be made by the public. The argument goes that the schoolman, through a lack of understanding of this principle, has unforgiveably abdicated professional responsibility. The situation is said to have come about this way: Through various means, the citizen has been given to understand that *all* educational decisions are within his province; that it is his privilege to decide not only what schools should attempt but all the means whereby goals shall be sought. It it for this reason that we now hear so many demands for specific courses, content, methods. Furthermore, it is claimed, many of the demands and protests of today are the harvest of the public relations programs devised to meet the demands and protests of yesterday—with yesterday's cure producing today's problem, ad infinitum.

An excellent case can be made for this interpretation. Much of the criticism of the First Wave was so absurd that schoolmen rightfully believed the citizen who came to look and see would immediately recognize the falsity of the charges. Thus, the public was urged to take an active part in education—without much thought of the specific role it was to play, and without sufficient attention to the proper division of labor between specialist and layman. Some of those citizens participating in study groups and advisory councils sponsored by schools may have the impression that their experience has equipped them with a professional's knowledge.

It may be true that the specificity of today's criticisms is the result of the public's having been invited to address itself to the details of education. If so, then the educators have done themselves a grave disservice. On the other hand, there are other explanations for the charges' having become more specific. Education is the only public enterprise over which voters exert direct control. The improvement of highways, police, fire, and other municipal or state services, all are financed through the decision of legislative bodies. But improvement in education is put directly to the voters, typically by means of a bond issue referendum. It may be that the public's interest in details is a perfectly logical outgrowth of its need to make detailed decisions. And when this decision-making obligation is combined with the citizen's general tax-paying obligation, perhaps it is not hard to see how the *circumstances* may serve to manufacture the criticism.

At least three additional explanations of the rationalistic type account for the more detailed demands of education's critics. One of these interpretations maintains that much of the criticism arises from differences in belief about the way people learn. A second accounts for disagreements in terms of the difficulties of social science research.

Still a third explanation attributes the criticism to the low status of professional education in our society.

Obviously, critics do espouse a number of approaches to learning. Recall the demands of such First Wave critics as Kitty Jones—heatedly echoed by the Second Wave's Council for Basic Education—that subjects be taught as separate studies. The reasons for the insistence are not precisely the same in the two cases, but both plainly rest on ideas of the learning process. Mrs. Jones built her case on the notion that integrated social studies instruction gives Socialists a better chance to put their ideas across. (Since it is the belief of many educators that more learning occurs when related subjects are presented in the perspective of their relationship, it seems to them that Mrs. Jones was demanding *less* effective teaching.) The Council for Basic Education, on the other hand, apparently subscribes to a theory of "mental discipline," holding that the mind is something which must be "trained" and that exposure to the established disciplines—in their logical organization—is the way to train it.[21] In accord with this belief, the Council advocates such specific practices as extensive drill and memorization. By contrast, those who profess little faith in these practices customarily do so out of a different conception of learning. This group holds that education does not consist of "training" a mind; that even if it did, logically presented subject matter might not be the best means of accomplishing the training; and that drill is not the way to produce maximum effects.

Some of these questions, about which much of the educational debate rages, are simple matters of fact. For example, questions regarding the effectiveness of drill can be and have been investigated. Why the quarrels continue, despite empirical evidence, is not explained by this notion that rival learning theories account for much educational criticism. Those who maintain that the difficulties of social science research explain today's educational criticism offer a better answer to why the battle continues quite apart from the evidence.

The physical scientist, working under laboratory conditions, can attain a great deal of precision. He can determine that acid turns litmus paper pink, by dunking a sheet of litmus in one acid after another. Or, he can learn that one form of skin fungus is transplantable, and others are not, by attempting to graft them on the same individual. In both cases, the investigator is able to control experimental conditions, making sure that it is not an extraneous substance which has pinked his litmus paper, or that his graft of a given fungus was successful only because of general susceptibility on the part of one individual.

Contrast this set of conditions with the problems of educational research. An investigator seeking to determine the most effective method of reading instruction cannot subject Johnny to three or four different methods and validly compare his results. The chemist can eliminate one source of possible error by using the same piece of litmus paper over and over. The educational investigator can use Johnny only once—success with a third reading method might represent a delayed success with the first. Further, the chemist can assume a degree of consistency or regularity with respect to litmus paper. But we cannot assume that most children learning to read react and behave similarly. As a result, the chemist can confidently predict certain results from a given procedure. He can say, "Acid turns litmus paper pink." The educational investigator, on the other hand, cannot be so unequivocal. By contrast, he may only be able to say: "X per cent of children attain a given level of reading ability in the shortest time, by Y method of instruction; M per cent attain this level quickest by N method; and P per cent, by Q method."

The failure of social science research to come up with unequivocal answers may indeed account for much educational criticism. Since the various problems in this type of research have to date precluded answers to many crucial questions about the educational process, the schoolman cannot always definitively defend his practice in terms of research. And since the variability of human beings leads to ambiguous and indecisive research conclusions, there are those who refuse to accept these conclusions as any evidence at all.

A final rationalistic interpretation of educational criticism sees the current attacks on schools as a direct outgrowth of the low status of education as a field of knowledge and as a profession. This group interprets most educational controversies as consisting essentially of challenges to the schoolman's claim to any sort of unique knowledge.*

* Oddly, this seems to be a relatively new feature in educational criticism, absent from the criticisms of 75 and 100 years ago. This is ironic, since it is only within the last 50 years or so that the educator *has* come to possess any knowledge not shared by the general public. Yet during the long period when teaching involved no special preparation and was largely a stop-gap vocation for the unfortunate, the public seems to have been less inclined to order the process directly.

In explaining critics' demands for drill, for example, advocates of this interpretation would stress the clear presumption that we *all* possess competence in the psychology of learning. And, they would add, this is just one way of saying that educators can tell the rest of us little that we don't already know. As one education professor puts it to his graduate classes, "You and I belong to the only profession in the world that the man in the street knows more about than we do!"

There are many obvious ways to support the claim of education's low status. In the next chapter we examine at length two common stereotypes of educators as individuals. As professionals with a claim to special knowledge, high school teachers are often seen as a species of subscholar, lacking sufficient mastery of their subjects to enter the "big leagues"—college teaching. The pedagogical part of their preparation is frequently viewed as a few gimmicks for handling the young, plus a lot of padding. Elementary teachers, whose preparation consists of more pedagogy, fare even worse. They are often thought of as vaguely superior college-bred baby-sitters.

As a body of knowledge, the field of education or pedagogy is quite new. Current criticism, goes the argument, is simply a trial—one phase which any new discipline must undergo. Charges comparable to those now leveled at education have earlier been aimed at many of the disciplines today accorded full respect. Opposition once confronted such now highly respected studies as the humanities, physical science, and history. The humanities were opposed on the basis that language and literature lacked sufficient merit and complexity to make them worthy of the scholar's concern. Centuries later, in another part of the world, some of the devotees of the then established humanities turned similar arguments against the sciences. The bitter struggle of the "Lost Cause" at Yale involved the claim that natural science did not warrant the scholar's attention. As recently as the late nineteenth century, many fought against admitting history to the public schools, on the grounds that it had little to contribute to the training and enlightenment of young minds.[22]

Some professions have undergone a similar process. The experience of the medical profession, for example, suggests that the trial period depends on the degree to which members possess knowledge not shared by the public at large—or, more accurately, on the public's *recognition* that the profession has such knowledge. Surgeons practicing in the late nineteenth century report that it was not uncommon for medical procedure to be determined by the families of patients rather than by the doctor—for a layman to provide the surgeon with detailed instructions on how to operate.[23]

In the light of such tradition-hallowed opposition of the established disciplines and professions to the new, the current hostility of the liberal arts specialist to the educationist is understandable. Moreover, not only is education itself a new discipline; it also rests largely on psychology and sociology—studies which are themselves new and still fighting for acceptance. But even granting the low status of education—and the public's conviction that its own competence to determine educational practice equals that of the educator—we still have not accounted for the many cases in which a critic's demands remain wholly unaltered by the facts. It remains to be explained why a number of critics have rejected, along with the judgment of the educator, *all* the evidence by which he arrived at it.

We have now examined the major explanations attempting to account for contemporary attacks on public education. Most, as we have seen, tend adequately to explain one or more specific instances of criticism, but they suffer from several shortcomings. Many of them are at least one step removed from the practical problem of attacks on schools. The individualistic interpretations are removed from the practical problem because *this* consists not of what causes Mrs. Jones or Mr. Zoll to attack schools, but what causes wide numbers of people to heed Mrs. Jones or Mr. Zoll. And what accounts for the audience may be quite different from what best explains the speaker.

A number of the explanations we examined are too specific to be practical. Derangement, for example, may explain some critics, but surely it cannot explain all. Warring theories of learning similarly may account for some complaints, but not all. The resulting difficulty is that insofar as these explanations suggest any remedies at all, they recommend a prohibitively expensive buckshot approach to preventing attacks on schools—a variety of measures no school system could possibly hope to carry out.

On the other hand, if some of the explanations are too narrow and specific to account for many critics, others suffer from a tendency grandly to reduce all the criticism to a single cause. We may be able to identify very general factors common to current criticism, but it is highly unlikely that any single explanation can at the same time account for Allen Zoll and Hyman Rickover.

The upshot of these and other difficulties is that all these explanations of educational criticism lack practical utility. Now, if the attacks on schools are serious, we need to view them—and the reasons for their occurrence—in such a way that we can do something about them.[24] And if we have been critical of the explanations examined, it has been with this purpose in mind. For each of the weaknesses to which we have pointed suggests a specific criterion which an adequate explanation for the attacks on schools must meet.

An adequate explanation must be practical, explaining the facts in a way that recommends a workable program for coping with them. It must deal directly with the problems that the attacks occasion for the schoolman—namely, it should focus on the reasons why so many people become critics rather than on why a particular individual comes to dislike schools. If it is to account for the beliefs and actions of a wide number of people urging a diversity of claims and demands, it will obviously have to be general in nature rather than highly specific. And finally, our explanation must avoid the temptation to explain everything in terms of a single cause. We hope that the two explanations advanced in the following chapter meet these requirements.

11. *Two Hypotheses*

As we saw in the preceding chapter, one can explain human behavior either by causes located within the individual or in terms of external conditions fostering certain actions. We believe that the causes of current attacks on education can be explained by two hypotheses, one of each type. The first—value cleavages between individuals—may offer the greater immediate potential for dealing with the problem. The second hypothesis—the educator's lack of power—seeks external causes and suggests a long-range goal for effectively dealing with attacks on schools.

Obviously, since values play a crucial role in our actions, and often provide the impetus to act at all, it is not surprising to find that conflicting beliefs about "what ought to be" account for a major portion of educational criticism. We are claiming something more, however: that these disagreements on educational values are derived from far more fundamental value cleavage. But first we must examine several assumptions:

1. An individual's educational values are related to his more general values.
2. Some values are held more dear than others, and our deepest commitments are to a highly generalized American Creed or faith in democracy.
3. A tendency toward logical consistency pushes us to resolve conflicts among our values. When such conflicts occur, the resolution seems usually to be in favor of the more generalized values.
4. Values have an important part in determining behavior.

Of course, all school criticism has something to do with value differences; what we are claiming is that fundamental, and far more general, values influence one's educational values. The relationship between them appears to be twofold: logical and psychological.

We must grant from the start that the direct, uncluttered relationship logicians have in mind when they speak of "logical implication" does not ordinarily characterize the relationship linking an individual's general with his educational values. Men who agree on general principles can even arrive at contradictory educational principles. The American axiom that all men should be granted equal opportunity logically rules out a denial of schooling to Negroes or Methodists or redheads. Yet when we ask what "equal opportunity" positively implies by way of educational values, there is no answer. Some think it is that "schools should provide all youngsters with as much education as they can absorb." To others, a commitment to equal opportunity implies only that schools admit impartially all youngsters meeting certain academic requirements. General values thus imply no specific educational values—hence, the relationship between the two is not so tight as that of logical necessity. On the other hand, logic *does* rule out such contradictions as simultaneous commitment to "equal opportunity" *and* to closing school doors to Methodists and redheads.

Not only *does* this qualified logical relationship usually exist, but we think it *ought* to. We tend to *feel* that our general values should dictate our beliefs about what schools ought to do. Virtually every serious discussion of education bears this out: sooner or later someone states the equivalent of "What one wants schools to do depends on what he thinks man and society should be."[1] More important, there seems to be a psychological connection between *specific* educational values and particular general values. Impressive evidence suggests such a high correlation that a man's school criticisms are often grounds for accurately assessing his whole value system, and vice versa. For example, after examining only a fraction of the We, the People! platform (see Chapter IV), one could predict with considerable accuracy the educational values of the group.

But we have further said that disagreements on educational values result from more fundamental values. So we must begin by asking how values are acquired. We know that often people acquire knowledge inductively. They move from the specific to the general—observing, for example, that a particular swan is white; that another one is white also, and so on—eventually coming to believe that "All swans are white." Of course, not all our knowledge is acquired by this process of generalization, but a substantial amount of it is.

Values, however, seem often to be acquired by a reverse process. For instance, when he first confronts it, a person who has given little thought to education will almost invariably invoke his general system of values—though not so self-consciously as any description is bound to suggest. The findings of anthropologists suggest some such deductive process of arriving at new values, rather than an inductive one based on experience. They tell us, for example, that values may even persist after the utter dissolution of the only culture in which they made sense, and despite changes rendering them wholly unrealistic and prohibitively expensive.[2]

That the process whereby we acquire specific values is a deductive one would account for the obvious tendency toward consistency among our valuations which many observers have noted. In *An American Dilemma,* Gunnar Myrdal says: "Most persons want to present to their fellows—and to themselves—a trimmed and polished sphere of valuations, where honesty, logic, and consistency rule. . . ."[3] Even those who, like William Graham Sumner, have attributed little rationality to man and his social arrangements, have seen a "strain toward consistency" in our collective valuations or mores.[4] Psychologists also have discussed the tendency—some even going so far as to suggest that the consistency of an individual's set of values is a measure of his emotional stability.[5]

Our devotion to consistency suggests that it is itself one of our primary values. Consistency requires that we try to resolve any conflicts among our values of which we are aware. The way in which we typically go about this resolution brings us to the second of the assumptions stated above, which is that our values are arranged in the form of a hierarchy.[6] Some of them we think much more important than others, and as a result we are more deeply committed to them. Thus, when we feel any two of our values conflict, the hierarchy of established priority determines which value is to be revised or dropped and which retained intact.

What are the particular values which enjoy top priority? We think that the deepest commitments of the people of the United States are to a specific set of principles, an "American Creed."[7] This creed consists in a number of fundamental tenets which are centrally important to our way of life. It is not confined to political beliefs; it is broad enough to define at least roughly all the "rules of the game" in the daily lives of Americans.

A number of people, from Bryce and De Toqueville on, have reported the existence of such a set of values and have noted our wide and pervasive commitment to it. Those concerned with the relationship of schools to society have written of its importance.[8] And Myrdal has claimed that the creed exerts tremendous influence on the thoughts and actions of Americans: To him, it represents "the national conscience"; it is "the *most explicitly expressed system* of general ideals" possessed by any Western nation, and it is "more widely understood and appreciated than similar ideals are anywhere else."[9] Not even commitments to religious values interfere with this allegiance—the requirements of democracy and those of Christianity having been successfully and almost totally equated in the mind of the public. Thus, a commitment to one actually *involves* a commitment to the other, and precludes the necessity of choosing which is the more deserving of primary allegiance.[10]

There is no "official" formulation of this influential creed, but its elements can be seen in two of the many presentations current:

1. The essential dignity of man, the importance of protecting and cultivating his personality on a fraternal rather than upon a differential basis, of reconciling the needs of the personality within the framework of the common good in a formula of liberty, justice, welfare.

2. The perfectibility of man; confidence in the possibilities of the human personality, as over against the doctrines of caste, class and slavery.

3. That the gains of commonwealths are essentially mass gains rather than the efforts of the few and should be diffused as promptly as possible throughout the community without too great delay or too wide a spread in differentials.

4. Confidence in the value of the consent of the governed expressed in institutions, understandings and practices as a basis of order, liberty, justice.

5. The value of decisions arrived at by common counsel rather than by violence and brutality.

A second formulation is somewhat less obscure. Its author refers to it variously as our "social faith," our "basic values," and "a general conception of democracy":

First of all, democracy affirms the worth and dignity of the individual. It declares that every human being is precious in his own right and is always to be regarded as an end, never as a means merely.

Second, democracy declares that . . . all men are created equally. . . . Regardless of class, creed, or color they should have the same rights, liberties, opportunities, and responsibilities.

Third, democracy regards political and civil liberty as the only dependable guardian of individual worth and equality.

Fourth, democracy rests on law and orderly process.

Fifth, democracy rests on basic morality. It can thrive only if elementary standards of decency and humanity in all public relations and in the conduct of all public affairs are observed.

Sixth, democracy rests on individual liberty.[11]

But if an overwhelming number of Americans subscribe to such a set of values, then wherein lie the troublesome disagreements? Even those who have proposed everything short of hanging for one of the authors just quoted would probably endorse his statement—at least until they knew its source. The major cleavages occur when we come to interpreting the creed, and to applying it. There are a number of people in the United States who would first want to argue not with the tenets of the creed but against the way we talk about it. These are the Birchers, or extreme conservatives—many of them active critics of the schools—who vehemently insist that we are not a *democracy* at all, but a republic. Still, even among these people the number who categorically deny allegiance to one or more elements of the American Creed might be extremely small.

The real difficulty arises from the fact that while generally agreeing to the creed, we do not agree on *priorities* among these basic values. For example, some Americans think the preservation of equal opportunity for all is the most important tenet of the creed, and others believe it is maximum freedom from governmental interference and restraint. Thus despite deference on the part of all to both equality *and* liberty, we clash over priorities when these two principles come into conflict.

What is more, despite tributes to the "American Tradition" and July Fourth oratory designed to convince us of unity, our disagreements over basic democratic ideology of course even predate our Constitution. *The Federalist Papers* of Hamilton, Madison, and Jay contain arguments still very much alive. And in the young nation, the immediate development of the Hamiltonian and Jeffersonian traditions foreshadowed an enduring dichotomy: ever since, there have been two distinct and opposing attitudes toward social and political affairs. And we have fought recurring battles over the question of how much power government should possess, and how much freedom from interference and restraint the individual must retain. Each period of history perceives this cleavage in different form—it arises over whether we should have a national bank, or whether some of us should be permitted to own others of us, or whether the government should act to prevent certain kinds of business combination. But ultimately it remains a battle over a single value disagreement: the proper priorities for individual freedom and governmental power. And this is only one of a number of priority questions dividing Americans with respect to the creed virtually all of them nominally accept.

An even greater chasm appears at another level: we disagree sharply over the operational implications of these basic tenets of democracy. The program one man wants to enact in order to put these basic tenets into effect is different from that of another. And even those who agree on priorities—for instance, on freedom of choice as *the* primary value in our way of life—may part company when it comes to adopting a specific plan of action. Does the axiom dictate, for example, that people should be "free" to purchase spoiled foods in a form disguised and undetectable? Perhaps there would be little argument here: few people would seek to reserve this particular freedom of choice for the consumer. But put the question another way—"Should sellers be free to offer us such foods?"—and argument comes quickly. For if government must then step in to establish and maintain certain standards, the freedom of the producer, processor, distributor of the food is curtailed. To some, this is a justifiable limitation of the businessman's prerogative. For others, despite having lost the battle fifty years ago, such a limitation still constitutes unwarranted governmental interference.

Differences at such a practical level, of course, are far more numerous than those at the level of fundamental values. This is so because the implications are endless, while the basic tenets are few. It is also the case because verbal agreement is often obtained when the actual implications of beliefs are not accepted—they remain unrecognized or ignored. For instance, two orators proposing diametrically opposed courses of action may swear allegiance to the same principles—sometimes with each declaring that *his* proposal is the only way to translate these principles into action. Similarly, two contenders for the same office repeatedly uphold identical values, while proposing opposite ways of realizing them.

Now, if we have seen that Americans clash over the question of value priorities, and that they disagree even more frequently over the operational implications of these tenets, the cleavages are even further multiplied when it comes to applying the American Creed to public education. One immediate example is obvious in the South today. One finds Southerners agreeing on the importance of equality of opportunity. But, they argue, the preservation of equal opportunity in education does not require integrated schools. But integration is just the most dramatic of a large number of conflicts over the implications of democratic ideology for the schools of a democratic society. As we saw earlier, one prominent current attack on education raises the question: Does our belief in equal opportunity obligate us to admit all youngsters to school? "If we provide a curriculum some children cannot keep up with, why must they be permitted to remain?" So runs the argument.

Still another conflict over the operational implications of the democratic faith concerns the question of grouping students according to ability. Schools have been attacked for denying equal opportunities to slow pupils by "segregating" them in special classes. Another heated issue, academic freedom, involves the implications of free speech. Although most people are willing to concede that the teacher's freedom in this respect is ideally more limited inside the public school classroom than it is outside, we have not decided where the limits should be drawn—thus, we still disagree on the implications of the basic right of free speech for schools and school personnel.

In the current criticism of education, another of our central values

—decision according to the will of the public—raises the question of the school board's function. Is the board an agency of representative government in which members are to exercise their own best judgment? Or is the board's task rather to mirror community opinion as closely as possible? Clearly we have not decided this issue, so it is unclear whether we are willing to let a board of education serve as a representative, decision-making body in any but the most narrow and limited sense. Apparently we are willing to entrust decisions to other elected officials. Final decisions rest with the members of legislatures and city councils, not with those who seek to advise them. But with a board of education, major decisions often result from what is in effect a "referendum"—only technically or formally are the decisions those of a representative body.

Thus, despite our near universal commitment to the principle of majority rule, basic conflicts surround the issue of what it actually *means* to the control of education. Ordinarily the battle is not fought in these terms. One rarely hears about heated controversies over such abstract questions as the general obligations and limitations of school boards. But if direct assaults on the broad question are rare, disagreements over derivative questions are myriad: If members of a community oppose the study of Communism in the schools, what is the board's obligation in the matter? Should the board actually authorize all that is taught? Must it actively select each and every textbook? If schools are supposed to carry out the will of the majority, can a citizen demand entrance to the classroom to see that this is being done? These questions where the point at issue is actually the implications of the democratic faith for the control of public institutions have been the nucleus of many attacks on schools.

As some of the above questions suggest, the role of the expert is a prominent aspect of our disagreement over democracy's implications for the operation and management of schools. General democratic theory holds that the public or its representatives determine policy and that administrators carry out these policies. In virtually all fields today, administrators are professionally prepared for their duties, and in many endeavors the lines between policy and administration are sharp and clear. In others, however—and education is one of these—there is severe disagreement over the end of the policy-making function and the beginning of the expert's prerogatives.

Almost every attack on schools involves the issue of the proper role of the expert. Because we have such widespread commitment of the principle of majority rule, there is little difficulty about where the privilege of over-all direction of the schools should lodge: the people determine the policies. But there is conflict over whether curriculum constitutes a technical or a policy question. If the public states its aim in the form "All children should learn Latin," then the curriculum becomes a policy issue. If, however, educational aims are more appropriately stated in the form "All children should learn how to think," then the question of what contributes to this end—including Latin—is a purely technical one.

The problem extends well beyond the determination of the curriculum which, incidentally, most educators consider a policy question for public determination. Various administrative practices—ability grouping of pupils, "skipping" or refusing to skip bright students—have been the objects of attack. We have also mentioned a few of the many questions of method which have been targets of criticism. Should reading be taught by the use of phonics? Should the introduction of cursive writing be delayed beyond the first year of school? Should geography, history, and perhaps other subjects be combined in a social studies course, or should each be taught separately?

But though such issues obviously exist, and can be traced to the far more fundamental disagreements in which they are rooted, we have yet to explain how values bring forth such a range of attacks as we have seen. To do this, we must show that they play a part in determining human action and behavior.

In taking the position that severe differences in values are a major factor in attacks on education, we are open to challenge from a number of sources. One such source is the psychologist who suggests that views and behavior are far more likely to be determined by emotion or other nonrational processes than by values. Another source of challenge is the work of biochemists suggesting that our mental lives are largely the product of physiochemical balance—which, if true, assigns a somewhat lesser role to rationality in the determination of our values. And from social theorists we hear that our values are determined largely by such conditions as our position on the economic ladder.

But in taking our stand, we are not claiming that all these psychologists, clinicians, sociologists, and others are mistaken about how human beings come to hold their values. Our concern is not how fundamental values *originally* come to be embraced, but rather the part they play in determining man's behavior and activities once they have been adopted. Hence, we make no claims for the forces underlying one's choice of his fundamental values; but we do assign these values significant status in subsequently determining his behavior.

We are here claiming at least a semirational basis of behavior: men act in accord with what they think to be true (their beliefs) or with their ideas of "what ought to be" (their values). It is not difficult to support the claim that beliefs determine our actions. Quite simply, our belief that it will rain determines our action in postponing a picnic or carrying an umbrella. Similarly, one can find evidence of the role of values in determining behavior. At the level of national activity, we can use the Supreme Court's school integration decision to show the determinative role of values. Some Southerners who did not really like the decision have nonetheless supported it out of deference to a value (perhaps the rule of law, or the right of all to equal opportunity, or both).

Many studies also show how values channel behavior along one path rather than another when there are alternative courses of action. An anthropologist, for example, has shown how values determined the very different use of land made by five cultures living under quite similar physical conditions. Several experiments have shown how values function to determine those whom we shall like, and vice versa, and who our friends will be. There is even evidence that our values determine so basic a choice as what we shall *see*.[12]

It is clear that in situations where there are alternatives, an individual's values are a major factor in his selections. But values also arouse us to action. They provide the momentum spurring us to act in returning a lost item to its owner or in going to the defense of a bully's victim. They can also serve to initiate more complicated, frequently repeated behavior—in the manner that a dedication to physical fitness has led to the establishment of whole industries.

Having now substantiated the assumptions of our claim that deep-rooted value cleavages underlie contemporary attacks on public education, we can return to the hypothesis: Disagreements over fundamental values produce the criticism. This requires us to show that critics embrace fundamental values at variance with those of many other Americans. Since few critics have written explicit formulations of the American Creed, we can only infer their values from their sociopolitical views.

Recall the positions taken by such organizations as America's Future, the Committee for Constitutional Government, and We, The People! Not only did their programs consist almost exclusively of proposals the American electorate *would* reject, but of proposals it *has* rejected. In general terms, all three groups want severely to restrict the powers of government; to curtail its sphere of activity as well as its spending; to "restore" an absolutely unfettered free-market economy; by various means (such as withdrawal from the United Nations), to return to an isolation which presumably would detach our fate from that of the rest of the world; and to make standard a particular version of Americanism, departures from which would be punishable as subversion. Specifically, the proposals designed to realize all but the last feature of this program would wipe out virtually all the major political decisions of the past thirty years. And since these decisions were made by elected (and reelected) governments, we may consider them as decisions acceptable to a majority of our citizens. These three groups—which we found typical of the organizational critics of First Wave attacks on schools—are then espousing sociopolitical values at variance with those of the majority.

It is difficult to test our hypothesis on *all* school critics who were active during the First Wave, since their sociopolitical views are not always available. But Mrs. Lucille Cardin Crain, for instance, in her *Educational Reviewer* and elsewhere, strongly suggests a position very similar to that discussed above, and the whole career of Allen Zoll associates him with a political posture that is even more extreme. We are not fully acquainted with the political views of Kitty Jones, but distinctly political echoes sound through many of the statements we examined. Recall, for example, Mrs. Jones's fear of governmental power, and her attempts to make standard her own version of Americanism and condemn all the rest.

It is even more difficult to show that the social and political positions of the Second Wave critics vary sufficiently from others' views to suggest cleavages at the level of fundamental values. The major national spokesman for the Second Wave—the Council for Basic Education—has specifically steered shy of those "large questions" that would call for expression of the group's version of the American Creed, or of derivative commitments.[13] In view of the organization's reluctance to take a stand on such issues, however, particular significance attaches to the way others appear to interpret CBE values. And in this connection it becomes even more noteworthy that those who finance the Council share that set of social and political values which characterizes the critics of the First Wave.

Remember also that one organization active in spearheading the Second Wave attack in Montgomery County has been a local "Conservative Club." The Club's declaration of principles recommends a series of steps which would differ very little from a program enacting the general demands of America's Future, the Committee for Constitutional Government, and We, The People! And also, we saw that as a part of its interest in education in Montgomery County, the Conservative Club imported two Council for Basic Education speakers: Mortimer Smith and Willmoore Kendall. We are not familiar with Mr. Smith's politics, but there is abundant evidence of Dr. Kendall's enthusiastic commitment to essentially the same values we have seen so often to recur among education's critics.

Let us now see whether our hypothesis offers as plausible an explanation for critics and charges as some of the individualistic explanations for educational criticism offered in Chapter X. You may recall, for instance, that many have sought to explain Allen Zoll in terms of his opportunism or, as a devil theory might have it, his cussedness. Yet we noted certain consistencies in Mr. Zoll's career: each of his remunerative activities has reflected a single orientation. Though this does not "prove" our case, it offers strong presumptive evidence to the effect that at each junction in his career Mr. Zoll's values played an important part in his decisions.

There is also a strong possibility that fundamental value differences may give rise to a great many of the educational criticisms from groups we suspiciously tag "vested interests." Despite the fact that the demands of many such groups obviously serve the personal interests of members—for example, reduced school costs jibe neatly with the aims of a taxpayers' association—perhaps we do them a serious injustice in questioning the sincerity of their purposes. There is much to suggest that a number of them have quite sincerely identified the public interest with their own—regardless of whether the rest of us share their particular conception of the public welfare. Under such circumstances, when sincerity is a genuine possibility, value differences offer the more economical explanation. This hypothesis does not require the additional, and possibly erroneous, assumption that these groups are surreptitiously plotting to enhance their interests at whatever cost to the public.

That criticism can be explained in terms of a "protest syndrome"—another highly cogent individualistic explanation of educational criticism—is also open to alternate interpretation. For whether or not the school critics to whom this explanation has been applied are emotionally driven to protest, their *other* complaints place many of them in the ranks of extreme political conservatism. Thus, perhaps the general orientation which leads to the conservatism is what also accounts for the educational values—regardless of what may explain the particular set of general values that initiates the chain. In a similar fashion, our hypothesis may also be consistent with the other psychological explanations of educational criticism outlined in Chapter X. For we have not contended that general values are necessarily an *ultimate* cause of attacks on schools.[14] We have maintained only that they are involved in the causal chain producing most attacks—and that, for the practical purposes which concern us, we can go no further in this chain. Actual causation might be: aberration leads to fundamental values leads to sociopolitical values leads to educational values leads to attacks on schools.

Nor does our hypothesis conflict with the sociological explanations of educational criticism discussed in Chapter X. In evidence for the theory that school criticism is cyclic or perennial, we saw that a number of current criticisms were offered at earlier periods in our history. We have seen that extreme value disagreements have existed ever since the nation was established. Hence, the early appearance of educational criticism tends to confirm our view: that it was the outgrowth of fundamental disagreements which were already evident.

But here we risk the danger of an explanation so broadly applicable that it accounts for everything and really explains nothing. Recall that we are trying to account for the *spurt* in educational criticism—the epidemic of attacks on schools since World War II. Have we just undermined our explanation of contemporary criticism in showing that it accounts also for earlier criticism? Perhaps not. For if we are right in attributing disagreements over educational values to more basic differences, then this follows: when the struggle over these basic values becomes more acute, conflicts in *educational* values are also intensified.

Certainly there is evidence that the chasm which divides Americans on fundamental values is broadening. To cite just one illustration, the famous Harvard Committee which sought universally accepted values as the grounds for general education gave up the task as totally impossible.[15] Furthermore, not only are the disagreements growing wider; we are also becoming more self-conscious about them. Since the War, we have focused a great deal of attention on the content of our basic national values. Recall, for example, the heated discussions occasioned by the Supreme Court's school integration decision, and by the phenomena of McCarthyism—more recently, John Birch-ism. These and many similar postwar events we could cite tend to confirm the view that educational conflict actually grows from far deeper conflict: for at the same time that the battle over educational values has intensified, disagreements over more general values have also been growing in number, in intensity, and in bitterness.

That *both* sociopolitical conflict and educational criticism are far more prevalent and intense today than at earlier periods lends credence to the theory that conflicts over schools mirror basic conflicts within society itself. This explanation, as we have just seen, is highly consistent with our hypothesis since it is these very conflicts over fundamental values which we are holding responsible for attacks on schools.

The third type of explanation frequently advanced to account for educational criticism—the rationalist interpretations examined in Chapter X—is similarly consonant with the view that value cleavages give rise to attacks on schools. For example, one such explanation attributes the attacks to our failure to decide what we want public schools to be. It makes sense to conclude that *fundamental* differences as to "what ought to be" are responsible for the delay of this rather important decision.

Several of the other rationalistic explanations for attacks on schools might appear to rule out our hypothesis, since they lay heavy emphasis on *factual* belief—not value commitment—as the basis of criticism.

Recall, for instance, those explanations attributing the attacks to a lack of information about what schools are doing, or to different beliefs regarding the nature of the learning process. Although values are not directly evident in such factual beliefs, they may still be operating to produce them, for our values play an important part in determining our "facts." They are a crucial factor in determining what we actually elect to see—rendering some facts quickly apparent, and erecting barriers to our perception of others.[16] Because of this dependence of facts on values, our view that value cleavages are responsible for attacks on schools is not inconsistent with the rationalist explanations of these attacks. We think ours is a bit more penetrating explanation, however, and that it serves better to account for such critics as the one who, confronted by one able and accomplished third-grader after another, continues to persist in his claim that "Johnny can't do nothing."

Thus none of the three types of explanation offered to account for current criticism invalidates our claim that the attacks on schools rise from deep-seated differences over values. We hope, moreover, that we have shown our explanation to be at least as plausible as those discussed earlier, and to account for a wider variety of cases than others. We believe that our explanation also has certain practical advantages over the others; and these advantages will be shown in Chapter XII.

Our second hypothesis—that the educator's lack of power accounts for current attacks on schools—is an entirely different type of interpretation than that just discussed. It seeks the cause of contemporary criticism in conditions rather than within individuals. Practically, it suggests long-range goals rather than immediate programs for solving the problem of attacks.

Strictly speaking, of course, an absence of anything cannot be a *cause*. But the educator's lack of power, either to prevent or to cope adequately with severe criticism, may provide the conditions permitting certain causes to operate effectively. Thus the educator's weakness may account for attacks on schools in the same sense that a weakened physical condition is responsible for certain infections or diseases.

Now, a group wielding power even approximately commensurate with that of potential adversaries usually finds fewer adversaries and less intense opposition than does the group which can readily be bested in any encounter. The educator's current lack of power poses a dilemma enclosing him in a vicious circle. On the one hand, without power he is subject to attack. On the other hand, he can obtain the necessary power only through recognition and concession on the part of the public—and a public so critical as to launch attacks is obviously unlikely to cede the power needed. The dilemma is not real, however, unless one views *power* only in a very limited sense—as specifically delegated authority. (The conception of power which critics apparently share is equally limited and unsatisfactory: speak of "power" for the educator, and they immediately assume you want to let him dominate and coerce the rest of us.)

In suggesting that the educator lacks power, we have a quite different meaning in mind. One good definition conceives power simply as "the production of intended effects."[17] Another asserts, "Power . . . denotes effective means of operation; ability or capacity to execute, to realize ends." This author—John Dewey—issues a specific warning against several connotations of the word *power*:

> Power . . . is either a neutral or an eulogistic term. . . . Granted an end which is worth while, and power . . . becomes an eulogistic term. It means nothing but the sum of conditions available for bringing the desirable end into existence. Any [group] . . . which will have nothing to do with power on the ground that all power is force and all force brutal and non-moral is obviously condemned to a purely sentimental, dreamy morals. It is force by which we excavate subways and build bridges and travel and manufacture; it is force which is utilized in spoken argument or published book. Not to depend upon and utilize force is simply to be without a foothold in the real world.[18]

It is such a view of power that we have in mind. For our purposes, educators need increased power simply in order to perform as educators. Despite the fact that the educator may exert considerable power over the immature, even in this kind of effectiveness he is limited, for he lacks control over many of the conditions which influence learning, and he possesses only in very small degree the various kinds of power which determine public decision in our society. What kind of power influences public decision? In order to determine which types the educator might effectively employ, let us examine a few of the most useful forms of power exercised by various groups in this country.

The most obvious form of power in any stable society is that exerted by the law, which specifically sanctions privileges for groups and institutions. The educator has certain legal privileges—his right to be an educator is established in most areas through state certification. With respect to some of the problems he may encounter, he has legal power to act, or to refuse to act, regardless of how he may be criticized for doing so. But by and large, the educator's legal power is far more circumscribed than that of other groups. Consider, for example, the doctor who decides that a child must have a blood transfusion. In many such cases where parents have refused, the doctor has obtained a court order for the transfusion. Now, try to imagine a case in which the educator could obtain a court order for his prescription that a child have remedial reading instruction or psychiatric care or anything else. We are not suggesting that the educator should have this power. (In fact, there are many good reasons why probably he should not.) Nevertheless the point of the analogy is an important one: Where other groups have or can obtain that legal power essential to carrying out the purposes of their endeavor, the educator lacks the power necessary to realizing his purposes—educating children. True, he can compel school attendance; but this is equivalent only to "leading the horse to water." To give the educator the legal power necessary to educating—in the sense that the doctor can resort, if need be, to the legal power necessary to healing—would involve the addition of a great many sanctions.

Political power is a form of power closely related to that of the law. In a stable society it is political power which largely determines legal power. Here too, if we define political power as capacity to achieve results through this specific means, educators individually and as a group are weak. Actually, the weakness is even more striking than it initially appears, in view of the strength that sheer numbers ordinarily bestow. Since democracy's formal criterion for the right to political power is that of numbers, the size of the educational profession should entitle it to a considerably greater voice in public decision than that of any other professional group. We have, for example, about six times as many schoolmen as doctors in this country. Yet, compare the complete success of the medical profession to date, in combating health and medical programs, with the relatively paltry achievements of educators in obtaining federal aid for education.

Still another measure of the educator's political power is the number of educators serving in state legislatures. As just one example, the 235-member Illinois General Assembly includes two educators: one teacher, one administrator.[19] This is probably about par for the course, since as of 1958 a total of 101 teachers were serving in their respective state legislatures. But fourteen legislatures contained no educators, and indeed in three states legal barriers prevented their election![20]

Economic power is another most effective means for realizing purposes in our society. If its funds were unlimited, for example, organized labor might very well win every industrial dispute simply by subsidizing members until demands had been met. Under comparable circumstances, of course, educators with the same assets could act similarly—though for a number of reasons they might not (and perhaps should not) choose to do so. But whether or not educators chose actively to wield economic power in this way, its very possession functions as power. The *capacity* to resort to an indefinite holdout operates as economic power whether or not a walkout occurs.

Now, to what extent can education count on this kind of economic power? The story of teachers' salaries is an old and mournfully familiar one. In view of the relatively limited finances of its members, it is not surprising that the education profession as a whole has comparatively limited economic resources. The membership fee in a professional organization is one index to the economic power the profession as a whole can exert. In 1956 a doctor paid $25 a year for membership in the American Medical Association. An architect's annual membership fee was $50 in the American Institute of Architects. And an educator paid $5 annual dues to the National Education Association.[21] Only the fact that there are a good many more teachers than doctors or architects enables the teaching profession, by comparison, to exert any sort of economic power at all. But note that even the considerable numerical superiority of the teachers did not swing the balance: for 1956 membership dues would have given the AMA a budget of $3,825,000, while giving the NEA—with four times the Medical Association's membership total—only $3,063,580.[22]

The economic power of most professional groups functions in two important ways. It is instrumental in enhancing the welfare of the group itself, and it is useful in improving the quality of the services the group renders. When a professional group is under attack as is education today, these two functions become linked. Increased economic power could be used simultaneously to improve education and the lot of the educator. For instance, funds might well be used for research into new means of carrying on the educational enterprise. As scientific evidence was amassed, attacks on certain practices could be expected to wane. Economic power would in this way work to improve both the quality of the services educators render and the conditions under which schoolmen work. It might also enable the profession to counterbalance some of the economic power that has proved an apparent factor in many contemporary attacks on schools.

One of the reasons why economic power is so important to the educational profession is its relationship to still another form: power over public opinion. The simplest and most inexpensive means of influencing public opinion are the media of mass communications. And the educator does not always have ready access to these media. In fact, at precisely the times when he may need them most—when an attack on schools is imminent or in full swing—they may well be closed to him. His prospects for added control over these means to influencing public opinion are dim, in view of the steady trend toward increasingly concentrated control. The number of newspapers in the nation is rapidly diminishing as smaller papers are sold to larger. Many of the latter also influence public opinion through their control of radio and television stations as well.[23] Our point is not that such control is always hostile to public education—though unmistakably it sometimes has been. The important thing is that if the power to influence public opinion is necessary to the educator in realizing his purposes, and if this power is limited to *other* groups, then it is obviously not available to him except with their approval.

Unfortunately the radio stations and television channels allocated to education do not seriously alter the situation. Experience has shown that education's access to the media only assures *potential* access to the public. In the main their audiences have been small,[24] and they seem fated to remain so: "Rhetoric 100" obviously has less appeal than Matt Dillon. Again, the fact that educators do not control mass communications media is not a constant disadvantage. It does mean, however, that at any time education's interests run counter to those of the group controlling a particular medium, education's viewpoint may be lost. It has been suggested, for example, that Goslin's lack of press support was an important factor in his eventual ouster from Pasadena.[25] We have called attention to an even more significant situation—that of education's archenemy, R. C. Hoiles, who owns a chain of newspapers. In more than one of the communities served by his dailies, the only paper published is that of Hoiles, and readers have been bombarded often with his view that public schools should be abolished.[26] (It is probably this lack of power over mass communications media which provided the major impetus for many school public relations programs and determined their techniques. The pamphlets and booklets were education's attempt to state its side of the story, since the standard mass media—radio, television, and press—were not always available.)

There is still another important form of power exerted by various groups in this country—the power of personal influence. If the standard means of influencing public opinion are not always open to the educator, perhaps this form of power might offer a partial substitute. Yet here, too, the educator is weak. The power of personal influence we refer to is not the kind which personality provides. There are educators who enjoy this kind of personal success, just as there are engineers and Presbyterians and Englishmen who have it. What we are talking about is the influence which accrues—or fails to accrue—by virtue of the educator's profession.

The members of some professions clearly have this power by virtue of their vocations. The doctor, for example, is surrounded by an aura of general sagacity that extends his influence far beyond his field of competence. As one sort of evidence, see the television doctor; he is invariably a respected figure whose advice is sought and heeded on a great variety of problems. Recently the military man has begun to enjoy a similar power of personal influence. The evidence consists not only of electoral ballots but also of the letterheads of big business. As one example, Admiral Rickover's recent criticisms of education have received wide attention, although his success with an atomic submarine certainly could not per se equip him with competence in pedagogy. It did, however, just as surely extend his influence beyond matters military.

Now, what of the educator's power of influence by virtue of *his* profession? It appears that while the doctor is fortunate in our stereotype of him, our picture of the educator tends to diminish, not to foster, his influence. He is often viewed either as a "lunkhead" or as an "egghead"—neither of which inspires much confidence. The female version of the "lunkhead" is typically the ex-coed who could not have graduated in another field. As a teacher of whatever age, she is hopefully marking time until she marries—and her efforts to attain this state lend ludicrous detail to the stereotype, as television has personified it for us in "Our Miss Brooks." The other "lunkhead" stereotype portrays the teacher as a well-intentioned but rather bumbling and ineffectual character (for example, television's Mr. Peepers). He is an individual driven to escape the rigors of the outside world. By virtue of his vocation he is a "lunkhead" because "He who can does; he who can't teaches."

The "egghead" label is more commonly reserved for the college teacher, but occasionally extended to the high school teacher who resists the "lunkhead" characterization. This stereotype shows the educator as an ivory-tower intellectual of considerable erudition. But since our society seems to perceive little real relevance of learning to its problems,[27] his very erudition serves to deny the educator influence. Apparently his learning in some mysterious way incapacitates him in dealing with matters of this world.* It is at this point that the two stereotypes reach common ground. For both the "lunkhead" and the "egghead" are expected to bungle practical affairs.

Thus the customary stereotypes hardly help the educator. The influence of the *members* of a profession must stem from the general prestige of the profession itself. And as the attacks on schools clearly show, the profession lacks this prestige. How is it acquired? There are probably numerous factors involved, but the one most pertinent to our purposes is the possession of technical knowledge. Education is making strides in this direction, despite difficulties in educational research and in spite of the fact that pedagogy is a new discipline. But progress is slow, and if public confidence that a profession possesses technical knowledge must provide the basis of its prestige, we have explored a great many implicit denials that educators possess any such knowledge.

* Obviously, many of the current administration's appointees represent a threat to this stereotype. Let us hope they will undermine it. Meanwhile, however, keep in mind that these professor-officials were appointed; they were not elected. And it was one of the nation's most prominent "eggheads" who failed to capture the successful party's nomination.

We have claimed that a group or institution which lacks power—the means necessary to realizing its purposes—is particularly vulnerable to attack. In examining the major forms of power exercised by various groups in our society, we have found that educators are comparatively weak with respect to each type—legal, political, and economic power; power over public opinion; and personal influence. Since such relative weakness introduces conditions conducive to attack, we must conclude that the educator's lack of power is a major factor in the extreme criticism. And to compound the misfortune, the very circumstances producing this susceptibility leave educators comparatively defenseless in combating attacks.

12. *Prevention and Cure*

We have met the critics, the aiders and abettors, and have seen evidence of bitter and unjust attacks on an institution most Americans consider vital to the nation's survival. Many of the attacks on schools have stemmed from charges that are not true, and demands that are unwarranted. Many have revealed disagreements among our citizens —disagreements of a magnitude that is far from reassuring.

Despite the fact that there are many severe critics of American education, it appears that a majority of citizens feel that schools are doing a passable, if not always exemplary, job. The last big national poll on education found 79 per cent of the public believing the things taught in the schools of 1950 equal to or more desirable than what was taught in 1930.[1] Of the California citizens polled in 1956, 82 per cent thought public schools were doing a job that was fair or better. In the state of Washington, 79 per cent of those polled thought today's high school graduate is at least as well educated as the graduates of their own day. And in Utah, 81 per cent of those asked were satisfied with the results achieved by their public schools.[2]

Yet such reassuring evidence serves only to underscore the problem of contemporary educational criticism. It demonstrates beyond all question that the critics are creating a commotion and degree of dissension out of all proportion to their numbers. Furthermore, in those communities where critics have been successful in their demands, it is at least reasonable to inquire whether their success has actually coincided with the wishes of the public—or whether it should rather be attributed to that kind of "government by intimidation" which we have explored.

We believe that value cleavages lie at the root of the problem and that there is a need for agreement if we are to prevent school attacks, or successfully meet those that get started. What we are really recommending then is some means of influencing values. There is nothing new, of course, in such an attempt. Ministers, teachers, and advertising men are just a few of the people who constantly seek to change the beliefs, attitudes, values, and behavior of others. In our private lives, all of us seek at one time or another to influence family and friends.

Basically, there are just two approaches to persuasion, the direct and the indirect. The direct approach is the ancient and time-tested one. Most of us turn to it in trying to persuade or "convert," and it is the advertising man's stock in trade. But social scientists are rapidly amassing evidence that the direct onslaught, no matter how subtle or "soft" the "sell," may be the least effective means of persuasion. Studies reveal that people refuse altogether to read or listen to ideas counter to their own.[3] Voting studies show that those who read and listen to campaign messages are precisely those least likely to be influenced, for they have already made up their minds.[4] Even the newest media of direct persuasion—the subliminal or subaudible message—seem to affect only those who are already convinced. Such a message may move a popcorn eater to want popcorn, but it can do no more.[5] And if a subliminal exhortation cannot create popcorn enthusiasts, it can hardly be expected to turn educational critics into stanch friends of the public school.

In short, the direct approach is not very effective. The group which needs persuading may never even get the message. And this in turn suggests that much of what the schoolman has done to try to prevent school attacks has been to no avail. If the investigators just cited are correct, then the typical school public relations program—the radio shows and announcements, the pretty brochures, the hard-won newspaper space—has had little effect on school critics.

Quite a different kind of evidence also suggests the ineffectiveness of present efforts to head off attacks on schools. As we have suggested, a large proportion of the schoolman's efforts to deal with criticism has consisted in presenting the facts. The assumption has been that facts persuade. Yet the evidence shows with growing clarity that this is not the case. Facts and attitudes apparently enjoy a remarkable independence of one another, and increased knowledge simply does not assure a change of attitude.[6] Often, those facts rendering an attitude ridiculous do not disturb it at all. It is even possible that we have got the relationship between facts and values just backward: it may be that the commitments or attitudes we have assumed to be built on facts are instead a necessary prerequisite to an individual's very acceptance of these facts.

But there is also evidence showing how attitudes and values *are* acquired. The studies of anthropologists have suggested that our basic values are socially determined by those around us. Others even influence our "facts." Not only do we unconsciously look to other people for what will be our interpretations of complex and unclear situations, but the views of those around us can even lead us to reverse our firm and *accurate* convictions about completely *obvious* situations.[7]

Thus the evidence corroborates what experience shows: that man is not the rational creature our institutions presuppose. Direct attempts to deal rationally with him generally do not succeed. He may simply choose not to listen, or if forced to confront facts he does not like, he may just deny them—irrespective of how strongly they can be supported. On the other hand, the work of social psychologists has shown that there *are* certain conditions under which facts can persuade. In effect, these men have suggested that there are *conditions* of rationality—that facts presented under certain circumstances will be accepted, while under other circumstances they will surely be rejected. It is this situation which leads us to propose an *indirect* approach to influencing, as the most promising means of preventing attacks on schools. The reason lies in what seem to constitute the conditions of rationality. If it is true that man's ability to operate rationally is limited by his environment, there may be a number of factors in the immediate environment making it all but impossible for him to adopt and modify attitudes objectively. When one's personal interests are seriously threatened, his perception of facts is likely to become distorted. If he is confronted with threats to his ego, these also will interfere with his accurate perception and interpretation of reality. And in the society at large there are a number of factors that impede clarity and rationality on the part of many of our citizens, for much of their lives. For example, interpreters of the current scene refer to the "displacement" and "dislocation" of modern man. Others speak of an "age of anxiety" and claim that suburbia, which houses an impressive segment of our population, might better be tagged "disturbia."

Life in contemporary America is hardly conducive to rationality. Yet we are committed to the view that man *is* rational, and this assumption is indeed fundamental to our whole political system. Therefore, if the system is to work, we must bring about those conditions that make rationality possible. The provision of such a set of circumstances is what we mean by the "indirect approach" to persuasion.

These consist in active group participation. Planned and conscious persuasion is not a necessary ingredient, and changes do not depend on the majority's bludgeoning of the recalcitrant few. Usually, the entire group simultaneously undergoes changes in values and behavior.

> Perhaps one might expect single individuals to be more pliable than groups of like-minded individuals. However, experience in leadership training, in changing of food habits, work production, criminality, alcoholism, prejudices—all seem to indicate that it is usually easier to change individuals formed into a group than to change any one of them separately.[8]

Now, it would clearly constitute enthusiasm gone wild to assume that we shall convert each destructive critic of public education by this or any other means. It does seem possible though that *some* of today's accusers could become defenders of the schools. The confirmed critic—and this describes most of those we have named in this book—is strongly committed to certain educational values, and to more general values he applies to education. To modify these values involves a process of replacing them with others. This two-part process of "reeducation" is more complex and difficult than the one-part process of instilling new values, and it is less assured of success.

There are many people, however, whose educational values are ill defined, and to the extent that they are held at all, are held without much conviction. This is in effect a "neutral" population, and the desired change involves the strengthening of incipient values, or the development of brand-new ones—"education," rather than "reeducation." This neutral group offers the best hope for averting future attacks on schools. For an extreme critic—no matter what his demands or how loudly and persistently he voices them—can cause trouble only when he influences the values of others. Hence, through building the kind of prior commitment which would preclude such influence, it may be possible to avoid the large-scale attacks that are the real problem.

An exclusive reliance on facts to build this commitment among the "neutral" population has not done the job. It seems equally true with the neutral population, as with the confirmed critic, that "tellin' ain't teachin'." Critics' values—and the neutral population's lack of them—simply block assimilation of the information presented.

Group methods, on the other hand, seem to offer a way to stimulate the value commitment which constitutes a prerequisite for knowledge. In this method participants undertake a problem or task requiring them to examine various facts for themselves. Participation evidently facilitates an entirely new view of the problem and of the facts. We need not discuss here the intricacies of the group we advocate for preventing attacks on schools. (A supplement following this chapter contains such detail, and suggestions on how to set up and carry out the project.) Some of the more general features of such a group might, however, be of interest.

There is nothing new, of course, in suggesting that schools establish citizen groups as a means of building community support. As we have seen, various parent advisory councils and citizen committees have been popular. It may be, however, that some of the features marking most of these councils and committees have prevented them from really succeeding. One of the major difficulties is the task typically assigned a citizen group. Often it is asked to propose solutions to problems or to recommend specific decisions to the board of education. This has been unfortunate since, by law, such groups have no authority and their advice has often been rejected by the agency which legally must make the decision, the board of education. Under such circumstances, it would not be surprising for members of the "advisory" council to question the worth of their efforts. And when such questions arise, the desired value commitment is unlikely to come about.

A citizens' group should be a fact-finding organization. Such a venture is less open to manipulation—and to charges of manipulation—

than are those involving the assignments typically given citizen committees. This is important because school-sponsored advisory groups usually include educators. Not infrequently, however, the professional member has been tempted to try strenuously to influence the outcome. The temptation may be understandable in view of his interest and knowledge, but it has been most unfortunate; the result has sometimes been bitter charges of manipulation and indoctrination. In *Progressive Education Is REDucation,* for example, Kitty Jones devotes eight full pages to the devious and nefarious nature of the "school workshop."[9] Although the fact-finding group may not be wholly exempt, either, from charges of manipulation (indeed, no assemblage of human beings has such immunity), it is far less vulnerable on this score. The facts sought are themselves less susceptible to manipulation, and the absence of an obligation to reach a concerted conclusion eliminates the occasion for it.

The fact-finding group may prove as effective in preventing attacks on schools as it has been in combating attacks on minority groups. Since preventing attacks on minorities seems similarly to be a matter of building certain value commitments, the measures most effective in the one case may also work best in the other.[10] The particular project used most extensively for antidiscrimination purposes is the community self-survey. These are the assumptions underlying this kind of fact-finding project:

—Individuals working together to discover facts, thereby influence themselves and one another to accept facts and values which otherwise they would reject or simply "not see."

—In two respects, facts are more acceptable when discovered for oneself, than when parcelled out to us: we are consciously more inclined to trust their accuracy and reliability, and consciously or unconsciously, we are more inclined to assimilate and retain them.

—The process of fact-finding develops on the part of the investigators, not only the knowledge sought, but also the commitments which create a sense of responsibility to act on the basis of this knowledge.

—The process of gathering the facts is at least as important as the tangible product of the efforts involved, since it is in the course of the *process* that the greatest effects may occur.[11]

These assumptions suggest a number of specifics for the community self-survey designed to prevent attacks on schools. The emphasis on the process itself is perhaps the most crucial feature. It also seems to be the feature most often overlooked in self-surveys which have so far been made of schools. By and large, such surveys have stressed product—the final report—rather than process. And the topic selected for investigation—typically, school-plant needs—has all but eliminated the opportunity for discovering any facts conducive to changes in values.

A carefully planned community self-survey of schools should serve to build the kind of commitment which greatly reduces the possibility of attacks on schools. If it is to serve this purpose, the focus on the process suggests that a number of people be involved in the study, including, of course, members of the "neutral" population as well as overt critics of education.

The project we have recommended provides a means of resolving major educational disagreements. There are other ways, however, of seeking to prevent and meet attacks on schools. The fact-finding group is just one of several possibilities for doing the job. Two others stem from a recognition of the inevitably political nature of educational problems.

There are a number of important respects in which education has been and must always be a political question and must remain so as long as there is political controversy. The matter of what schools should teach is in part political. We can agree generally that we want schools to transmit our national heritage. But, obviously, they cannot transmit everything, and one's view of just what is worth saving is determined by one's political orientation. We happen to agree fairly widely on what constitutes the good man. So there would be little controversy over whether to transmit a knowledge of George Washington or, for example, of the members of Murder Incorporated. But we do not agree on what constitutes the good society. Thus the selection of just what to preserve for posterity becomes a political question.

In the day-to-day management of schools, political questions also loom large. Questions such as segregation and the sources and legal uses of school funds are eminently political in nature. We argue them openly as politics and elect governments on the basis of their views on these matters. But there is still another important sense in which education is a political question. We have seen that a number of the schools' most bitter detractors espouse programs which are primarily political. They have coupled a specific educational position with a political one. Hence, even if it were possible to divorce educational and political concerns, the weapons critics have chosen make such a separation currently impossible. Many of them, as we have seen, have carried the battle into legislative halls. First and foremost, they are political pressure groups.

One method of dealing with these critics, then, might be to seek the same sort of governmental regulation currently urged for the control of pressure groups *recognized* as political—a control which many legislators believe essential to preserving the public's interests.[12] This would surely be a logical step, and it might well be a desirable one. But it probably would not be enough. In view of the inability of Congress to reach an effective solution for the parallel problem of lobbyists, it seems unlikely that this kind of state and national legislation could be passed—or that measures passed would prove wholly successful.

A third possibility is simply to accept the relationship between politics and education. For example, we might seek openly political school board elections to avoid hidden political ties. If it would accomplish nothing more, this recognition would serve to lay out the issues more clearly, and thereby allow the voter to make a more intelligent choice. Recognition of education as a political matter might conceivably lead to increased national attention for schools. It might thus foster whatever assistance and improvement an informed electorate desires, as an outgrowth of increased awareness that our national fate is inextricably tied to that, for instance, of Mississippi.

Recognition of the strong ties linking education to politics might also mean that it is time for the education profession to make itself heard in the same way that other professions contribute a loud, clear voice on matters of public policy. But regardless of what the profession might choose to do, in the long run the answer to the problem of illegitimate school criticism must come from the American people as a whole. We can only hope that by exposing the hidden ax hacking away at our schools we can alert the people. Ultimately, it is they who must act against the dangers which could destroy public education—and with it our whole way of life.

Supplement

HOW TO CONDUCT A COMMUNITY SELF-SURVEY

Of course, no single effort is going to be enough, and we are not suggesting the community self-survey will forever guarantee tranquillity. Many other efforts of various types would have to follow it, in order to prevent future outbreaks of attack. The survey does, however, seem to be the best first step. We think it could be used as a means of meeting school attacks, as well as a means of preventing them—though prevention is obviously the best cure.

What follows attempts to answer some of the questions which might occur in planning and executing a community self-survey. Our suggestions consist largely in direct adaptations of the surveys designed to deal with discrimination. Descriptions of these discrimination surveys would be most helpful in planning the fact-finding project described here.[1]

Why Should This Approach Succeed When Others Have Failed?

Those who first attempted to combat the rash of postwar criticism assumed that information alone would do the job. But that enlightening information seems not to have "reached" the critics and "neutralists" for whom it was intended. These people lacked the commitment necessary in order to assure a real hearing for the information.

Later efforts to meet and/or prevent the attacks rightfully assumed that the problem was a bit more complex and the solution more difficult than merely disseminating information. Many recognized that the desired commitment was likely to come about only under special conditions. They suggested a group setting because of its effectiveness in modifying members' values. But the potential effectiveness of such a setting has often been undermined by various factors: the composition and size of the group; an exclusive concern with the outcome or product of group endeavors, and insufficient attention to the process; asking the group to go through the motions of decision-making, when decisions actually were being made elsewhere; and alleged or actual manipulation of parent and citizen committees. A community fact-finding project can offer the advantages of a group setting, while minimizing or completely avoiding these disadvantages. By encouraging the development of those common values which would establish common spheres of rationality, the community self-survey might turn the present school debate to valuable and constructive purposes.

Organizing and Initiating a Community Self-Survey

If the purpose of the fact-finding project is to broaden agreement on values, obviously nothing is to be gained by limiting participation to those who already have the desired commitment. This means that the project should include active critics of the schools as well as those we have called "neutralists." In the interests of obtaining broad support and presenting the project for what it should be—a completely honest investigation—it is well to enlist diverse groups as sponsors.

Although such obviously interested organizations as parent-teacher groups or local citizens committees for the schools could initiate the survey, it might ultimately be more desirable if the impetus came from a group with a less specific and partisan interest in education. Local civic or service organizations such as the League of Women Voters might prove the most desirable originators and organizers. Various groups—service, social, and civic clubs, and organizations representing employers, labor, industry—might serve as sponsors for the survey. Groups having a direct and primary concern with schools may of course be invited to join in the sponsorship, but it is necessary that such "vested interests" do not dominate the sponsoring group.

Representatives of the several sponsoring organizations compose the committee that plans and administers the survey. Ideally, this group is large enough to represent various community interests and small enough to facilitate interaction among members. The number might range from fifteen to twenty-five, plus several consultants—school personnel and research specialists. Again, it is neither necessary nor desirable that all members of this group be enthusiastic supporters of local school policy and practice.

Other Personnel and Division of Labor

The sponsoring committee plans the survey, but participants are by no means limited to this group. In the first place, a survey of the proportions necessary to achieve our purposes is an extensive undertaking which requires a director and coordinator, as well as a policy-making group. Ideally, there would be a survey director who could devote several hours each day to coordinating and supervising the survey. The director must be an accomplished administrator, preferably with some knowledge of social science research methods and data analysis.

Once under way, the survey includes a number of subcommittees, chaired by the various members of the sponsoring committee. It is these subcommittees, involving many additional participants, which actually collect the data and record it. Although the sponsoring committee must decide such broad questions as the kind of information to be obtained, and how it is to be reported to the community, as many decisions as possible should be left to the subcommittees.

At every stage throughout the survey, interaction among all those participating is crucial. From the start, steps must be taken to assure that participants see themselves as a group rather than as individuals who happen simultaneously to be embarked on the same task. Furthermore, the group must be sufficiently attractive for members to value their participation in it. And one of the best attracting features is a group cohesiveness, or *espirit de corps.*[2] One of the reasons, after all, for conducting the survey in the first place, is its potential for changing the participating members. The desired value commitments emerge primarily from the process and not the product.

Facts to Be Found

If we are correct in claiming that attacks on schools stem from disagreements over values, then it is values with which the survey should be concerned. A survey of projected building needs may never lead to an examination of values, or in fact to any considerations except those which concern a census taker. A survey designed to prevent attacks on schools might instead be concerned with determining whether schools enjoy the approval and support of the community, or whether people disapprove of what is being done.

Furthermore, the survey should seek to determine not just *whether* there is community support, but also which aspects of the school program are favored and which are not. The survey should, therefore, inquire into the various features of public education: curriculum, extracurricular activities, student service provisions, adult and community services, and school personnel. For purposes of dividing the work and administering the survey, a separate subcommittee might assume responsibility for each of these features.

Methods of Gathering Data

There are various means of obtaining information. If the sponsoring committee or subcommittees desire, there is no reason why official reports and records or analyses of newspaper coverage should not be used. But it is particularly important to make personal interviews the primary source of data, for the very process of asking and responding to a series of questions often leads to change in questioner and respondent alike. Only one major precaution need limit the methods of data collection. If the survey is to be effective, there must be broad participation. Thus, investigation methods must be suitable for untrained research workers.

Interview Questions

The experience of professional opinion surveyors has shown that devising adequate questions involves much skill. For this reason, it would be valuable to have on the sponsoring committee, or available as a consultant, a person with this kind of experience. Short of such help, there are a number of sources offering guides for preparing interview questions.[3] Here are some of the major points ordinarily suggested.

Although given our purpose, questions must stimulate reconsideration of values, direct questions should be avoided. The blunt "Do you approve of our teachers?" specifically invites the respondent to formulate and announce a position; thus it minimizes the chances for a change in values. Furthermore, such a question is less likely to yield an accurate picture of an individual's values than would several more specific, derivative questions.

Open-ended questions (such as our example) complicate the task of interviewing, and later, that of reporting and interpreting replies. All three jobs are greatly simplified by multiple-choice questions asking respondents to select an answer from among stated alternatives.

Preparing Research Methods and Workers

The subcommittees charged with investigating each specific feature of the schools should work out their own research methods, including the interview questions they will use. After the sponsoring committee has approved these instruments, the various subcommittees will proceed to carry out the actual research.

It is important that *everyone* in the group understand the project as a whole, and initial meetings should be used to this end. Later, the workers engaged in their various tasks will need specific instruction. This is particularly important for the interviewers, who should together review the instrument they will use, and practice one or more interviews.

Publicizing the Survey

Two publicity patterns have been used in community self-surveys investigating discrimination: early and deferred publicity. Some surveys have deliberately avoided publicity until all the facts were in—on the grounds that awareness of the investigation might bias the replies of those interviewed. Others have felt that this possible disadvantage is more than offset by the concern that publicity itself may stimulate. If the purposes of the project are primarily to evoke value commitment, early publicity seems desirable since the very news of the survey might lead to an examination of values. In fact, it might even be desirable to supplement standard publicity channels with personal visits to community leaders not otherwise involved in the project.

Analyzing the Information Gathered

In order to involve as many people as possible, and at the same time to avoid overburdening volunteers, a separate group should analyze the information gathered. Devices such as tabulating sheets reduce the drudgery of assembling quantitative data. Codes for recording any qualitative responses must be devised with the aid of specialists. Statistical computations and detailed analysis will have to be performed under the direction of specialists in this area.

The Final Survey Report

The sponsoring committee must take final responsibility for the content of the survey report. The subcommittees which investigated the various questions, however, are obviously best equipped to prepare the report for their areas, and it will further serve the primary purposes of the project for them to do so.

Despite the fact that changes on the part of survey workers are expected to be far greater than the change produced in others, the potential effects of the report itself should not be underrated. If the survey has involved a number of people—with at least some of them known and respected figures—the suspicions that have sometimes accompanied school surveys in the past may be avoided. If some of the survey workers have been people not sympathetic to local schools, general reception of the report will be enhanced. With this in mind, survey findings should be presented in readable form, as vividly as possible.

The Survey Follow-Up

Community self-surveys of discrimination have often been followed by various projects designed to modify the circumstances revealed in the course of the investigation. It is entirely possible that similar projects might follow the community self-survey on attitudes toward schools. It goes without saying, of course, that such projects must be the *outgrowth* of the survey. If the initial plans for the investigation include a program of follow-up action, suspicions will be unavoidable: this is a fact-finding project—the facts may or may not call for action.

After the survey, school officials can follow it up in several ways. If the survey has been successful in stimulating a consideration of values and leading to commitment, then many of the present school public relations programs can function effectively. A number of the techniques we have deemed ineffective as an *initial* means of preventing school attacks can be effective once the fact-finding group has done its work. The community self-survey stimulates agreement on fundamental values. If such agreement can safely be assumed, public relations techniques can then serve to sustain school support.

Assessing the Results of the Survey

It would be difficult to find a way of measuring the changes actually attributable to the survey. Outside a laboratory, it is almost impossible to ascribe one event or condition to another. But passage of a school bond issue by a substantial majority; formation of a citizens group primarily concerned with constructively aiding schools; or increased attendance at parent-teacher meetings and school board meetings might all indicate the success of the survey. A successful community self-survey should prevent invalid educational criticism and encourage the development of such a strong and widespread feeling of "psychological ownership" of local schools that any severe attack on them would be virtually impossible.

APPENDIX I

QUESTIONNAIRE SENT CRITICS

DIRECTIONS: Please answer the questions in the column on the left, first—by placing a check in the appropriate box. In connection with any question in this column to which your answer is YES, please answer the parallel question (or questions) in the righthand column.

Has Your Organization Investigated or Otherwise Looked Into . . .	*Yes*	*No*	*If So, Did You Conclude the Situation in Public Schools to Be Generally* UNDESIRABLE *with Respect to . . .*	*Yes*	*No*
1. School textbooks?	☐	☐	*a.* Subversive authorship or intent?	☐	☐
			b. Other unsuitable material?	☐	☐
2. The loyalty of teachers?	☐	☐	*a.* Disloyalty and/or lack of patriotism?	☐	☐
3. The curriculum in our schools?	☐	☐	*a.* Un-American and/or anti-Christian topics taught?	☐	☐
			b. Courses in "life adjustment" and/or other nonessentials?	☐	☐
			c. An impractical and/or "soft" curriculum?	☐	☐
4. The beliefs and activities of teachers?	☐	☐	*a.* Questionable beliefs?	☐	☐
			b. Questionable political and/or private activities?	☐	☐
5. Teaching methods?	☐	☐	*a.* The use of "Progressive" education methods?	☐	☐
6. The aims of educators and schools?	☐	☐	*a.* Aims inconsistent with the American Tradition?	☐	☐
			b. Aims inconsistent with the proper scope of education?	☐	☐
7. Religion in the schools?	☐	☐	*a.* Godlessness in schools?	☐	☐
			b. Sectarianism in schools?	☐	☐
8. The education given American teachers?	☐	☐	*a.* A lack of the kind of preparation needed?	☐	☐
			b. Too little emphasis on subject matter?	☐	☐
9. The costs of public education?	☐	☐	*a.* Too much money being spent on schools?	☐	☐
			b. Money spent on the wrong things?	☐	☐
10. The policies and practices of school administrators?	☐	☐	*a.* Policies and/or practices inconsistent with sound education?	☐	☐
			b. Aimlessness or lack of policy?	☐	☐
11. Teacher organizations?	☐	☐	*a.* A lack of interest in sound education?	☐	☐
			b. A lack of devotion to the American Tradition?	☐	☐
			c. A desire of these groups to control society?	☐	☐
			d. Domination by anti-intellectual elements?	☐	☐

APPENDIX II

IDENTIFICATION OF INDIVIDUAL RESPONDENTS

(EXHIBIT II)

Miss Marilyn Allen is a writer who devotes a large part of her efforts to pointing out the threat to this country posed by Jewish citizens. *Alien Minorities and Mongrelization* is perhaps her most well-known book. Mrs. Haskell, who replied at Miss Allen's request, identifies herself only as a parent who has studied "the adverse situation, in the public schools. . . ."

Dr. George Benson is president of Harding College. See Chapter VII, pp. 118-120, for a discussion of some of his views and activities.

Dr. Arthur Bestor is a professor of history at the University of Illinois. See Chapter VI for a discussion of his views and those of the Council for Basic Education of which he was a founder.

William F. Buckley, Jr., is a writer (*God and Man at Yale*) and the editor of *National Review*. Chapter VIII contains a number of quotations from the magazine (including its editorial policy) and several from Buckley's own column "The Ivory Tower."

Frank Chodorov is a writer and has served as editor of *Human Events*. His views on public education were expressed in his pamphlet "Private Schools: The Solution to America's Educational Problem," published by Zoll's Council for American Education.

Dr. L. Victor Cleveland is a former high school teacher and college professor. For eleven years he edited a publication known as *The High Way*. Presently Dr. Cleveland is working on an "Anti-Evolution Compendium" which to date numbers eight volumes.

Dr. Lee De Forest was a renowned scientist and writer with more than 300 patents to his credit. He had been a teacher, and a writer—having written an autobiography entitled *Father of Radio*. He was a member of The National Advisory Board of We, The People!

General Pedro A. del Valle is a retired Marine Corps officer. He is active in the Defenders of the American Constitution, Inc. (See Exhibit I for the educational criticism of this organization.) He is a member of the Advisory Committee of the "United States Day" Committee, Inc., and of the Advisory Board of We, The People!

Homer Dodge is a registered lobbyist representing the Committee for Constitutional Government.

Dr. Medford Evans was formerly a professor at Louisiana's Northwestern State College. See Chapter VIII for a discussion of some of his views and activities.

Miss Rosalie Gordon is Secretary of America's Future. For some of Miss Gordon's views, as expressed in her several printed works, see Chapter IV.

Dr. Alfred P. Haake is a former professor of economics. He was a founder of the American Economic Foundation (see Exhibit I for the educational criticism of this group), and he has served on the Executive Committee of the National Small Business Men's Association, and the American Economic Association. He is on the National Advisory Board of We, The People!

Wallace Hall is an attorney and a former teacher. He has served as president of Patriotic Education, Inc., and of the Sons of the American Revolution. He is a past Commander of the American Legion.

Dr. Lewis Haney is a professor of business administration at New York University. He served as a member of the Consulting Staff of the *Educational Reviewer.*

Robert Cyrus Hoiles is the millionaire owner of a newspaper chain. His idea that public schools should be abolished altogether has been referred to several times in this book.

J. Curtis Hoyt is the man who served as president of the Pascack Study Group on Education which attacked the Hillsdale, New Jersey, high school several years ago. See Chapter III.

John G. Keenan is the editor of the publication *Counterattack.* P. Speroni, who answered for Mr. Keenan, is identified on the reply as his secretary.

Dr. Willmoore Kendall is a professor of political science at Yale. For a discussion of his views and activities, see Chapter V and Chapter VIII.

Dr. Willford I. King is a retired professor of economics. He has been president and chairman of the board for the Committee for Constitutional Government.

Dr. Russell Kirk is a professor at Long Island University. For a discussion of his views and activities, see Chapter VIII.

The Honorable J. Bracken Lee is former Governor of Utah. He has served on the National Advisory Board of We, The People!, as National Chairman of For America, as Director of the National Committee to Repeal the Sixteenth Amendment, and as an official of the Congress of Freedom, Inc.

Robert T. Le Fevre has served as executive director of the Congress of Freedom, Inc., and of the "United States Day" Committee. He is the director of the Freedom School in Colorado—an institution "dedicated to the libertarian philosophy of individualism." [Among the instructors at the school have been Frank Chodorov, R. C. Hoiles, Leonard Read (president of the Foundation for Economic Education), and Rose Wilder Lane (editor of the National Economic Council's book review publication)]. Mr. Le Fevre is on the Advisory Committee of the "United States Day" Committee and on the advisory boards of Patriotic Education, Inc., and We, The People!

Conde McGinley is the publisher of the fervently anti-Semitic *Common Sense.* Mr. McGinley considers himself an authority on Communism, which his publication also opposes.

Donald MacLean is executive secretary of the De Mille Foundation for Political Freedom.

Dr. Walton Manning is a professor of education at the University of Miami.

Dr. Felix Morley is a columnist for the *Nation's Business.* For a discussion of his views and activities, see Chapter VIII.

Dr. Charles W. Pavey is a physician. He is on the board of directors of the Association of American Physicians and Surgeons, an organization which has vigorously opposed federal aid to schools and that distributed Rudd's *Bending the Twig* to state medical associations. Dr. Pavey is a member of the We, The People! National Advisory Board.

Colonel Eugene C. Pomeroy, retired, is an active member of the Defenders of the American Constitution. He is on the National Advisory Board of We, The People!

Edward Regentin is Superintendent of Sanilac County (Michigan) Schools. He is active in the Michigan Association for Rural Education.

Colonel Augustin G. Rudd is a retired Army officer. For a discussion of his views and activities, see Chapter IV.

Mrs. Cornelia Dabney Tucker is active in the Supreme Court Security League of Charleston, South Carolina.

Eugene Van Der Hoeven is Superintendent of Schools in Wheelock, North Dakota.

Admiral Homer N. Wallin, retired, is president of National Sojourners (see Exhibit I for the educational criticism of this organization), and past National Commander of the Heroes of '76. He is a lecturer and has written several pamphlets—among them, "Loss of American Freedom and Culture Through Education."

John R. Williams is a recent graduate of the public schools of Fargo, North Dakota. He is reported to have opposed alleged subversion in the high school he attended.

Mrs. Arnold Zube is a former school board member living in Fargo, North Dakota. She reports that she is "not a member of any organization in regard to schools. . . ."

NOTES

CHAPTER 1

1. Authorship of the poem is attributed to Marjorie Niles Kime. Since the Minute Women credit bears the date "July-August, 1958," presumably the piece initially appeared in that publication. The date under the Committee for the Preservation of the Constitution credit is "September 11, 1958."
2. Signed "Dorothy M. Seeger, Sec'y. of Beverly Hill Freedom Club" and reproduced by permission. The undated reply was postmarked Feb. 26, 1959. Miss Seeger states that the questionnaire, originally addressed to Club President Elfreida Kirchoff, was given her for reply by Mrs. Kirchoff.
3. "Home Rule," *CBE Bulletin* #8 (March, 1957), p. 15.

CHAPTER 2

1. From a formulation by Virgil Rogers included in his address to the 1951 General Assembly of the National Education Association.
2. Rudolf Flesch, *Why Johnny Can't Read—and What You Can Do About It* (New York: Popular Library, 1956), pp. 12 and 9.
3. *Ibid.*, p. 9.
4. Reported by William H. Burton, in "Scientific Criticism Aids Education," *National Association of Secondary-School Principals Bulletin*, 42:242 (December, 1958), p. 174. The professor in question is Dr. Joel Hildebrand. His exact statement was, "I shall not hesitate to criticize 'units' of pseudo-science, even though the unit organization is shown to be superior by 225 studies."
5. Cited in "The Secretary's Letter" of the American Association of School Administrators, March 12, 1954.
6. The critic who made the claim was Mortimer Smith in "How to Teach the California Child," *Atlantic*, 202:3 (September, 1958). Smith's misinformation was pointed out by Arthur F. Corey in "California Schools Do Educate," *Atlantic*, 202:6 (December, 1958), p. 63.
7. "What Went Wrong with U.S. Schools: An Interview with Prof. Arthur Bestor, University of Illinois," *U.S. News & World Report*, XLIV:4 (Jan. 24, 1958), p. 69.
8. Quoted in "To Protest Montgomery Curriculum," *Washington (D.C.) Post*, Sept. 10, 1948.
9. Compare the statement of one of the organizations to be discussed in Chapter V, the Montgomery Conservative Club: "We believe that the merit of the principles we champion lies in the principles themselves, and is not dependent on how the principles fare in an election or in a Gallup Poll. . . ." (The Club's "Declaration of Principles," p. 4.) Even more blatant is the statement of the Foundation for Economic Education, discussed in Chapter

VII: "Since we are convinced that right and wrong cannot be determined by a show of hands, we do not and will not advocate basing such decisions upon the vote of the majority." (From the Foundation's descriptive leaflet entitled "The Study of Freedom" [undated], p. 4.)

10. Both titles appear in *Roots of Political Behavior*, a book of readings compiled by Richard C. Snyder and H. Hubert Wilson (New York: American Book Company, 1949). Authors of the two articles named are Harvey Fergusson and Walton Hamilton, respectively.
11. House Select Committee on Lobbying Activities, *Conference of American Small Business Organizations*. House Report No. 3232, Eighty-first Congress, Second Session (Washington: United States Government Printing Office, 1950), p. 15. The "CASBO" referred to in the quotation is, of course, the organization whose name titles the report. Italics added.
12. House Select Committee on Lobbying Activities, *General Interim Report*. Eighty-first Congress, Second Session (Washington: U.S. GPO, 1950), p. 65.
13. From notes taken by observers at the annual meeting of We, The People! held in Chicago in September, 1958 (from the files of the Defense Commission).
14. This definition of a "front" group is that of the late Frank Buchanan, who was Chairman of the House Select Committee on Lobbying Activities, Eighty-first Congress. The statement is quoted from Representative Buchanan's article "Lobbying and Its Influence on the Public Schools," *The Nation's Schools*, 48:1 (July, 1951), p. 25.
15. Letter to the editor of the *Tri-Boro* (New Jersey) *News*, from Mayor John F. Doud of Hillsdale, May 23, 1956.

CHAPTER 3

1. Suggested by this citizen—Mrs. Kitty Jones—in her article "The Tenafly Story," *National Republic*, XLII:2 (June, 1954), p. 7.
2. Her support is apparent from her participation in a rally sponsored by the New Jersey Anti-Communist League. She is reported to have become active in the Englewood Anti-Communist League in 1950. By October of 1953, the names of Cartwright and Jones were so linked that a newspaper, making a specific criticism of Tenafly schools, printed a disclaimer: "This criticism has no connection with the Jones-Cartwright attacks" (*Tenafly Press-Journal*, Oct. 22, 1953).
3. Kitty Jones, "Report to Stillman Home-School Association and MacKay Home-School Association on the Columbia Public Relations Workshop" (Tenafly: Kitty Jones, April 1, 1953).
4. Kitty Jones, "What Do We Want for Our Children?" (Tenafly: Kitty Jones, May, 1953).
5. Kitty Jones, "Facts from a 'Grass-roots Citizen'" (Tenafly: Kitty Jones, September, 1953).
6. Kitty Jones, "How 'Progressive' Is Your School?" (Tenafly: Kitty Jones, September, 1953).
7. In a statement headed "What IS the Educational Aim of Our Superintendent?" The fictional administrator is a character in the book *How We Fought for Our Schools*, by Edward Darling (New York: W. W. Norton and Company, 1954).
8. Quoted in the *Northern Valley Tribune*, Jan. 29, 1954.
9. Mr. and Mrs. T. A. Jones, "Superintendent Approves Communist Works

for School Use" (Tenafly: Mr. and Mrs. T. A. Jones, Jan. 18, 1954).

10. Englewood Anti-Communist League, Frederick G. Cartwright, president; Frederick H. Grein, vice president; "Fellow Citizens" (undated). The date of distribution, however, was March 30, 1954.
11. This is the book referred to in Footnote 7.
12. According to statements quoted by Kathleen S. Backus, in "Sex Teaching Row Tied to Bond Vote," *Bergen* (County, N. J.) *Evening Record*, May 24, 1956.
13. It should be noted that Hoyt claimed his "letters were sent only to school board members and to members of the study group. He expressed surprise than any other citizen had received a printed letter."—"Regional School Defends Courses Against Surprise Attack Shortly Before Bond Issue Referendum," *Hillsdale* (N. J.) *Local*, May 24, 1956.
14. The high school has its own board of education. None of Mr. Hoyt's three children were then in schools served by this board. But Hoyt told reporters that his interest was personal, and his concern a selfish one: ". . . the high school is not good enough for his daughter who is scheduled to enter in September" (*Bergen Evening Record*, May 25, 1956).
15. See Robert Safaldo, "School Critics Like Anonymity," and "Group to Continue Sex-Education Row," *Bergen Evening Record*, May 24, 1956, and May 25, 1956, respectively.
16. Although no surname appears on the letter, which is simply addressed "Dear Joan," Mrs. Jones's address is given in the upper righthand corner. The letter is dated Sept. 17, 1956.
17. This is according to the program accompanying the invitations that bore the heading "American Seminar on Education—conducted by Mrs. Kitty Jones."
18. Arnold Forster and Benjamin Epstein, *The Troublemakers: An Anti-Defamation League Report* (Garden City, New York: Doubleday and Company, Inc., 1952), p. 78.
19. *The Tablet* (Brooklyn, N. Y.), March 9, 1957.
20. Letter to the editor from Mrs. Katherine V. Jones, *Bergen Evening Record*, May 10, 1957.
21. The article analyzed had disagreed with Holman Harvey's "Do School Pupils Need Costly Palaces?", *Reader's Digest*, 71:425 (September, 1957), pp. 37-42. Mrs. Jones's letter appeared in the *Tablet* on Dec. 21, 1957.
22. *Ibid.*
23. *Progressive Education Is REDucation* (Boston: Meador Publishing Company, 1956). Edward K. Meador runs a small publishing business under the name "Meador Publishing Company." He and his employees—reported to have totaled four in 1956—have printed such other books as Marilyn L. Allen's *Alien Minorities and Mongrelization*.
24. Lillian Boudier, "Olivier Is Reinstated by St. Landry Board," *Baton Rouge Morning Advocate*, June 9, 1957. Some time after the publication of the Olivier-Jones book, the board—now with a different membership—voted in a contested decision to reinstate him. The purpose of the reversal, plainly stated by the board, was to let Olivier complete a final year that would make him eligible for retirement. He was reinstated on condition that he was to spend this final year on sabbatical leave.
25. During her campaign for school board membership, Mrs. Jones made a public statement to the effect that school maintenance costs could be lowered and that she, owing to a "background" in engineering, was in a position

to advise how this might be accomplished. Reported by Melvin Englehardt, of the NEA Safety Commission, who was present at the gathering at which Mrs. Jones made the statement.

26. Points 1 through 8 are suggested in *Progressive Education Is REDucation*, pp. 196-197. Point 9 is suggested by the "Report to the Stillman Home-School Association and MacKay Home-School Association." Point 10 is suggested in "Is This What Is Meant by 'The Best Possible Educational Program'?" Points 11 through 16 are suggested in "How 'Progressive' Is Your School?"

CHAPTER 4

1. Statement made by Zoll to a group in Michigan. Quoted by John Bainbridge in "Save Our Schools," *McCall's*, LXXIX:12 (September, 1952), p. 84.
2. Reported by Arthur Morse in "Who's Trying to Ruin Our Schools?" *McCall's*, LXVIII:12 (September, 1951), p. 102.
3. All Guardians of American Education quotations come from the following of the group's publications: a news release entitled "Nationwide Radical Propaganda System Operating in Public Schools" (dated "For Release Monday, April 7, 1941"); an undated brochure titled "What Is It?"; and *Undermining Our Republic* (New York: Guardians of American Education, Inc., 1941).
4. According to a GAE list, these articles were: Irene C. Kuhn's "Your Child Is Their Target"; William Fulton's "Let's Look at Our Foundations"; E. Merrill Root's "Our Academic Hucksters"; Irene C. Kuhn's "Why You Buy Books That Sell Communism"; E. Merrill Root's "Smog All Around the Clock"; John T. Flynn's "Who Owns Your Child's Mind"; and J. B. Matthews' "Communism and the Colleges."
5. Augustin G. Rudd, *Bending the Twig* (Chicago: The Heritage Foundation), 1957; and Augustin G. Rudd, *Bending the Twig*, published by the New York Chapter of the Sons of the American Revolution, and printed by American Book-Stratford Press, Inc., New York, 1957. Subsequent quotes from the book are cited from the Sons of the American Revolution issue.
6. Commission on the Social Studies in the Schools, A. C. Krey, Chairman, *Conclusions and Recommendations* (New York: Charles Scribner's Sons, 1934).
7. For Rugg's own very eloquent defense and refutation of the accusations, see his *That Men May Understand* (New York: Doubleday, Doran and Company, Inc., 1941).
8. The magazine was the *Social Frontier*, later retitled *Frontiers of Democracy*.
9. According to the magazine's last editor, Harold Rugg, in *Foundations for American Education* (Yonkers-on-Hudson, N.Y.: World Book Company, Inc., 1947), p. 581.
10. The organization in question is the John Dewey Society. The membership figure cited is the estimate of Dr. I. N. Thut, who for several years following World War II served as the group's executive secretary.
11. Willard E. Givens, "Keeping the Record Straight" (two-page mimeographed correction prepared in answer to an earlier claim to this same effect, made in the Oct. 15, 1951, issue of the *Educational Reviewer*).
12. According to Dr. Givens, the claim was actually initiated even prior to 1940, by General Amos Fries, in *Bulletin of the Friends of the Public*

Schools. It was subsequently repeated by George Washington Robnett, of the Church League of America. The *Reviewer*, and later Colonel Rudd, may have taken it from either of these two sources (interview with Dr. Givens, April, 1959).

13. Quoted on an advertising sheet for *Bending the Twig*, announcing its availability from the Bookmailer, Box 101, New York 16, N. Y. Mrs. Jones's comments are stated to have appeared in the *Tablet*, June 22, 1957.
14. "For the Record," *National Review*, V:6 (Feb. 8, 1958), p. 122.
15. "Colorado Bucks the Tide," the *Nation*, Feb. 28, 1953, p. 179.
16. "Student Charges C.U. Defends 'Pro-Red' Texts." Article in unidentified, undated Denver newspaper, mailed to the Defense Commission, Dec. 22, 1953.
17. "Look Who's Here!" editorial in the *Denver Post* (undated article mailed to the Defense Commission, Dec. 22, 1953).
18. Single-page letter addressed "To Those Interested in Education," signed by Donner, dated May 12, 1952. A stamp in the upper righthand corner urges "DO NOT DESTROY—HAND TO A FRIEND."
19. Memorandum from the Defense Commission files, dated March, 1951.
20. *Ibid.* See also "The Attacks on Modern Education," *The Facts*, VI:5 (May, 1951), published by the Anti-Defamation League.
21. The House Select Committee on Lobbying Activities of the Eighty-first Congress, *General Interim Report* (Washington: U.S. GPO, 1950), p. 22.
22. Arnold Forster and Benjamin Epstein, *The Troublemakers* (New York: Doubleday and Company, Inc., 1952), p. 208.
23. Rosalie M. Gordon and Cortland G. Smith, editors, *All-American Books*, II:4 (Fall, 1956), p. 7.
24. Statement on cover of pamphlet entitled "America's Future, Inc." (New Rochelle, New York: The Corporation, undated). Statements in the pamphlet appear to suggest that it was written in 1957.
25. Rosalie M. Gordon, editor, *All-American Book Digest*, I (New Rochelle, N.Y.: America's Future, Inc., 1956).
26. New Rochelle, N.Y., America's Future, 1956. The quoted statement appears as a sort of supratitle on the pamphlet's cover.
27. First published by America's Future as a pamphlet, in 1957. (Published in book form in 1958 by Devin-Adair Company, New York.)
28. *Ibid.*, p. 20.
29. On the front cover, for example, of the pamphlet "America's Future, Inc." Proposed copy for an AF pamphlet, however, shows beyond much doubt the continuity of the two America's Future organizations. House Select Committee on Lobbying Activities, Hearings, Part V, *Committee for Constitutional Government* (Washington: U.S. GPO, 1950), p. 461.
30. *General Interim Report*, p. 51.
31. Hearings, Part V, *op. cit.*, p. 113.
32. *Ibid.*, p. 41. (Quoted from a memorandum prepared by Dr. Willford I. King, President of CCG.)
33. *General Interim Report*, p. 50.
34. Figures in this paragraph are based on a count of names listed by the NEA Research Division in a memorandum entitled "Committee for Constitutional Government" (Washington: National Education Association, January, 1951).
35. Hearings, Part V, *op. cit.*, pp. 40, 41, 122, and 131.

36. *General Interim Report*, p. 30.
37. Hearings, Part V, *op. cit.*, p. 63. (Quoted from an undated statement signed "Committee for Constitutional Government, Inc., Willford I. King, Chairman.")
38. *Ibid.*, p. 57. (Quoted from the first report submitted by Dr. King in accord with the requirement that registered lobbyists submit quarterly reports.)
39. *Ibid.*, pp. 39-40. (Quoted from a memorandum prepared by Dr. King.)
40. *Ibid.*, pp. 155 and 131.
41. *Ibid.*, p. 130.
42. *Ibid.*, p. 125.
43. Quoted in NEA Research Division memorandum, "Committee for Constitutional Government," p. 14.
44. Hearings, Part V, *op. cit.*, pp. 124-125. (Quoted by Edward Rumely, from John T. Flynn's *The Road Ahead.*)
45. "We, The People! Sponsors *Liberty Lobby*." Memorandum prepared Sept. 20, 1957, by a participant at the We, The People! convention. From the files of the Defense Commission.
46. *Ibid.*
47. San Francisco: Liberty and Property, 1957.
48. The figure is that of Gordon D. Hall. Quoted by Thomas Burke Carson in "An Evening with an Anti-Right Wing Rabble-Rouser," *National Review*, VI:12 (Nov. 8, 1958), p. 305.
49. We, The People! "Program for Freedom" (Chicago: The Association, 1957), pp. 10-11.
50. *Ibid., passim.*
51. Hearings, Part V, *op. cit.*, pp. 155-156 and 100-101.
52. John Fischer, "Gwinn and Bear It" ("The Editor's Easy Chair") *Harper's Magazine* 217:1299 (August, 1958), pp. 14-15.

CHAPTER 5

1. Attributed to Bernard De Voto by Edgar Lane, in "Educators and Lobbyists," the *Antioch Review*, XI:3 (September, 1951), reprint, p. 10.
2. The critic referred to is Professor Arthur Bestor who, in a March 22, 1952, letter to the University of Illinois' president, said: "I have never had any correspondence or other contact with groups like those sponsored by Mr. Allen A. Zoll, groups that I think can properly be characterized as enemies of public education. . . ."
3. Roger B. Farquhar, "3R's, Parents Say," *Washington* (D.C.) *Post*, March 19, 1948.
4. According to a letter to the editor from a member of the group, W. W. Barrow, *Washington Post*, May 9, 1951.
5. "Montgomery Board Receives Petition Seeking Changes in Present Curriculum," *Washington Post*, July 3, 1948.
6. "Sauter Charges School Frill: Spending Plan in Montgomery," *Washington Post*, June 5, 1948.
7. "Attorney Hits Montgomery School Books," *Washington Post*, June 16, 1948.
8. "Attorney Withdraws Textbook Charges," *Washington Post*, Aug. 11, 1948, and "Miles Reports Commie Charge," *Ibid.*, Sept. 7, 1948.
9. The group was the Silver Spring, Md., Post of the Veterans of Foreign Wars, according to an anouncement in *Washington Post*, Sept. 13, 1948.

10. "Miss Moody Reinstated—Victory for Parents," *Parents League Bulletin*, I:1 (Nov. 1, 1950).
11. According to notes taken at the meeting, March 29, 1951, in the Bethesda (Md.) County Building. From the files of the Defense Commission.
12. Geri Hoffner, "Expert Says Anti-Schools Plan Evident," *Minneapolis Tribune*, May 9, 1951.
13. "Educators Deny Attack Charges," *Baltimore Sun*, July 6, 1951.
14. Drew Pearson, "Maryland Merry-Go-Round," *Maryland News*, Oct. 15, 1954.
15. *Ibid.*
16. "Cumulative Minor Disagreements Caused School Board to Drop Norris," *Washington Post & Times Herald*, April 7, 1957.
17. "Showdown Is Expected This Week on Norris," *Washington Star*, April 7, 1957.
18. Quoted in "Citizen Group Urges Clear School Policy," *Washington Post & Times Herald*, April 9, 1957.
19. Jean Jones, "Montgomery in School Budget Trouble," *Washington Post & Times Herald*, Nov. 30, 1957.
20. Montgomery County Conservative Club, "Declaration of Principles" (undated. Distributed Jan. 30, 1958, at a meeting of the Club, according to an article titled "Anti-School Revolt Urged by Speaker," in the *Montgomery County Sentinel*, Feb. 7, 1958), p. 3.
21. The impression was created by announcements made at the meeting, according to notes taken by an observer. From the files of the Defense Commission.
22. Dorothy Waleski, "Spotlight Turns on School Group," *Montgomery County Sentinel*, Dec. 5, 1957.
23. "Anti-School Revolt Urged by Speaker," *op. cit.*
24. Quoted in "Biographies and Views of Candidates for Board of Education," compiled by the Citizens' Information Committee on School Board Elections, and printed in the *Suburban Record*, Sept. 25, 1958.
25. The School Board Elections Committee, Montgomery County Council of PTA's. Quoted in "Board's Record on 23 of 277 Resolutions Decided on Split Vote," the (Montgomery County) *Tribune*, Sept. 26, 1958.
26. "Better Schools Unit Names Yost President," *Washington Post & Times Herald*, March 21, 1959.
27. "Citizens Back Fundamental Education," *Washington Post & Times Herald*, May 10, 1960.
28. "Reese Veto Over School Money Killed," and "School Budget Power Taken from Manager," *Washington Post & Times Herald*, Sept. 30, 1959, and July 8, 1960, respectively.
29. "Giveaway School Texts Obsolete, Whittier Says," (Washington) *Evening Star*, March 7, 1959.
30. "Conservative Club" (editorial) *Montgomery County Sentinel*, Feb. 7, 1958.
31. The first and third paragraphs are quoted from the Lobbying Committee's report, *Conference of American Small Business Organizations*, pp. 14 and 16. The second paragraph appears in the Committee's *General Interim Report*, p. 36.
32. According to the reports of local residents. From a memorandum dated Nov. 17, 1957, Defense Commission Files.
33. According to reports of local residents. Defense Commission files.
34. "Report of Evaluation Committee, School District #4, Douglas County, Oregon," signed by Harold E. Schmeer, Chairman, undated.

CHAPTER 6

1. The first example is from "The Seven Deadly Dogmas of Elementary Education," *CBE Bulletin* II:7 (February, 1958), p. 9; the second is from *CBE Bulletin* III:6 (January, 1959), p. 5; the third is from "Crisis in the Colleges," *CBE Bulletin* #12 (July, 1957), p. 3.
2. "CBE Reviews," CBE Bulletin #7 (February, 1957), p. 6. The book in question is *They've Got Your Number,* by Robert Wernick (New York: W. W. Norton and Company, 1956).
3. *Descriptive Leaflet, Council for Basic Education,* p. 1 (undated, but we received a copy through the mails in December, 1958, when this revision of an earlier "descriptive leaflet" was apparently distributed.)
4. All are quoted from "The Seven Deadly Dogmas of Elementary Education," *CBE Bulletin,* II:7 (February, 1958), pp. 3ff.
5. See "Snobs, Slobs, and Shibboleths," *CBE Bulletin,* II:8 (March, 1958), p. 2.
6. Quoted from the *Descriptive Leaflet, Council for Basic Education,* pp. 1-2.
7. All statements are from *CBE Bulletins.* The book referred to, *Reading: Chaos and Cure,* is by Sibyl Terman and Charles C. Walcutt (New York: McGraw-Hill Book Company, Inc., 1958).
8. First edition of the *Descriptive Leaflet, Council for Basic Education.* Undated.
9. "Report of the Annual Meeting of the Council for Basic Education," *CBE Bulletin,* III:4 (November, 1958), p. 5.
10. *Certificate of Incorporation of Council for Basic Education,* Bylaws, Article VII, Section 3, p. 8.
11. "Report of Harold L. Clapp," *CBE Bulletin,* II:4 (November, 1957), p. 7; "Report of the Annual Meeting of the Council for Basic Education," *CBE Bulletin,* III:4 (November, 1958),p. 3; and "Report . . ." *CBE Bulletin,* IV:3 (November, 1959), p. 11.
12. In November, 1958, a CBE staff member disclaimed local affiliates. The public statement appeared in "Speaking of Names . . ." *CBE Bulletin* #8 (March, 1957), p. 11.
13. "Will You Help the Cause of Basic Education?" *CBE Bulletin,* III:6 (January, 1959). The service was advertised this way: "Do you have friends—parents, teachers, school board members—who might be interested in learning about the Council and its activities? If so, send us their names, and we will be happy to forward to them a small kit of Council material." The January, 1961, *Bulletin* adds: "Let us know if you would like to have your name used when we mail the material." (p. 8).
14. According to the following announcement on a three-page document mimeographed on CBE letterhead: "The foregoing statement was prepared for the editorial page of the *Des Moines* (Iowa) *Sunday Register,* and appeared there in slightly abridged form September 2, 1956."
15. "Report of Mortimer Smith," *CBE Bulletin,* II:4 (November, 1957), p. 13.
16. Commission for the Defense of Democracy Through Education, "The University Bookman," Information Sheet, 1960.
17. "Announcement," *CBE Bulletin,* II:10 (May, 1958), p. 4.
18. "The Council's Basic Curriculum Study and Related Plans for the Future," *CBE Bulletin,* II:12 (July, 1958), p. 1.
19. *Ibid.,* p. 3.

20. The book sanctioned is *A Fourth of a Nation* (New York: McGraw-Hill, 1957).
21. The quote is from Clifton Fadiman's article in the August, 1958, issue of *Holiday*.
22. The article, with Maxine Livingston as co-author, was entitled "More Schools for the Money." It appeared in *Parents' Magazine*, January, 1957.
23. The first article by Holman Harvey, *Reader's Digest* (September, 1957), pp. 37-42; the second article by Dorothy Thompson; and the third by Clifton Fadiman—both appeared in *Reader's Digest* (October, 1958), pp. 47-48 and 49-52.
24. "Who Is Being Unfair?" *Reader's Digest* (January, 1959), pp. 196-198, a statement by the editors of the magazine.
25. House Select Committee on Lobbying Activities, Hearings, Part VIII, *Foundation for Economic Education* (Washington: U.S. GPO, 1950), p. 185.
26. See the Committee's report, *Ibid.*, pp. 104, 182, and 183.
27. "California Again," *CBE Bulletin*, II:10 (May, 1958), p. 10. The original statement, almost identically worded, appeared in "All Is Not Gold . . ." *CBE Bulletin*, II:7 (February, 1958), p. 11.
28. "Can Good Education Be Bought?" *CBE Bulletin*, II:1 (August, 1957), p. 15 (quoted from a report of a study), and "After a Quarrel, a Proposal," *CBE Bulletin* #12 (July, 1957), p. 12. (Quoted from a Bestor article—and, through repetition, compounding the logical error therein.)
29. "Scholarship and Federal Aid," *CBE Bulletin*, III:1 (August, 1958), p. 10. The individual quoted is John R. Stalnaker, president of the National Merit Scholarship Corporation.
30. *Human Events*, XV:2 (January 13, 1958), p. 4.
31. Chamber of Commerce of the United States, "Editorial Comment on: Defeat of Proposed Federal Intervention in Schools Construction; Local and State Responsibility for Meeting School Needs" (undated).
32. "Tax Groups Blast U.S. School Aid," *Washington Post & Times Herald*, April 21, 1955.
33. National Commission for the Defense of Democracy Through Education, *Institute for Social Science Research, American Enterprise Association, Inc., and Roger Freeman*. Defense Circular No. 3 (Washington: The Commission, undated), p. 1.
34. Drew Pearson, "Weeks Contrasts with Cabinet" ("Washington Merry-Go-Round"), *The Washington Post*, Jan. 17, 1953.
35. By George C. S. Benson and John M. Payne (Washington: American Enterprise Association, Inc., May, 1958).
36. See, for example, "Can Our Schools Get by with Less? A Critical Review of Roger A. Freeman's *School Needs in the Decade Ahead*" (Washington: National Education Association, October, 1958).
37. The three paragraphs quoted are from pages 28, xxvii, and xxvi, respectively, *School Needs in the Decade Ahead.*
38. *Human Events*, XV:43 (Oct. 27, 1958).
39. "Freeman Study on School Needs," *NEA Journal*, 47:6 (September, 1958), p. 356.
40. Honorable Ralph W. Gwinn, "Propaganda for Federal Aid to Education Exposed and Exploded," *Congressional Record*, Appendix, pp. A8208 and A8210.

41. *CBE Bulletin*, II:12 (July, 1958), p. 13.
42. "Prof. Else to Take Part in Study of Curriculum," *Ann Arbor* (Michigan) *News*, July 10, 1958.

CHAPTER 7

1. The sum of $114,000 was promised initially; an additional $15,000 was provided in the spring of 1957, according to the report of CBE's first executive secretary; $100,000 was promised for general operation in 1959 (some of which is doubtlessly represented in the initial $114,000 promise); and an additional $15,000 was promised to finance the citizens' manual mentioned earlier, according to the 1958 report of CBE's treasurer.
2. Robert Skaife, "Neo-Conservatives Are on the March with 'Sound Education' as Battle Cry," *Nation's Schools*, 59:5 (May, 1957), p. 55.
3. Reported by the Fund to Wilmer S. Rich, for *American Foundations and Their Fields* (New York: American Foundations Information Service, 1955). Quoted in the Seventh Edition, p. 42.
4. National Commission for the Defense of Democracy Through Education, *Institute for Social Science Research, American Enterprise Association, Inc., and Roger Freeman*, Defense Circular No. 3. (Washington: The Commission, undated), p. 7.
5. House Select Committee on Lobbying Activities, Eighty-First Congress, Second Session, Hearings, Part VIII, *Foundation for Economic Education* (Washington: U.S. GPO, 1950), p. 12. ($80,000 of this sum was reportedly a loan.)
6. House Select Committee on Lobbying Activities, Eighty-first Congress, Second Session, Hearings, Part IV, *National Economic Council* (Washington: U.S. GPO, 1950), p. 133.
7. According to the quarterly financial reports filed by registered lobbying organizations, plus contributions not reported but discovered by the Lobbying Committee, the National Economic Council received $32,453.74, between 1947 and 1950, from the Volker Fund (and/or William Volker and Company). During the same period, Mr. Lammont DuPont contributed $34,513.50 (Hearings, Part IV, pp. 161 and 157, respectively).
8. House Select Committee on Lobbying Activities, Eighty-first Congress, Second Session, *General Interim Report* (Washington: U.S. GPO, 1950), p. 50.
9. *Ibid.*
10. Hearings, Part VIII, pp. 111 and 113.
11. We have not, as it well may appear, ridden roughshod over these replies and distorted them. One may discover this for himself by reading the four letters and the memorandum appearing on pages 134-138 of the Hearings, Part VIII.
12. Hearings, Part VIII, p. 3. (Quoted from the 1950-1951 edition of FEE's *Some Facts About the Foundation for Economic Education.*)
13. Foundations for Economic Education, "The Study of Freedom" (undated), p. 2.
14. The two articles were written by T. Robert Ingram and August W. Brustat, respectively. They appeared in the November, 1957, and May, 1956, issues of the *Freeman*.
15. Excerpted from pages 2-4 of a reprint from the *Freeman*, titled "Today's School 'Problem'" by Bettina Bien of the FEE Staff (September, 1957, issue). Quoted passages are not consecutive in the original.

16. Quoted by Robert A. Skaife, in a speech entitled "The Enemies and the Critics of the Schools—Their Current Efforts," delivered at the NEA Convention, June 29, 1954 (p. 2.).
17. See minutes of annual meeting, May 14, 1946. Hearings, Part VIII, p. 27. (FEE was incorporated in March, 1946.)
18. Hearings, Part VIII, p. 129.
19. *Ibid.*, pp. 129, 166, 167, 168.
20. *Ibid.*, p. 92.
21. *Ibid.*, p. 35.
22. In a memorandum describing a conference with Mr. Luhnow. Hearings, Part IV, p. 238.
23. The anticipations are revealed in a letter written by the FEE president. (Hearings, Part VIII, p. 50) It is impossible to know what contributions and purchases have been made subsequent to July, 1950, when these hearings took place. The recipient (FEE) is not a registered lobbying organization, so contributions are not listed with Congress. (Even if it *were* a registered group, the total—but not the *sources*—of contributions over $500 would be all the information published in the *Congressional Record.*) The only other source of information would be the *American Foundation News.* Insofar as this periodical is an indication, the Volker Fund seems to have followed consistently the principle of not "mixing personal publicity with charity."
24. Gene Grove, "Inside the John Birch Society," I, *New York Post,* May 22, 1961; and Maxine Block, editor, "Hart, Merwin K(imball)," *Current Biography,* Second Annual Compilation (New York: H. W. Wilson Company, 1941), pp. 368-369.
25. In "The Attacks on Modern Education" (*The Facts,* VI:5, May 1951), the Anti-Defamation League reported, "This Hart group has not been active for some time. . . ." (p. 1). In "They Sow Distrust" (*Nation's Schools,* 47:1 January, 1951) Robert A. Skaife reported that the Parents' Council "acted as a distributing agency for literature prepared by Merwin K. Hart, Maj. Augustin G. Rudd, and others" (p. 28).
26. Hearings, Part IV, p. 96.
27. *Ibid.*, pp. 60-61. In his testimony before the House Lobbying Committee, NEC President Hart approved a list of stands as an accurate summary of his organization's lobbying interests. The list was compiled from an analysis of various NEC statements. The stands we have listed were excerpted from the lengthy summary compiled by the Lobbying Committee staff.
28. Anti-Defamation League, *op. cit.*, p. 1.
29. See Merwin K. Hart, "Palestine—Chapter III: The Conquest of Zion," *Economic Council Letter* No. 186 (March 1, 1948), p. 2.
30. Merwin K. Hart, "The Eichmann Trial," *Economic Council Letter* No. 501 (April 15, 1961), pp. 3-4. Quoted passages not consecutive in the original. The publishing body, the National Economic Council, Inc., requests that its address be cited along with quotations from the *Economic Council Letter.* The council's current address, therefore, is The Empire State Building, New York 1, N.Y.
31. The six titles listed are, respectively, those of the following issues of the *Economic Council Letter:* No. 414 (Sept. 1, 1957); No. 408 (June 1, 1957); No. 403 (March 15, 1957; it should be noted that this issue was prepared by Rosalie Gordon, Secretary of America's Future); No. 338 (July 1, 1954); No. 357 (April 15, 1955); and No. 437 (Aug. 15, 1958).

32. It should be noted that it is not clear in all gifts and/or purchases whether the money comes from the William Volker Fund or William Volker and Company. NEC President Hart reported checks from both organizations (Hearings, Part IV, p. 133).
33. Merwin K. Hart, "Now Make Us a King," *Economic Council Letter* No. 162 (March 1, 1947), p. 1.
34. *Ibid.*, p. 4.
35. Rose Wilder Lane, editor, *Economic Council Review of Books*, IV:3 (March, 1947).
36. Merwin K. Hart, "Political Medicine," *Economic Council Letter* No. 206 (Jan. 1, 1949), p. 3; Merwin K. Hart, "The Impending Battle of Capitol Hill," *Economic Council Letter* No. 204 (Dec. 1, 1948); Rose Wilder Lane, editor, *Economic Council Review of Books*, VI:2 (February, 1949), pp. 1 and 4; Merwin K. Hart, "This Business of 'World Government,'" *Economic Council Letter* No. 216 (June 1, 1949), p. 4; Rose Wilder Lane, editor, *Economic Council Review of Books*, VI:6 (June, 1949), p. 4; Merwin K. Hart, "Who Is Looking Out for Capital?" *Economic Council Letter* No. 208 (Feb. 1, 1949).
37. The author of the first mentioned is Sir Ernest Benn. NEC apparently published the American edition of the pamphlet. (See *Economic Council Review of Books*, VI:3, March, 1949, p. 4.) Cecil Palmer wrote the second publication. It was apparently available from NEC. (See Hearings, Part IV, p. 456.)
38. See Hearings, Part IV, pp. 389-392 and 452-453.
39. *Ibid.*, p. 133.
40. Harold W. Knight, "Whooping It Up for Adam Smith," *Nation*, 175 (Aug. 2, 1952), p. 88; Cabell Phillips, "Wide Anti-Red Drive Directed from Small Town in Arkansas," *New York Times*, May 18, 1961; "Meet the Press," May 21, 1961 (Washington: Merkle Press, Inc.); and Murray Illson, "Norman Thomas Hits Birch Group," *New York Times*, April 20, 1961.
41. Philip S. Rose, "Arkansas Crusader," *Saturday Evening Post*, 216, Part 4 (June 3, 1944), p. 19.
42. Knight, *op. cit.*, p. 87.
43. *Ibid.*, p. 89.
44. "Forty-three on Policy Unit of 'For America,'" *New York Times*, Nov. 14, 1954.
45. George S. Benson, "Arkansas, a Relatively 'Poor' State, Can and Should Get Along by Herself," *Congressional Digest*, XXV:2 (February, 1946), p. 45.
46. George S. Benson, "Extract from a Statement Filed with the House Committee on Education and Labor," *Congressional Digest* XXVIII:11 (November, 1949), p. 287. (The equating of a socialist economy with a totalitarian political system—very marked in the second of these quotations—is not unusual in the circles Dr. Benson frequents.)
47. "Matters Financial," *CBE Bulletin*, IV:1 (September, 1959), p. 6.
48. "Prof. Else to Take Part in Study of Curriculum," *Ann Arbor* (Michigan), *News*, July 10, 1958.
49. Another advantage and attraction of this plan which seems clear time and again from testimony at the Hearings is that it provided for donor anonymity. Under the Lobbying Act of 1946, grantees must report the amount and source of any contribution in excess of $500. But if $10,000 is received for *purchases*, as many of these organizations interpreted the Lobbying Act

they were not required to report the sum or its source. In fact, the executive secretary of the Committee for Constitutional Government refused to provide the Lobbying Committee with the names of purchasers of mass quantities on the grounds that this violated CCG's rights, as a *publisher*, under the Bill of Rights. (Dr. Rumely was cited for contempt, for this refusal.) (See the following pages of the Hearings, Part V, *Committee for Constitutional Government:* 45, 167-168, 170, 171, 253, 271-273, and 485.)

50. Hearings, Part IV, pp. 120-121, 93, 157.
51. Hearings, Part VIII, p. 13. Although the "Earhart Foundation" is separate and distinct from the Relm Foundation, and was established 31 years prior to the latter, the two have certain features in common:
    1. All officers of the two foundations are identical (Wilmer Rich, *op. cit.*, pp. 238 and 254).
    2. Both are housed in the same building (*Ibid.*).
    3. According to a statement of Richard Earhart, who is credited with having established the Relm Foundation (and whose initials, along with those of the co-founder, are generally thought to have produced the name RE LM), the funds for both foundations come from the same source (Defense Commission files).
52. National Commission for the Defense of Democracy Through Education, *op. cit.*, p. 7.
53. *American Foundation News*, VII:1 (September 15, 1958), p. 4.
54. Reported in an NEA Information Center "Memo from New York," dated March-April, 1960, p. 3.
55. "Report of the Annual Meeting of the Council for Basic Education," CBE *Bulletin*, IV:3 (November, 1959), p. 12.
56. "Public Education and Free Enterprise," *CBE Leaflet No. 5*, undated.

CHAPTER 8

1. America's Future, Inc., "Textbook Evaluation Committee" (undated), p. 3. Subsequent quotations not otherwise noted also are taken from this prospectus.
2. *Ibid.* Here again it seems to be suggested that parents and teachers too have been tainted, and, as products of this educational system, cannot judge things for themselves—*ergo*, the need for someone to do it for them. Compare this with the similar Council for Basic Education implication cited on page 87. An earlier textbook review group—still another ideological predecessor of the AF Committee—also stressed the esoteric problems in distinguishing the subversive from the nonsubversive. Its sponsor, Allen Zoll, is said to have reported in all seriousness, "'Once . . . we had to have a book reviewed eight times before we got a good analysis.'" (Quoted by Arthur D. Morse, in "Who's Trying to Ruin Our Schools?" *McCall's*, LXVIII:12, September, 1951, p. 102.)
3. "An Interim Report," *America's Future: A Weekly Review of News, Books and Public Affairs*, II:23 (June 3, 1960), p. 7.
4. See Russell Kirk's *Textbook Evaluation on "Magruder's American Government," revised by William A. McClenaghan* (New Rochelle: America's Future, Inc., Feb. 19, 1960), p. 1; and A. H. Hobbs' *Textbook Evaluation Report on "Social Living," by Paul H. Landis* (New Rochelle: America's Future, Inc., May 27, 1960), p. 1. Professor Hobbs begins with the statement, "When Mr. Jack Schwartzman reviewed the 1949 edition of this

textbook . . ." Mr. Schwartzman's review appeared in the July 15, 1951, issue of the *Educational Reviewer* (III:1), pp. 4-6.

5. Quotations are taken from the following reviews respectively: Medford Evans, *Textbook Evaluation Report on "American Problems Today," (Second Edition). By Robert Rienow* (New Rochelle: America's Future, Inc., Jan. 12, 1960), p. 1; Charles Callan Tansill, *Textbook Evaluation Report on "National Governments and International Relations." By Frank A. Magruder* (New Rochelle: America's Future, Inc., Nov. 23, 1959), p. 3; Neil Carothers, *Textbook Evaluation Report on "Man, Money and Goods" by John S. Gambs* (New Rochelle: America's Future, Inc., Sept. 23, 1959), p. 3; Marie R. Madden, *Textbook Evaluation Report on "Economics and You." By Sol Holt* (New Rochelle: America's Future, Inc., June 9, 1960), p. 5.
6. "An Interim Report," *op. cit.*, pp. 6-7.
7. *Ibid.*, and *Progress Report "Operation Textbook"* published by America's Future, Inc., pp. 5-6 (New Rochelle: The Corporation, undated).
8. E. Merrill Root, *Textbook Evaluation Report on "Guide to Modern English." By Richard K. Corbin and Porter G. Perrin* (New Rochelle: America's Future, Inc., Dec. 4, 1959), p. 1.
9. "Textbook Evaluation Committee," p. 9.
10. *The Minute Women of the U.S.A., Inc.*, No. 30 (September-October, 1958), p. 1.
11. Farrar and Rinehart, 1934.
12. "Bimetallism," *Experimenting with Our Money*, pp. 9 and 14.
13. "Who Profits by Inflation?" *Experimenting with Our Money*, pp. 16, 21, and 22.
14. Reported in *National Review*, VIII:19 (May 7, 1960), p. 290.
15. "Insubstantial Pageant," *National Review*, V:11 (March 15, 1958), pp. 253-255.
16. Medford Evans, "Why I Am an Anti-Intellectual," *Human Events*, XIV:4 (Jan. 26, 1957). (We have not just inferred these traits. A form of each term we cite is specifically used by Dr. Evans in his article.)
17. "An Open Letter to Dr. Oppenheimer," *National Review*, III:10 (March 9, 1957), pp. 225-235.
18. William Cuthbert Brady, "Conservatives Debate on Oppenheimer at Harvard." Quoted in the *Congressional Record* for June, 1958 (Washington: United States Government Printing Office, 1958), Appendix, pp. A5339 and A5340.
19. "The Editors of NATIONAL REVIEW Believe:" *National Review*, I:1 (Nov. 19, 1955), p. 8.
20. By John Fischer, "Why Is the Conservative Voice So Hoarse?" ("The Editor's Easy Chair") *Harper's Magazine*, 212:1270 (March, 1956), p. 20.
21. "The Liberal Line . . ." *National Review*, I:10 (Jan. 25, 1956), p. 10. The two premises quoted are not consecutively stated in the original.
22. "What Are We Going to Do with the Willmoore Kendalls?" ("The Ivory Tower") *National Review*, IV:22 (Dec. 7, 1957), p. 521.
23. *National Review*, IV:9 (September, 1957), p. 212.
24. *Ibid.* (The book alluded to is John Wesley's *NEA: The First Hundred Years*, New York: Harper & Brothers, 1957).
25. "Lenin and the Naked Ladies. Part II" ("From the Academy") *National Review*, IV:12 (Sept. 28, 1957), p. 280.

26. *Academic Freedom* (Chicago: Henry Regnery Company, 1955), p. 42.
27. "Lenin and the Naked Ladies. Part II," *op. cit.*, p. 280.
28. "The New School" ("From the Academy"), *National Review,* V:1 (Jan. 4, 1958), p. 18.
29. The quotations appear in Kirk's "From the Academy" column: "Totalitarian Liberalism at MSU," *National Review,* IX:8 (Aug. 27, 1960), p. 117; "Behold Behemoth," *National Review,* I:11 (Feb. 1, 1956), p. 24, and "Universities or Matrimonial Bureaus," *National Review,* V:23 (June 7, 1958), p. 545.
30. The four quotations appear, respectively, in the following "From the Academy" columns: "The New School," *op. cit.*, p. 18; "School Libraries," *National Review,* V:15 (April 12, 1958), p. 353; "Riverside Restoration," *National Review,* I:3 (Dec. 7, 1955), p. 25; and "Accreditation," *National Review,* III:13 (March 30, 1957), p. 308.
31. "Macauleyflowers" ("From the Academy") *National Review,* IV:14 (Oct. 12, 1957), p. 330.
32. William Montgomery McGovern and David S. Collier (Chicago: Henry Regnery Company, 1957).
33. *Ibid.*, p. 10.
34. *Ibid.*, p. 16. (In the interests of accuracy, it should be noted that we have quoted the full statement of *neither* the radical nor the conservative position.)
35. *Ibid.*, p. 26.
36. According to Revilo Oliver, in *National Review,* III:8 (Feb. 23, 1957), p. 181.
37. According to Owen Frisby, then a member of the Northwestern chapter, in " 'Students for America,' " *National Review,* XLII:5 (September, 1954), pp. 5-6.
38. The label is quoted by Robert A. Skaife, in "The Conflict Continues," *Nation's Schools,* 53:3 (March, 1954), pp. 45-46. It is credited to the University of Virginia's *Cavalier Daily.*
39. Mr. and Mrs. Theodore A. Jones. "Is This What Is Meant by 'The Best Possible Educational Program'?" (Tenafly: Mr. and Mrs. Theodore A. Jones, October, 1953), p. 8.
40. E. Merrill Root, *Collectivism on the Campus* (New York: The Devin-Adair Company, 1955) and *Brainwashing in the High Schools* (New York: The Devin-Adair Company, 1958).
41. *Brainwashing in the High Schools,* p. 10.
42. *Ibid.*, p. 263. (Italics in the original.)
43. *Ibid.*
44. "False Statements about Evanston Township High School, found in *Brainwashing in the High Schools,* Devin-Adair, 1958," undated.
45. See, respectively, John H. Haefner, "Attack on Evanston Texts Found to Be Unfair, Unfrank," *Chicago Sun-Times,* Nov. 23, 1958, and *Brainwashing in the High Schools,* by E. Merrill Root, Devin-Adair, the *Christian Century,* Jan. 28, 1959.
46. "Poet Out of His Age," *National Review,* V:14 (April 5, 1958), p. 330. (Root's review of Roy Campbell's *Collected Poems,* Chicago: Henry Regnery, 1958).
47. "Speakers Rap 'Collectivism' in Education," *Evening World-Herald* (Omaha, Neb.), Oct. 1, 1953.

48. According to a letter of Jan. 27, 1959, to this writer, on the letterhead of the Citizens' Foreign Relations Committee.
49. According to Robert J. Donovan in "John Birch Society Accused: Charge That Eisenhower Is a Red Roils Congress," *New York Herald Tribune*, March 31, 1961.
50. Harrisburg, Pa.: The Stackpole Company, 1951.
51. *Collectivism on the Campus*, p. 245.
52. Dr. George Benson, for example, devoted four issues of his column "Looking Ahead," to Dr. Hobbs's book. (Prepared for Aug. 12, 19, 26, and Sept. 2, 1953, according to copies sent us by the author.)
53. *The Claims of Sociology*, p. 9.
54. *Ibid.*, p. 11 (italics in the original).
55. *Ibid.*, p. 7.
56. Harrisburg, Pa.: The Stackpole Company, 1953.
57. *Social Problems and Scientism*, p. 406.
58. *Collectivism on the Campus*, pp. 323, 329, and 330.
59. Root's criticism appears in *Brainwashing in the High Schools*, p. 226. Professor Tansill's *Back Door to War* was published by the Henry Regnery Company of Chicago, in 1952.
60. See Don Olesen, in "GU Disavows Tansill's Race Talk," *Washington Post & Times Herald*, Oct. 19, 1955. Cf. a release from the Religious News Service, "Georgetown to Act Against Negro-Hating Professor," dated Oct. 21, 1955.
61. Religious News Service, *op. cit.*
62. Quoted by Anne Crutcher in a letter to the editor of the *Washington Post & Times Herald*, Oct. 18, 1955.
63. According to D. H. Wilson in a letter to the editor of the *Washington Post & Times Herald*, Oct. 27, 1955.
64. Olesen, *op. cit.*
65. *Ibid.*
66. New York: W. Neale, 1933.
67. Quoted in NEA Research Division memorandum, "Operation America, Inc." (Washington: NEA, Dec., 1953), from Operation America's *Report No.* 3 of July 10, 1952.
68. *Ibid.* Also taken from *Report No.* 3.
69. NEA Research Division, *op. cit.* Cited from Operation America *Report No.* 7, Aug. 4, 1952, p. 1; and "Members of Two Parties Weigh Plan for Third," *Chicago Tribune*, Aug. 8, 1952.
70. John Bainbridge, "Danger's Ahead in the Public Schools," *McCall's*, LXXX:1 (October, 1952), p. 116. (Mr. Bainbridge quotes Mrs. Suzanne Silvercruys Stevenson, founder of the organization.)
71. *Ibid.* The statement also appears in an article titled "The Major Objectives of the Minute Women," in the February, 1951, issue of the organization's newsletter, *The Minute Women of America, Inc.* Reprinted in a "Series of Reports" taken from the *Houston Post* (issues of Oct. 11-28, 1953), p. 1.
72. According to Ralph O'Leary, in the *Houston Post*, *op. cit.* (Article titled "Caller Tipped Search for an 'Example,'" p. 6.)
73. "Dr. Ella Lonn Joins Consulting Staff," *Educational Reviewer*, IV:2 (Oct. 15, 1952), p. 8.
74. We have been unable to find a statement of the official function of the consulting staff. This function has been inferred from the occasional state-

ment, following a review, that "The above review of——— is not approved by———, of the Consulting Staff." (See, e.g., *Educational Reviewer* III:4, April 15, 1952, p. 9.)

75. Published by New York's Fordham University Press, in 1930. The foreword quoted (pp. ix-x) was written by Moorhouse I. X. Millar, S.J. (Father Millar credits the quotation, from which we have quoted excerpts only, to Holdsworth, in *Some Lessons from Our Legal History.*)
76. *Educational Reviewer,* IV:2 (Oct. 15, 1952), p. 3. (The subject of Dr. Madden's review is *The American Way of Business—The Role of Government in a System of Free Enterprise.* Problems in American Life Series, Unit No. 20, NEA. The authors are Oscar Lange, Abba P. Lerner, and Archie W. Troelstrup.)
77. *Educational Reviewer,* III:4 (April 15, 1952), pp. 7 and 9. (The subject of Dr. Madden's review is *Politics in Action: The Problems of Representative Government.* Problems in American Life Series, Unit No. 18, NEA. The authors are Arthur N. Holcombe and James E. Downes.)
78. "The State of the Nation," *Nation's Business,* 45:4 (April, 1957), pp. 23-24.
79. "This Session Tests Congress' Belief in Democracy" ("The State of the Nation") *Nation's Business,* 47:2 (February, 1959), p. 26.
80. "The State of the Nation" *Nation's Business* 44:1 (January, 1956), pp. 17-18.
81. "The State of the Nation" *Nation's Business* 46:9 (September, 1958), p. 23.
82. *Ibid.* and "This Session Tests Congress' Belief in Democracy," *op. cit.,* p. 26.
83. According to Harvey H. Springer, in an article titled "Dr. J. B. Matthews' Subject to Be 'Christ and Communism' at I.C.C.C. Congress in Brazil," the *Western Voice,* XXII:5 (Aug. 7, 1958), p. 1.
84. "Communism and the Protestant Clergy," *Look,* 17:23 (Nov. 17, 1953). (The statement was the opening sentence of an article Dr. Matthews wrote for the *American Mercury.*)
85. Gordon D. Hall, "How Reliable Is Protestantism's Accuser?" *Christian Register,* 132 (November, 1953), p. 16.
86. Paul Hutchinson, "The J. B. Matthews Story," the *Christian Century,* 70, Part 2 (July 29, 1953), p. 865.
87. *Ibid.*
88. Springer, *op. cit.*
89. The book is Matthews's *Partners in Plunder* (New York: Covici, Friede, 1935.)
90. House Select Committee on Lobbying Activities, *Conference of American Small Business Organizations.* Report of the Committee, the Eighty-first Congress, Second Session (U.S. GPO, 1950), p. 15.
91. *Ibid.,* p. 3. (Quoted from CASBO's letterhead.)
92. *Ibid.,* p. 55. (Quoted from an article titled "A Declaration," in the *Educational Reviewer,* I:1, July 15, 1949.)
93. Reported by Robert A. Skaife in "They Want Tailored Schools," the *Nation's Schools,* 47:5 (May, 1951), p. 37.
94. "School Committee Examines Textbook Reviews," the *Nation's Schools,* 48:4 (October, 1951), pp. 110-112.
95. "Speakers Rap 'Collectivism' in Education," *op. cit.*
96. In an address delivered by Mrs. Crain at the May 6, 1953, meeting of the Freedom Club of Downtown Chicago, according to notes taken at the meeting. From the files of the Defense Commission.

97. Arthur D. Morse, "Who's Trying to Ruin Our Schools?" *McCall's*, LXVIII:12 (September, 1951), p. 109.
98. Robert J. Donovan, *op. cit.*
99. "An Interim Report," *op. cit.*, p. 6.
100. *Ibid.*
101. "George A. Membrez, Jr.: Biographical *Fact Sheet,* 1960." National Commission for the Defense of Democracy Through Education, December, 1960.
102. Hans F. Sennholz, "The Phantom Called 'Monopoly,'" the *Freeman,* X:3 (March, 1960), pp. 39-40 and 46.
103. The quotations are taken from the following of Dr. Sennholz' articles, respectively: Hans F. Sennholz, "Slums and Mansions," the *Freeman,* VIII:8 (August, 1958), p. 28; "In Another Recession," the *Freeman,* VIII:4 (April, 1958), p. 7; and "The European Economic Community," the *Freeman,* X:1 (January, 1960), p. 57.
104. Anthony Trawick Bouscaren, "Immigration Policy Too Lenient Toward the Enemy," *The Cross and the Flag,* (February, 1960), p. 4.
105. Published by Henry Regnery, 1958.
106. Rosalie Gordon, "Before It Is Too Late," *America's Future: A Weekly Review of News, Books and Public Affairs,* 1:5 (April 17, 1959), p. 6.
107. Anthony T. Bouscaren, "The UN Congratulates Itself," the *Freeman,* V:14 (August, 1955), p. 607.
108. Anthony T. Bouscaren, "Can Anyone Strike Back?" *National Review,* 1:15 (Feb. 29, 1956), p. 19.
109. Anthony T. Bouscaren, "The Double Standard in Education," the *Freeman,* V:12 (June, 1955), p. 519.

CHAPTER 9

1. For this and other features of the committee's investigation, see the address of Robert M. Hutchins to the National Press Club, Washington, D.C., Jan. 26, 1955. (Mimeographed copies distributed by the Fund for the Republic.)
2. Fred M. Hechinger, "Education 1954-55: A Newscast," *The Saturday Review,* XXXVII:37 (Sept. 11, 1954), p. 21.
3. States in which there have been moves to reduce professional requirements include New York, Michigan, Indiana, and Virginia. The last-named is the state that considered abolishing them altogether, according to a gleeful and detailed account entitled "Another Bright Spot," *CBE Bulletin,* II:9 (April, 1958), p. 3.
4. See, e.g., the story in *Life,* 29:24 (Dec. 11, 1950), pp. 95-96.
5. National Commission for the Defense of Democracy Through Education, *The Pasadena Story* (Washington: National Education Association, June, 1951); and David Hulburd, *This Happened in Pasadena* (New York: The Macmillan Company, 1951).
6. National Commission for the Defense of Democracy Through Education, *Houston, Texas: A Study of Factors Related to Educational Unrest in a Large School System* (Washington: National Education Association, December, 1954), p. 16. The book in question was Frank Magruder's *American Government.*
7. *Ibid.* The speakers were Clarence Streit and Stringfellow Barr.
8. Commission for the Defense of Democracy Through Education, "State of the Nation in Regard to Attacks on the Schools and Problems of Concern

to Teachers" (Washington: National Education Association, December, 1955).

9. See, e.g., Robert M. Hutchins, "Are Our Teachers Afraid to Teach?" *Look* (March 9, 1954). The Hutchins article was substantiated by a survey of 72 colleges, which reported faculty unwillingness to speak out on controversial issues, for fear of professional reprisals. (*New York Times,* May 10, 1951.) More recently, the same sort of situation has been suggested in an extensive study made by Paul Lazarsfeld and Wagner Thielens, Jr. See *The Academic Mind* (Glencoe, Ill.: The Free Press, 1958).
10. Springfield, Mo., is one of the communities in which the core program—frequent victim of critics' demands—was all but eliminated following vigorous attack. Los Angeles is one of a number of communities where content related to the United Nations and to Communism has been dropped from social studies courses following criticism. Recently, the most noticeable change in methods to follow critics' demands has been the return in many communities to the phonetic introduction of reading instruction.
11. John Bainbridge, "Danger's Ahead in the Public Schools," *McCall's,* LXXX:1 (October, 1952), pp. 98 and 108. The town was Sapulpa.
12. See the charges against Olivier, quoted in *Progressive Education Is REDucation,* p. 178.
13. Defense Commission, *Houston, Texas . . . ,* p. 47. The quotes are from a stenographic record of a Sept. 9, 1953, broadcast by Joe Worthy, on "Worthy Speaks Out."
14. Report in the *New York Times,* May 10, 1951.
15. Fay L. Corey, *Values of Future Teachers: A Study of Attitudes Toward Contemporary Issues* (New York: Teachers College, Columbia University, 1955), p. 122.
16. August J. Wiesner, Jr., "Englewood, N.J." *The Public-School Crisis* (reprinted from *The Saturday Review of Literature,* Sept. 8, 1951), p. 4.
17. John Bainbridge, "Save Our Schools!" *McCall's,* LXXIX:12 (September, 1952), p. 104.
18. "Proposed National Commission on the Defense of Democracy Through Education," *National Education Association Addresses and Proceedings,* 79 (Washington: The Association, 1941), p. 778.
19. Harold C. Hand and Charles W. Sanford, in *The Bulletin of the National Association of Secondary-School Principals,* XXXVII:194 (April, 1953), pp. 460-488.
20. Aside from the obvious academic allusions intended in the titles of the early Bestor and Bestor-inspired pronouncements, the student of wit or behavior should be able to find aspects of significance in this assortment: "The Emperor's New Clothes, or *Prius Dementat*" (Speech by Professor Harry Fuller, May 10, 1950); "The Bewildered Botanist, or Academic *Envoûtement*" (Dean Willard Spaulding's reply to Fuller, Jan. 8, 1952); "Aimlessness in Education, or, *Ex Nihilo Nihil Fit*" (speech by Professor Arthur Bestor, Feb. 7, 1952).
21. William Clark Trow, "Academic Utopia? An Evaluation of *Educational Wastelands,*" *Educational Theory,* IV:1 (January, 1954), pp. 16-17.
22. Arthur D. Morse, "Who's Trying to Ruin Our Schools?" *McCall's,* LXVIII:12 (September, 1951), p. 102. Interestingly, Zoll prepared a 12-page "Confidential—Not for Publication or Distribution" memorandum ("An

Analysis by Allen A. Zoll of the article entitled 'Who's Trying to Ruin Our Schools?' " undated), denying the numerous allegations of Morse, and at one point loyally defending his alma mater. But Zoll never filed suit for libel against Morse or *McCall's*—and certainly many of Morse's allegations might well have been libelous if false. It is possible that Zoll was awaiting the decision in a suit filed against *McCall's* by Mrs. Lucille Cardin Crain, based on the Morse article. Mrs. Crain lost the suit. The decision for the magazine, handed down in this case late in 1955, augured ill for the plan to sue which Zoll had announced in his confidential memo.

23. See Robert A. Skaife's article, "They Oppose Progress," the *Nation's Schools* 47:2 (February, 1951), pp. 31-33, for details on these three charges.
24. Both quoted statements appear as headings in Zoll's pamphlet "Progressive Education Increases Delinquency" (New York: National Council for American Education, undated), pp. 2 and 9.
25. George E. Axtelle, "Public Relations and Educational Statesmanship: Next Steps," *Progressive Education*, 27-28 (May, 1951), pp. 214-216. That there is much to be said for Professor Axtelle's point of view is underscored by the way in which industrial public relations methods were apparently translated in some locales. Hamlin tells that within the framework of public relations, many schools concentrated on obtaining community support through the athletic program: the production of bigger and better teams as an avenue to public support and approval (Herbert M. Hamlin, *Citizens' Committees in the Public Schools,* Danville, Ill.: The Interstate Printing Company, 1952, p. 7).
26. Differences in the means appropriate to replying to criticisms of the earlier and later period can be partially illustrated by the changing emphases of the only national organization established primarily to meet attacks: the NEA's Defense Commission. Instead of the many articles prepared earlier to expose the background and methods of critics, commission efforts are now more often devoted to investigating problems arising within a school system itself (in contrast to troubles stemming from public criticism). On the whole, the Commission has said little in reply to individual Bestor-type charges—possibly owing to the fact that professors of education, as major targets of the academically oriented charges, have themselves stepped forth in considerable number to reply.
27. Writing in early 1954, Dr. Skaife reported the National Council for American Education "dormant," the *Educational Reviewer* discontinued, and the *Bulletin* of the Friends of the Public Schools no longer being issued. Robert A. Skaife, "The Conflict Continues," the *Nation's Schools,* 53:3 (March, 1954), pp. 44-49.
28. The Defense Commission had taken this position from the start (See *Defense Bulletin* No. 38, February, 1951, p. 3). For more recent urgings to the same effect, see, e.g., the articles of B. C. Willis ("Using the Criticism of Public Schools for Constructive Purposes," *Elementary School Journal,* 55: September, 1954, pp. 13-23); B. C. Korn ("Answering the Critic," *Wisconsin Journal of Education,* 17: November, 1956, p. 7); and M. S. Marshall ("Criticisms of Education," *Science Education,* March 1957, pp. 154-160).

CHAPTER 10

1. John T. Flynn, "To Get Rich Scare the Rich" ("Other People's Money"),

New Republic, LXXXVIII:1136 (Sept. 9, 1936), p. 129. The two paragraphs are not consecutive in the original.

2. For details of these and other Zoll activities, see Arnold Forster, *A Measure of Freedom* (Garden City, New York: Doubleday and Company, Inc., 1950), pp. 74-79, and Robert A. Skaife, "They Oppose Progress," the *Nation's Schools,* 47:2 (February, 1951), pp. 31-33.
3. The phrase is Mr. Flynn's. It appears in "The Deluded Liberals" ("Other People's Money"), *New Republic,* LXXXIX:1144 (Nov. 4, 1936), p. 18.
4. John Bainbridge, in an article titled "Save Our Schools!" *McCall's,* LXXIX:12 (September, 1952), pp. 89 and 100.
5. Quoted by Bainbridge, *ibid.,* p. 89.
6. The phrase and the theory as outlined here are those of Professor Harry Broudy of the University of Illinois.
7. This is the renowned study reported by T. W. Adorno, Else Frenkel-Brunswik, *et. al., The Authoritarian Personality* (New York: Harper & Brothers, 1950).
8. See, for example, Douglas Rugh, "The Scapegoat Value of American Public Education," *School and Society,* 74:1908 (July 14, 1951), pp. 20-22.
9. C. Winfield Scott, "Why All the Fuss?" *Phi Delta Kappan,* 34:9 (June, 1953), p. 365.
10. These underlying factors, plus two others (conformity and tabloid thinking), are advanced by expert Gordon W. Allport in *ABC's of Scapegoating* (Anti-Defamation League, 1948 Revised Edition), pp. 16-19.
11. Statement of Professor Archibald W. Anderson of the University of Illinois.
12. The following statement is attributed to Socrates: "The children now love luxury; they show disrespect for elders and love chatter in place of exercise. Children are now tyrants, not the servants, of their households. They no longer rise when elders enter the room. They contradict their parents, chatter before company, gobble up dainties at the table, cross their legs, and tyrannize over their teachers."
13. The statements are from the following: a complaint raised in Cincinnati, according to Arthur D. Morse, in "Are Our Schools as Bad as They Say?" *Household,* 53:4 (April, 1953), p. 19; from the minutes of the Harvard faculty, quoted by Dr. Marvin Glock, in the *Euclid* (Ohio) *Educator,* V:3 (March, 1958), p. 2; an editorial in the *New York Sun,* Oct. 5, 1902, quoted by Morse, *op. cit.,* p. 19; statement of the Chicago Board of Education, according to Morse, *ibid.;* and Charles A. Richmond, "Present Educational Discontent," *North American Review,* CCXXIV:834 (March-April, May, 1927), p. 67.
14. The title first appeared in *Century Magazine,* according to Henry Steele Commager, in "Victims of Success," *The Saturday Review,* XLI:18 (May 13, 1958), p. 12. The modern use of the title was made first in critic Lynd's article in the March, 1950, issue of the *Atlantic Monthly,* later served as the title of his book, published by Little, Brown & Co. in 1953.
15. According to an analysis of entries in the *Education Index,* reported by C. Winfield Scott and Clyde M. Hill, in *Public Education Under Criticism* (New York: Prentice-Hall, Inc., 1954), p. 3. As the authors note, listings in this index include only articles appearing in professional periodicals. Their use of the count suggests, however, that the ratios in periodicals of general circulation may be comparable.

16. Statement made by Dr. Oppenheimer on the CBS television program "The Great Challenge," Feb. 22, 1959.
17. Frederic W. Terrien, "The Sociology of the Attacks on the Schools," *California Journal of Secondary Education,* XXVIII:3 (March, 1953), p. 138.
18. The latter reference is to Earl Conrad's book *The Public School Scandal* (New York: The John Day Company, 1951).
19. "Teachers Can Be Wrong" (editorial) *Champaign Urbana* (Illinois) *Courier,* Feb. 5, 1959.
20. Professor William H. Cartwright, in "What's the Shooting All About?" *NEA Journal,* 44:8 (November, 1955), p. 477.
21. As evidence of this point of view on the part of the Council, see: "What Do We Mean by 'Basic'? Some Notes for a Definition," *CBE Bulletin,* Reprint Series No. 1 (June, 1958), p. 2; "The Seven Deadly Dogmas" (from the same publication), pp. 11-12; and "Two Recent Books," *CBE Bulletin* II:10 (May, 1958), p. 12.
22. For a brief discussion of the twelfth century struggle of the Humanists against the Scholastics, see R. Freeman Butts, A *Cultural History of Western Education* (New York: McGraw-Hill Book Company, Inc., 1955), Chapters V–VII, *passim*. The Humanist position in the "Lost Cause" battle at Yale is outlined in the faculty's report of 1828. For the objections to admitting history to United States public schools, see Butts, *op. cit.*, p. 500. See also Stuart G. Noble, A *History of American Education* (New York: Farrar and Rinehart, Inc., 1938), p. 320.
23. See, for example, Robert T. Morris's *Fifty Years a Surgeon* (New York: E. P. Dutton and Company, Inc., 1938), pp. 83-84.
24. Some might here object that if we want truth—if we really want to know what is causing the criticism—we ought to be concerned only with accuracy and not with the utility of explanations. But it is obvious that there are a number of valid approaches to explaining human behavior, and for our purposes some are far more fruitful than others. It is not inconsistent with the interests of accuracy to insist on applicable explanations. It is even possible that this insistence best serves the interests of truth, for an explanation which suggests remedies is one that can be tested, and is thereby shown true or false.

CHAPTER 11

1. Witness, for example, the statements of two of education's critics: ". . . any real discussion about those needs ["a child's 'real needs' "] . . . requires certain judgments—philosophical, historical, esthetic—about the nature of man and society" (Albert Lynd, *Quackery in the Public Schools* [Boston: Little Brown & Co. 1953], p. 184). And, "A debate over abolition of report cards stems from fundamental views about competition, incentives and rewards, not only in school but in life. . . ." (Howard Whitman, "Speak Out Silent People: The Struggle for Our Children's Minds," *Collier's,* 133:3 [Feb. 5, 1954], p. 25).
2. See, for example, Laura Thompson, "Attitudes and Acculturation," *American Anthropologist,* 50 (1948), pp. 200-215, and Evon Z. Vogt, *The Homesteaders: A Study of Values in a Frontier Community* (Cambridge: Harvard University Press, 1955).
3. Gunnar Myrdal, *An American Dilemma* (New York: Harper & Brothers, 1944), p. 1027.

4. See his *Folkways* (Boston: Ginn and Company, 1940), pp. 5-6, 34 and 39.
5. See, for example, Karen Horney, *The Neurotic Personality of Our Time* (New York: W. W. Norton and Company, Inc., 1937), and Lowry W. Harding, "Experimental Comparisons Between Generalizations and Problems as Indices of Values," *Journal of General Psychology*, 38:1 (January, 1948), pp. 31-50. For an anthropologist's similar conclusions, see Raymond Firth, "The Study of Values by Social Anthropologists," *Man*, 53 (October, 1953).
6. Myrdal, *op. cit.*, speaks also of a hierarchy in valuations.
7. So labeled by Myrdal, *op. cit*. Interestingly, it also seems that all the values we hold *most* important are highly generalized values. Myrdal notes without explaining, "In Western culture people assume, as an abstract proposition, that the more general . . . valuations are morally higher. . . ." (p. 1028). Perhaps one of the criteria we unconsciously apply in determining our most precious values is precisely a criterion of generality! This might explain our evident fondness for generalizing and our reluctance to modify our generalizations.
8. See James Bryce, *The American Commonwealth* (New York: The Macmillan Company, 1896), and Alexis De Tocqueville, *Democracy in America* (translated by Henry Reeve. London: Saunders and Otley, 1838, Third Edition). For an example of the discussions of educational sociologists, see George S. Counts, *Education and American Civilization* (New York: Teachers College, Columbia University, 1952).
9. Myrdal, *op. cit.*, p. 3.
10. Myrdal claims Christianity, the Enlightenment, and English law to be the roots of the American Creed. By way of illustrating the contemporary relationships of religion and the creed, he states, "Political leaders are continuously deducing the American Creed out of the Bible" (*op. cit.*, p. 11).
11. The first formulation is cited despite its lack of clarity, as it is the statement of the creed used by Myrdal (*op. cit.*, p. 8), hence a formulation to which he felt Americans would subscribe. Myrdal attributes the statement to Charles E. Merriam, in "The Meaning of Democracy," *Journal of Negro Education*, X:3 (July, 1941), p. 309. The second formulation of the creed is compiled from Counts, *op. cit.*, pp. 281-284.
12. The studies cited are those, respectively, of: John L. Landgraf, "Land-Use in the Ramah Area of New Mexico: An Anthropological Approach to Areal Study," *Peabody Museum Papers*, Vol. 42, No. 1 (Cambridge: Harvard University Press, 1954); Joseph A. Precker, "Similarity of Valuings as a Factor in Selection of Peers and Near-Authority Figures," *Journal of Abnormal and Social Psychology*, 47:2 (April, 1952), pp. 406-414; Helen Richardson, "Community of Values as a Factor in Friendships of College and Adult Women," *Journal of Social Psychology*, XI (1940), pp. 303-312; and E. Jacobson, W. W. Charters, Jr., and S. Lieberman, "The Use of the Role Concept in the Study of Complex Organizations," *Journal of Social Issues*, VII:3 (1951), pp. 18-27; and Leo Postman, Jerome S. Bruner, and Elliott McGinnies, "Personal Values as Selective Factors in Perception," *Journal of Abnormal and Social Psychology*, XLIII:2 (April, 1948), pp. 142-154.
13. See "Report of Harold L. Clapp," *CBE Bulletin*, II:4 (November, 1957), p. 11.
14. Very possibly value cleavages explain the great majority of critics, while psychological phenomena might better account for the leaders. But since it

is the support leaders garner—rather than the views they espouse—that is responsible for education's difficulties, it would seem the more practical approach to concentrate on the rank and file.

15. The Committee reported that we should have to settle for "cooperation on the level of action irrespective of agreement on ultimates." Report of the Harvard Committee, *General Education in a Free Society* (Cambridge: Harvard University Press, 1945), p. 41. Many sociologists have called attention to the number and nature of the value cleavages characterizing our society. Some have even concluded that the situation may lead to the complete downfall of the West. See, e.g., Karl Mannheim, *Man and Society in an Age of Reconstruction* (New York: Harcourt, Brace, and Company, 1951).
16. Postman, Bruner, and McGinnies, *op. cit.*
17. Bertrand Russell, *Power* (New York: W. W. Norton and Company, 1938), p. 35.
18. John Dewey, "Force and Coercion," *Characters and Events,* Vol. II (New York: Henry Holt and Company, 1929), p. 784.
19. According to the *Illinois Blue Book,* 1957-1958, Charles F. Carpentier, editor. pp. 156 and 158.
20. National Association of Secretaries of State Teachers Associations, "Teachers Serving in State Legislatures," Information Service Report No. 19, Sept. 5, 1958, *passim.*
21. NEA Research Division, "Dues of Professional Associations," December, 1956, p. 4. (In 1957, NEA dues were raised to $10 yearly.)
22. Figures for both organizations were arrived at by multiplying their membership fees (*Ibid.*) by the number of members in each organization (as reported in the *Encyclopedia of American Associations,* Detroit: Gale Research Company, 1956, pp. 144 and 173).
23. See Raymond B. Nixon, "Implications of the Decreasing Numbers of Competitive Newspapers," *Communications in Modern Society* (Urbana: University of Illinois Press, 1948) and Morris L. Ernst, *The First Freedom* (New York: The Macmillan Company, 1946), p. 152.
24. According to a study of the audience of a Pittsburgh educational TV station, for example, only 10 per cent of the total sample reported that they watched the station regularly. Those reporting "some degree of viewing" had risen from 39 per cent of those sampled in 1955, to 73 per cent of those sampled in 1957. These figures were taken from a study by Lewis Diana and Howard Rowland, *The WQED Audience: An Analysis of Three Audience Surveys* (Department of Sociology, University of Pittsburgh, May 10, 1947), as reported in the National Association of Educational Broadcasters' Fact Sheet Service, Series IV, No. 12; Audience Studies (undated).
25. David Hulburd, *This Happened in Pasadena* (New York: The Macmillan Company, 1951), p. 44.
26. Lewis C. Fay, "'Abolish Public Schools' Says Owner of Newspaper Chain," the *Nation's Schools,* 50:2 (August, 1952).
27. E.g., see Bruce Bliven, "Lean Days for Ideas," *The Saturday Review,* XXXIX:35 (Sept. 1, 1956), pp. 15 ff.; John Cogley, "The Eggheads," *Commonweal* LVII:7 (Nov. 21, 1952), p. 158; and the articles comprising the XI:3 (1955) issue of the *Journal of Social Issues,* "Anti-Intellectualism in the United States" (S. Stansfeld Sargent and Theodore Brameld, editors).

CHAPTER 12

1. Elmo Roper, "What U.S. Thinks About Its Schools," *Life,* XXIX (Oct. 16, 1950), p. 11.
2. All the studies cited are summarized in the NEA's *Public Opinion Polls on American Education* (Washington: The Association, May, 1958), pp. 10-12.
3. See, e.g., the study of W. S. Robinson, "Radio Comes to the Farmer," in *Radio Research* (New York: Duell, Sloan & Pearce, Inc., 1941), pp. 224-294.
4. Lazarsfeld, Berelson, and Gaudet, as reported in *Handbook of Social Psychology* (Cambridge: Addison-Wesley Publishing Company, Inc., 1954), Vol. II, p. 1095.
5. Al Geller, "Truth About These 'Invisible' Ads," *Science Digest,* 42:6 (December, 1957), pp. 16-18. Cf. C. I. Hovland, A. A. Lumsdaine, and F. D. Sheffield, *Experiments on Mass Communication* (Princeton: Princeton University Press, 1949). The investigators found that motion pictures had some modifying effects, but, according to Hovland in the *Handbook of Social Psychology* (Vol. II, p. 1093), "basic approach or avoidance tendencies which constitute general attitudes were most difficult to change. . . ."
6. Kurt Lewin and Paul Grabbe, "Conduct, Knowledge, and Acceptance of New Values," in *Resolving Social Conflicts* (New York: Harper & Brothers, 1948), pp. 62-63.
7. The classic experiment suggesting the size of this influence was conducted by Muzafer Sherif. A brief account, entitled "Group Influences upon the Formation of Norms and Attitudes," is found in *Readings in Social Psychology* (New York: Henry Holt and Company, Revised Edition, 1952), pp. 249-262. See also S. E. Asch, "Effects of Group Pressure upon the Modification and Distortion of Judgments," *Ibid.,* pp. 2-11.
8. Kurt Lewin, *Field Theory in Social Science* (New York: Harper & Brothers, 1951), pp. 227-228.
9. *Progressive Education is REDucation,* pp. 106-113.
10. Striking parallels suggest a number of similarities between attacks on schools and attacks on minority groups. The similarities extend to the behavior of aggressors in both kinds of attack, the conditions that appear conducive to such aggression, and the reactions of the subjects or victims of both kinds of attack. Consider, e.g., the predominating emotionality and intensity exhibited by many aggressors in both situations; the aggressor's strong tendency to reject entirely any facts undermining his position; and his pronounced conviction of the complete reliability of his stereotypes. If such similarities lend credence to psychological interpretations of those who attack schools or minorities, it still appears that aggressors in both situations typically act in conformance with their own values and that a logical relationship binds these values together and then links them to the individual's behavior. Thus, altering the content of the values offers hope of preventing attacks—irrespective of the ultimate explanation for the initial value pattern.
11. See Ronald Lippitt and Marian Radke, "New Trends in the Investigation of Prejudice," *The Annals of the American Academy of Political and Social Science,* 244 (March, 1946), pp. 167-176; Alfred J. Marrow and John R. P. French, Jr., "Changing a Stereotype in Industry," *Journal of Social Issues,* I:3 (Summer, 1945), pp. 33-37; and John Harding, "Some Basic Principles of Self-Surveys," *Journal of Social Issues,* V:2 (Spring, 1949), p. 28.
12. See, e.g., the *General Interim Report* of the House Select Committee on

Lobbying Activities, Eighty-first Congress, Second Session (Washington: U.S. GPO, 1950), pp. 66-67.

SUPPLEMENT

1. These two sources are probably the finest available on how to carry out the recommended fact-finding project: Margot H. Wormser and Claire Selltiz, *How to Conduct a Community Self-Survey of Civil Rights* (New York: Association Press, 1951), and the "Community Self-Surveys: An Approach to Social Change" issue of the *Journal of Social Issues* (V:2, Spring, 1949). The following are excellent sources of information on the rationale of the project and some of its more general features: Kurt Lewin, *Resolving Social Conflicts* (New York: Harper & Brothers, 1948), and Kenneth D. Benne and Bozidar Muntyan, *Human Relations in Curriculum Change* (Illinois Secondary School Curriculum Program Bulletin No. 7, Springfield, Ill.: Office of the Superintendent of Public Instruction, June, 1949).
2. Theodore M. Newcomb, in "Attitude Development as a Function of Reference Groups: The Bennington Study," and Ferenc Merei, in "Group Leadership and Institutionalization" (pp. 420-430 and 318-328, respectively, in *Readings in Social Psychology*) offer substantiation for our claim. Sources suggesting how to develop a group offering this attraction to members include the following: Christopher Sower, John Holland, *et al.*, *Community Involvement* (Glencoe, Ill.: The Free Press, 1957); Herbert Thelen, *Dynamics of Groups at Work* (Chicago: The University of Chicago Press, 1954); and Ronald Lippitt, J. Watson, and B. Westley, *The Dynamics of Planned Change* (New York: Harcourt, Brace & Company, 1958).
3. Two good sources are Marie Jahoda, Morton Deutsch, and Stuart W. Cook, *Research Methods in Social Relations* (New York: The Dryden Press, 1951), pp. 160-175 and 431-462; and William J. Goode and Paul K. Hatt, *Methods in Social Research* (New York: McGraw-Hill Book Company, Inc., 1952), pp. 132-145.

INDEX